Kaplan Publishing are constantly fir
ways to make a difference to your st
exciting online resources really do o
different to students looking for exam success.

This book comes with free MyKaplan online resources so that you can study anytime, anywhere. **This free online resource is not sold separately and is included in the price of the book.**

Having purchased this book, you have access to the following online study materials:

CONTENT	AAT	
	Text	Kit
iPaper version of the book	✓	✓
Progress tests with instant answers	✓	
Mock assessments online	✓	✓
Material updates	✓	✓

How to access your online resources

Kaplan Financial students will already have a MyKaplan account and these extra resources will be available to you online. You do not need to register again, as this process was completed when you enrolled. If you are having problems accessing online materials, please ask your course administrator.

If you are already a registered MyKaplan user go to www.MyKaplan.co.uk and log in. Select the 'add a book' feature and enter the ISBN number of this book and the unique pass key at the bottom of this card. Then click 'finished' or 'add another book'. You may add as many books as you have purchased from this screen.

If you purchased through Kaplan Flexible Learning or via the Kaplan Publishing website you will automatically receive an e-mail invitation to MyKaplan. Please register your details using this email to gain access to your content. If you do not receive the e-mail or book content, please contact Kaplan Flexible Learning.

If you are a new user register at www.MyKaplan.co.uk and click on the link contained in the email we sent you to activate your account. Then select the 'add a book' feature, enter the ISBN number of this book and the unique pass key at the bottom of this card. Then click 'finished' or 'add another book'.

Your Code and Information

This code can only be used once for the registration of one book online. This registration and your online content will expire when the final sittings for the examinations covered by this book have taken place. Please allow one hour from the time you submit your book details for us to process your request.

Please scratch the film to access your MyKaplan code.

Please be aware that this code is case-sensitive and you will need to include the dashes within the passcode, but not when entering the ISBN. For further technical support, please visit www.MyKaplan.co.uk

COSTS AND REVENUES

Qualifications and Credit Framework

AQ2013 Level 3 Diploma in Accounting

British Library Cataloguing-in-Publication Data

A catalogue record for this book is available from the British Library.

Published by
Kaplan Publishing UK
Unit 2, The Business Centre
Molly Millars Lane
Wokingham
Berkshire
RG41 2QZ

ISBN: 978-1-78415-394-6

We are grateful to the Association of Accounting Technicians for permission to reproduce past assessment materials and example tasks based on the new syllabus. The solutions to past answers and similar activities in the style of the new syllabus have been prepared by Kaplan Publishing.

CONTENTS

Introduction   v

Unit guide   vii

The assessment   xvii

Study skills   xix

Terminology for CSTR   xxiii

STUDY TEXT AND WORKBOOK

Chapter		Study Text	Workbook Activities Answers
1	Principles of cost accounting	1	n/a
2	Cost classification	11	337
3	Inventory	37	340
4	Labour	83	345
5	Expenses	111	346
6	Basic variance analysis	121	347
7	Overheads	141	348
8	Job, batch and service costing	185	351
9	Process costing	197	352
10	Marginal costing	245	355
11	Short-term decision making	263	357
12	Long-term decision making	297	361
Mock Assessment Questions		369	
Mock Assessment Answers		381	
Glossary		389	
Index		I.1	

INTRODUCTION

HOW TO USE THESE MATERIALS

These Kaplan Publishing learning materials have been carefully designed to make your learning experience as easy as possible and to give you the best chance of success in your AAT assessments.

They contain a number of features to help you in the study process.

The sections on the Unit Guide, the Assessment and Study Skills should be read before you commence your studies.

They are designed to familiarise you with the nature and content of the assessment and to give you tips on how best to approach your studies.

STUDY TEXT

This study text has been specially prepared for the revised AAT qualification introduced in September 2013.

It is written in a practical and interactive style:

- key terms and concepts are clearly defined

- all topics are illustrated with practical examples with clearly worked solutions based on sample tasks provided by the AAT in the new examining style

- frequent activities throughout the chapters ensure that what you have learnt is regularly reinforced

- 'pitfalls' and 'examination tips' help you avoid commonly made mistakes and help you focus on what is required to perform well in your examination

- practice workbook activities can be completed at the end of each chapter.

WORKBOOK

The workbook comprises:

Practice activities at the end of each chapter with solutions at the end of the text, to reinforce the work covered in each chapter.

The questions are divided into their relevant chapters and students may either attempt these questions as they work through the textbook, or leave some or all of these until they have completed the textbook as a final revision of what they have studied

ICONS

The study chapters include the following icons throughout.

They are designed to assist you in your studies by identifying key definitions and the points at which you can test yourself on the knowledge gained.

Definition

These sections explain important areas of Knowledge which must be understood and reproduced in an assessment

Example

The illustrative examples can be used to help develop an understanding of topics before attempting the activity exercises

Activity

These are exercises which give the opportunity to assess your understanding of all the assessment areas.

Quality and accuracy are of the utmost importance to us so if you spot an error in any of our products, please send an email to mykaplanreporting@kaplan.com with full details.

Our Quality Co-ordinator will work with our technical team to verify the error and take action to ensure it is corrected in future editions.

UNIT GUIDE

Cost and revenues covers both knowledge and skills.

Principles of Costing (Knowledge)

4 credits

Providing Cost and Revenue Information (Skills)

4 credits

Purpose of the unit

The purpose of this unit is to ensure that students know and understand the role of costing in an organisation, and how organisations use cost and revenue information to aid management decision-making.

This unit builds on the knowledge and skills that students develop at Level 2 in the Basic Costing unit (BCST) and prepares them for the Level 4 Budgeting unit (BDGT) and Financial Performance (FPFM). Together, these three units develop students with an underpinning understanding of cost and management accounting principles and the ability to apply relevant techniques.

Costs and revenues also links into the wider development of students, by linking their growing knowledge and skills of cost and management accounting to those being developed in financial accounting. This is primarily through the connections to the Level 2 units Processing bookkeeping transactions (PBKT); Control accounts, journals and the banking system (CJBS); Computerised accounting (CPAG); and Work effectively in accounting and finance (WKAF). The unit also links to the Level 3 unit Accounts preparation (ACPR) and to the Level 4 unit's Financial performance (FPFM) and Internal control and accounting systems (ISYS).

Learning objectives

On completion of this unit the learner will be able to:

- Understand the nature and role of costing systems within an organisation
- Record and analyse cost information
- Apportion costs according to organisational requirements
- Analyse deviations from budget and report these to management
- Be able to use information gathered from costing systems to assist decision-making

Learning Outcomes and Assessment criteria

The unit consists of five learning outcomes which are further broken down into Assessment criteria. These are set out in the following table with Learning Outcomes in bold type and Assessment criteria listed underneath each Learning Outcome. A K indicates a knowledge criteria and an S indicates a skill criteria. Reference is also made to the relevant chapter within the text.

To perform this unit effectively you will need to know and understand the following:

		Chapter
1	**Understanding of the nature and role of costing systems within an organisation**	
1.1K	Explain the purpose of internal reporting and providing accurate information to management	1
1.2K	Explain the relationship between the various costing systems within an organisation	1
1.3K	Identify the responsibility centres, cost centres, profit centres and investment centres within an organisation	1
1.4K	Explain the characteristics of different types of cost classifications and their use in costing	2
1.5K	Explain the differences between marginal and absorption costing	7, 10

Chapter

2 Record and analyse cost information

2.1S Record cost information for materials, labour and expenses in accordance with the organisation's costing procedures — 3, 4, 5

2.2S Analyse cost information for materials, labour and expenses in accordance with the organisation's costing procedures — 3, 4, 5

2.3K Define the various stages of inventory — 3, 9

2.4S Value inventory using these methods — 3

- First in first out (FIFO)
- Last in first out (LIFO)
- Weighted average

2.5K Describe the behaviour of these costs: — 2

- Fixed
- Variable
- Semi-variable
- Stepped

2.6S Record cost information using these costing systems: — 1, 2, 8, 9

- Job
- Batch
- Unit
- Process
- Service

3 Apportion costs according to organisational requirements

3.1S Attribute overheads costs to production and service cost centres in accordance with agreed bases of allocation and apportionment: — 7

- Direct
- Step down method

		Chapter
3.2S	Calculate overhead absorption rates in accordance with suitable bases of absorption:	7
	• Machine hours	
	• Labour hours	
3.3S	Make adjustments for under and over recovered overhead costs in accordance with established procedures	7
3.4S	Review methods of allocation, apportionment and absorption at regular intervals and implement agreed changes to methods	7
3.5S	Communicate with relevant staff to resolve any queries in overhead cost data	7
4	**Analyse deviations and report these to management**	
4.1S	Compare budget costs with actual costs, noting any variances	6
4.2S	Analyse variances for management reports	6
4.3S	Provide information for budget holders of any significant variances, making valid suggestions for remedial action	6
4.4S	Prepare management reposts in an appropriate format, presenting these within the required timescales	6, 11, 12
5	**Be able to use information gathered from costing systems to assist decision-making**	
5.1S	Prepare estimates of future income and costs for decision making using:	11, 12
	• Relevant costs	
	• Break-even analysis	
	• Margin of safety	
	• Target profit	
	• Profit-volume analysis	
	• Limiting factors	
	• Payback	
	• Discounted cash flow	

		Chapter
5.2K	Explain the effect of changing activity levels on unit costs	2
5.3S	Calculate the effect of changing activity levels on unit costs	2
5.4K	Identify factors affecting short-term and long-term decision making	11, 12

Delivery guidance

The AAT have provided delivery guidance giving further details of the way in which the unit will be assessed.

Understand the nature and role of costing systems within an organisation (LO1; AC 1.1K-1.5K).

Students need to understand different ways in which organisations record, analyse and report costs and revenues. Such costs and revenues are often treated differently from one business sector to the next, depending on the accepted practice within the business sector the organisation operates in, and on the specific measurement rules chosen by the individual organisation. They are expected to have a basic appreciation of the treatment of costs in different sectors (for example, a civil engineer would use job costing for an infrastructure project; whereas a petrol refinery would use process costing).

Effective internal reporting usually requires organisations to produce segmented reports. Students are, accordingly, expected to be able to produce basic profit and loss statements by product line.

Students should be able to comment on compliance with organisational policies, such as those for inventory control, and labour payment rates. They must be able to understand the significance of these different ways of dealing with cost and revenue information, and indirectly demonstrate knowledge by skill by applying them in relevant circumstances.

Management needs accurate information, based on an understanding of cost behaviour. This information will be used for short-term decision making (for example, break-even analysis techniques, and limiting factor decision making); It will equally be used for long-term decision making (for example, investment appraisal techniques); planning (for example, forecasting changes in profitability as activity levels change); and control (for example, through flexible budgeting and variance analysis).

Students need to understand the relationship between various costing and accounting systems in an organisation. This includes the relationship between the materials costing system and the inventory control system; the relationship between the labour costing system and the payroll accounting system; and the relationship between the overheads costing system and the accounting system. This involves understanding and being able to deal with cost accounting journals for these areas.

They need to understand and be able to recognise and explain the difference between cost, profit and investment centres. They need to be able to identify which of these applies to different parts of an organisation. They also need to know and understand the principles behind cost objects and direct/indirect costs; and know the makeup of the elements of cost (for example, prime cost and production cost).

Students should be able to advise on the most appropriate costing principles and methods to use within an organisation. They should understand the circumstances in which marginal costing is more appropriate (for example, short term decision making), and those in which absorption costing is more appropriate (for example, mainstream cost plus pricing) or is a requirement (for example, statutory financial reporting).

Students need to know and understand the principles of marginal (variable) and absorption (full absorption) costing. They should understand the causal effects on reported profits, and closing inventories in any one accounting period due to the choice of costing principle; but that over the life of an organisation there is no effect on overall reported profits.

They should understand the difference between product costs and period costs. Students should be able to indirectly demonstrate knowledge, through the application of skills, by making calculations of product costs and reported profits using both principles.

Record and analyse cost information (LO2; AC 2.1S-2.6S)

Students must be able to record inventories in inventory records, and deal with labour cost calculations (for basic pay, overtime and bonuses) in payroll calculation sheets and in other methods of presentation.

Students must be able to interpret and explain the processes set out above.

Students should know and understand the reasons behind, and the implications of, classifying the costs of inventory at different stages. This includes understanding the recording of different stages of processed inventory in the accounting records, and that equivalent unit calculations (see below) are made in this context.

They must be able to identify and explain the principles behind First in First out (FIFO), Last in First out (LIFO) and Weighted Average Cost (AVCO) methods of inventory control and valuation.

Although inventory control is no longer explicitly stated in the revised standards its understanding and application is implied; Students should be able to undertake calculations for FIFO, LIFO and AVCO methods of inventory control and valuation, including analysis of the closing balance. Calculation tasks based on LIFO are now specifically included for internal management accounting purposes; although excluded under IAS for external reporting. They should be able to advise management what the effects on reported profits and inventory values are of using each method in different circumstances, such as when reorder costs are increasing or decreasing.

They should know, understand and be able to analyse the different methods that organisations use to control inventories, such as inventory buffers, lead times, minimum/maximum order quantities and the Economic Order Quantity (EOQ). Calculations may be required for all of these, including EOQ, and they need to know the formulae for these methods.

They need to be able to identify how particular costs would be classified, based upon their short term cost behaviour, and the implications of cost behaviour for cost recording, reporting and analysis. Cost classifications are made up of fixed, variable, semi-variable and step-fixed costs.

They should appreciate that such a classification of costs holds only in the short term, and that in the long term (by definition) all costs are variable. Students should be able to undertake calculations based on cost behaviour (fixed, variable, semi-variable and step-fixed costs), including using the high/low method.

They should be able to undertake calculations using Job, Batch, Unit, Process and Service costing systems. **Note:** Calculation tasks will now be set on Job, Batch and Unit based systems.

An understanding is required of appropriate organisational costing systems – and students should be aware that the choice of system depends on the business sector of the organisation; for example, a shipbuilder is likely to use job costing whereas a chemical manufacturer is likely to use process costing. Process and job costing systems represent the extreme ends of a continuum, and many organisations need a combination of these two elements (as in batch costing).

Process costing will be examined to the following extent:

- students should be able to explain and prepare calculations for normal loss; abnormal loss; and abnormal gain

- there will be no more than two processes. The associated T accounts (for example the scrap account) will not be required – just the process account itself

- process accounts will be required, covering the terms under the first bullet point, where there is no closing work in progress. This will include scrap sales revenue

- unit cost calculations for equivalent units where there is closing or opening work in progress, but not both and not including process losses

- neither by-products nor joint products will be examined.

Apportion costs according to organisational requirements (LO 3; AC 3.1S-3.5S)

Students need to be able to identify, explain and make calculations for both the direct and step down bases of allocation and apportionment of overheads. They should appreciate, and be able to explain, the difference between allocations and apportionments.

They should be able to allocate costs to responsibility centres where these have entirely incurred the relevant cost. They should be able to make primary apportionments to responsibility centres where these have shared the benefits of the relevant cost.

They should then be able to make secondary apportionments from cost centres to profit/investment centres using either the direct or step down methods.

Students should be able to undertake calculations on an appropriate basis leading to final budgeted overhead absorption rates, and must be able to identify, interpret and make calculations of under and over recovery (absorption) of overheads.

They must know and understand different bases of absorption. These are confined to machine hours, direct labour hours, and direct labour % add on methods (a variant of the direct labour hours basis) for manufacturers; and to appropriate volume bases (e.g. miles travelled for a bus company) for service sector organisations. They should be able to choose the most appropriate basis for a particular organisation, and to justify their choice of basis.

They should understand the significance of under and over recoveries and how they are recorded in the organisation's statement of profit or loss (income statement). Students should recognise the arbitrary nature of these methods under traditional costing systems, and the need to review and perhaps change them as the organisation changes over time (e.g. as a company adds more automation, it may be appropriate to change from a labour hour to a machine hour basis of absorption).

Students should be able to consult with staff in operational departments as well as with specialist accounting and management personnel. They may be examined by a brief 'report', memo or email as set out below.

Analyse deviations from budget and report these to management (LO 4; AC 4.1S-4.4S)

Students should be able to identify and calculate variances for:

- direct materials.
- direct labour.
- fixed overheads.
- sales revenue

The sub-division of these variances into price and usage elements will not be examined. Students should be able to reconcile the budgeted and actual costs and revenues, using the variances set out above.

'Budget costs and revenues' refers to both fixed and flexed budgets. Students are expected to be competent in using either approach, and in identifying the causes of variances from both. Flexed budgets will not involve semi-variable cost calculations. Students will not be asked to calculate the sub-variances, but will be expected to answer discursive tasks that require knowledge of their sub-variances.

Students should be able to explain the meaning and significance of the above variances. This includes being able to explain the likely causes and effects of each, and should be able to advise management of ways of addressing significant deviations from budget; for example, an adverse material variance may be resolved by reducing the amount of materials wasted or buying it at a cheaper price.

Students should be able to prepare reports in an appropriate format and present these to management within the required timescales. Students may be asked in any task to produce a written report, memo, or e-mail to advise of their findings.

Be able to use information gathered from costing systems to assist decision-making (LO 5; AC5.1S-5.4K).

Students should be able to identify and explain relevant (avoidable) and irrelevant (unavoidable) costs in the context of short-term decision making. They should be able to categorise costs as direct or indirect, and as relevant or irrelevant. They should appreciate that in the long term all costs are relevant (avoidable).

They should be able to identify and explain the principles underpinning break-even (CVP) analysis. This includes identification, explanations and calculations of break-even units; break-even revenue; margin of safety units; margin of safety revenue; margin of safety %; target profit units; and target profit revenues.

Students should be able to identify and explain the principles underpinning limiting factor decision making for a single limiting factor. Knowledge of linear programming for multiple limiting factors is not required.

Students should be able to undertake calculations for payback, net present cost, net present value and internal rate of return. Calculations for discounted payback and accounting rate of return are not required. Tasks requiring students to make basic internal rate of return calculations will now be set.

Tasks requiring students to explain the principles of discounted cash flow will no longer be set. Discursive tasks will be concerned with interpreting the meaning of investment appraisal criteria (including their own results) rather than discussing the underpinning principles.

Students must be able to identify, explain and understand the effects of changes in activity levels on unit product and service costs, revenues and profits. This requires an understanding of cost behaviour as set out in the cost classifications above.

Students need to be able to identify, explain and make calculations based upon different types of short term cost behaviour. They should be able to produce short term forecasts based on short term cost behaviour classifications, and long term forecasts based on all costs being purely variable.

THE ASSESSMENT

The format of the assessment

The assessment will comprise ten independent tasks. Students will normally be assessed by computer-based assessment.

Task	Learning outcome	Assessment criteria	Maximum marks	Title for topics within task range
1	1, 2	1.1K 1.2K 2.1S 2.2S 2.3K 2.4S	16	Inventory control
2	1, 2	1.1K 1.2K 2.1S	16	Cost accounting journal entries
3	1, 2	1.1K 1.2K 2.1S 2.2S	12	Calculation of direct labour costs
4	3	1.3K 3.1S	18	Overhead allocation and apportionment
5	3	1.5K 3.2S 3.3S 3.4S 3.5S	15	Overhead absorption/Choice of costing principles
6	1	1.1K 1.2K 2.5K 5.2K 5.3S	20	Activity effects/segmental reporting

Task	Learning outcome	Assessment criteria	Maximum marks	Title for topics within task range
7	1, 2	1.1K 1.4K 2.5K 5.1S 5.2K 5.3S 5.4K	16	Break-even (CVP) analysis
8	1, 2, 5	1.1K 1.2K 1.3K 1.4K 2.1S 2.2S 2.6S 5.1S 5.2K 5.3S 5.4K	16	Limiting factor decision making/Types of costing systems
9	4	4.1S 4.2S 4.3S 4.4S	16	Variance analysis
10	1, 5	1.1K 5.1S 5.4K	20	Capital investment appraisal

Time allowed

The time allowed for this assessment is **2 hours 30 minutes.**

STUDY SKILLS

Preparing to study

Devise a study plan

Determine which times of the week you will study.

Split these times into sessions of at least one hour for study of new material. Any shorter periods could be used for revision or practice.

Put the times you plan to study onto a study plan for the weeks from now until the assessment and set yourself targets for each period of study – in your sessions make sure you cover the whole course, activities and the associated questions in the workbook at the back of the manual.

If you are studying more than one unit at a time, try to vary your subjects as this can help to keep you interested and see subjects as part of wider knowledge.

When working through your course, compare your progress with your plan and, if necessary, re-plan your work (perhaps including extra sessions) or, if you are ahead, do some extra revision/practice questions.

Effective studying

Active reading

You are not expected to learn the text by rote, rather, you must understand what you are reading and be able to use it to pass the assessment and develop good practice.

A good technique is to use SQ3Rs – Survey, Question, Read, Recall, Review:

1   **Survey the chapter**

Look at the headings and read the introduction, knowledge, skills and content, so as to get an overview of what the chapter deals with.

2   **Question**

Whilst undertaking the survey ask yourself the questions you hope the chapter will answer for you.

3 Read

Read through the chapter thoroughly working through the activities and, at the end, making sure that you can meet the learning objectives highlighted on the first page.

4 Recall

At the end of each section and at the end of the chapter, try to recall the main ideas of the section/chapter without referring to the text. This is best done after short break of a couple of minutes after the reading stage.

5 Review

Check that your recall notes are correct.

You may also find it helpful to re-read the chapter to try and see the topic(s) it deals with as a whole.

Note taking

Taking notes is a useful way of learning, but do not simply copy out the text.

The notes must:

- be in your own words
- be concise
- cover the key points
- be well organised
- be modified as you study further chapters in this text or in related ones.

Trying to summarise a chapter without referring to the text can be a useful way of determining which areas you know and which you don't.

Three ways of taking notes

1 Summarise the key points of a chapter

2 Make linear notes

A list of headings, subdivided with sub-headings, listing the key points.

If you use linear notes, you can use different colours to highlight key points and keep topic areas together.

Use plenty of space to make your notes easy to use.

3 Try a diagrammatic form

The most common of which is a mind map.

To make a mind map, put the main heading in the centre of the paper and put a circle around it.

Draw lines radiating from this to the main sub-headings which again have circles around them.

Continue the process from the sub-headings to sub-sub-headings.

Highlighting and underlining

You may find it useful to underline or highlight key points in your study text – but do be selective.

You may also wish to make notes in the margins.

Revision phase

Kaplan has produced material specifically designed for your final examination preparation for this unit.

These include pocket revision notes and a bank of revision questions specifically in the style of the new syllabus.

Further guidance on how to approach the final stage of your studies is given in these materials.

Further reading

In addition to this text, you should also read the 'Student section' of the 'Accounting Technician' magazine every month to keep abreast of any guidance from the examiners.

Terminology for CSTR

There are different terms used to mean the same thing – you will need to be aware of both sets of terminology.

UK GAAP	IAS
Final accounts	Financial statements
Trading and profit and loss account	Statement of profit or loss
Turnover or sales	Revenue or Sales revenue
Balance sheet	Statement of financial position
Fixed assets	Non-current assets
Net book value	Carrying amount
Tangible assets	Property, plant and equipment
Stock	Inventory
Trade debtors	Trade receivables
Trade creditors	Trade payables
Long term liabilities	Non-current liabilities
Capital	Equity
Profit and loss balance	Retained earnings
Net profit	Profit for the year

Principles of cost accounting

1

Introduction

This chapter considers the basic principles of management accounting and management information. It contains fundamental principles that the rest of the course is built on.

ASSESSMENT CRITERIA

Explain the purpose of internal reporting and providing accurate information to management (1.1K)

Explain the relationship between the various costing systems within an organisation (1.2K)

Identify the responsibility centres, cost centres, profit centres and investment centres within an organisation (1.3K)

Record cost information using these costing systems (2.6S):

– Unit

CONTENTS

1 Management accounting
2 Terminology – cost objects, cost units and responsibility centres
3 The cost card

1 Management accounting

1.1 Introduction

The purpose of **Management accounting** is to provide information for use within an organisation.

Internal users, such as the departmental managers, will require a variety of information to ensure the smooth running of their department.

1.2 The aims of management accounting

The aim of management accounting is to assist management in the following areas of running a business:

- **Decision making**

  Management accountants use management information to make informed decisions about the future.

- **Planning**

  Management accountants provide the information for the creation of short, medium and long term plans; for example, a short term plan is the preparation of annual budgets.

- **Co-ordinating**

  Planning enables all departments to be co-ordinated and to work together.

- **Controlling**

  The comparison of actual results with the budget helps to identify areas where operations are not running according to plan.

  Investigating the causes, and acting on the results of that investigation, helps to control the activities of the business.

- **Communicating**

  Preparing plans that are then distributed to departmental managers helps to communicate the aims of the business to those managers.

- **Motivating**

  Plans and budgets should include targets to motivate managers (and staff) and improve their performance.

  If the target is too difficult, however, it is likely to demotivate and the target is unlikely to be achieved.

1.3 Management information

A management accountant's main objective is to provide information to managers to enable the correct decisions to be made. The information provided may be the same as that required for financial accounting but there are no regulations that need to be applied.

Management information needs to have the attributes of good information. It needs to be:

- **Fit for purpose** – management information needs to be **accurate**, **relevant** and **complete**. The reason the information is required will determine how accurate it needs to be. For example, if the cost of a single item is required then pounds and pence will be needed for accuracy but the costs for a division or department of an organisation may be accurate to the nearest thousand pounds. Information needs to be complete enough to enable managers to make decisions. Ensuring that information is complete does not mean that all information should be provided to all managers. Managers only require information that will be relevant to their decisions.

- **Cost-effective** – the value that the information is going to provide the organisation with should exceed the cost of collating it.

- **Timely** – information should be available when it is required. To improve timeliness management information systems can be installed into organisations. These are computer packages that allow reports to be produced and data to be extracted with ease.

Management information can be produced in **any format** that is useful to the business and tends to be produced frequently, for instance **every month.**

1.4 Cost accounting

Cost accounting is usually a large part of management accounting. As its name suggests, it is concerned with **establishing costs**. It developed within manufacturing businesses.

Cost accounting is primarily directed at enabling management to perform the functions of **planning, control** and **decision making:**

(a) determining costs and profits during a control period

(b) valuing inventory of raw materials, work in progress and finished goods, and controlling inventory levels

(c) preparing budgets, forecasts and other control data for a forthcoming control period

(d) creating a reporting system which enables managers to take corrective action where necessary to control costs

(e) providing information for decision-making such as pricing.

Items (a) and (b) are traditional **cost accounting roles**; (c) to (e) extend into management accounting.

Cost accounting is not confined to the environment of manufacturing, although it is in this area that it is most fully developed. **Service industries, central and local government, and accountancy and legal practices** make use of cost accounting information. Furthermore, it is not restricted purely to manufacturing and operating costs, but also to administration, selling and distribution and research and development.

Be prepared for non-manufacturing scenarios in the computer based assessments.

 2 **Terminology – cost objects, costs units and responsibility centres**

2.1   Cost object

A **cost object** is anything for which costs can be ascertained. Cost units and cost centres, described below, are types of cost object.

2.2   Cost units

To help with planning, control and decision making, businesses often need to calculate a cost per unit of output.

A key question, however, is what exactly we mean by a 'unit of output', or '**cost unit**'. This will mean different things to different businesses but we always looks at what the business produces.

- A car manufacturer will want to determine the cost of each car and probably different components as well.

- In a printing firm, the cost unit could be the specific customer order.

- For a paint manufacturer, the unit could be a litre of paint.

- An accountancy firm will want to know the costs incurred for each client. To help with this it is common to calculate the cost per hour of chargeable time spent by staff.

- A hospital might wish to calculate the cost per patient treated; the cost of providing a bed for each day or the cost of an operation.

2.3 Responsibility centres

> ### Q Definition
>
> A responsibility **centre** is an individual part of a business whose manager has personal responsibility for its performance

The main responsibility centres are:

- Cost centre

- Revenue centre

- Profit centre

- Investment centre

A **cost centre** is a production or service location, function, activity or item of equipment whose costs are identified and recorded. A **cost centre** is a part of a business for which costs are determined.

- For a paint manufacturer cost centres might be: mixing department, packaging department, administration, or marketing departments.

- For an accountancy firm, the cost centres might be: audit, taxation, accountancy, word processing, administration, and canteen. Alternatively, they might be the various geographical locations, e.g. the London office, the Cardiff office, the Plymouth office.

- Cost centre managers need to have information about costs that are incurred and charged to their cost centres. The performance of a cost centre manager is judged on the extent to which cost targets have been achieved.

A **revenue centre** is a part of the organisation that earns sales revenue. It is similar to a cost centre, but only accountable for revenues, and not costs.

- Revenue centres are generally associated with selling activities, for example, a regional sales manager may have responsibility for the regional sales revenues generated.

- Each regional manager would probably have sales targets to reach and would be held responsible for reaching these targets.

- Sales revenues earned must be able to be traced back to individual (regional) revenue centres so that the performance of individual revenue centre managers can be assessed.

A **profit centre** is a part of the business for which both the costs incurred and the revenues earned are identified.

- Profit centres are often found in large organisations with a divisionalised structure, and each division is treated as a profit centre.

- Within each profit centre, there could be several costs centres and revenue centres.

- The performance of a profit centre manager is measured in terms of the profit made by the centre.

- The manager must therefore be responsible for both costs and revenues and in a position to plan and control both.

- Data and information relating to both costs and revenues must be collected and allocated to the relevant profit centres.

Managers of **investment centres** are responsible for investment decisions as well as decisions affecting costs and revenues.

- Investment centre managers are therefore accountable for the performance of capital employed as well as profits (costs and revenues).

- The performance of investment centres is measured in terms of the profit earned relative to the capital invested (employed).

Activity 1

A cost centre is defined as:

A   A unit of product or service for which costs are accumulated

B   A production or service location, function, activity or item of equipment for which costs are accumulated

C   Costs that relate directly to a unit

D   Costs that contain both a fixed and a variable element

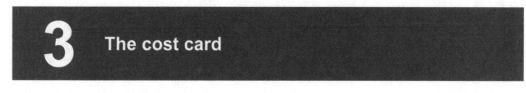

3 The cost card

3.1 Cost cards

A cost card is used to show the breakdown of the costs of producing output based on the classification of each cost.

A cost card can be produced for one unit or a planned level of production. The cost card below is an example of a cost card for a planned level of production i.e. in total.

The following chapters are aimed at being able to build up the total or unit cost.

	£
Direct costs	
Direct materials	250,000
Direct labour	120,000
Direct expenses	10,000
Prime cost *(Total of direct costs)*	380,000
Variable production overheads	15,000
Marginal production cost *(total of direct and variable costs)*	395,000
Fixed production overheads	35,000
Absorption cost *(total production cost)*	430,000
Non-production cost (e.g. administration overhead; selling overhead)	20,000
Total cost	450,000

Note: The terminology in this cost card will be explained during your cost and revenues studies.

4 Summary

In this introductory chapter we looked at some of the basic principles and terminology used in cost and management accounting.

You need to be aware of the difference between **cost units** (individual units of a product or service for which costs can be separately ascertained) and **cost centres** (locations or functions in respect of which costs are accumulated).

Answers to chapter activities

Activity 1

A cost centre is defined as:

B   A production or service location, function, activity or item of equipment for which costs are accumulated.

Cost classification

2

Introduction

This chapter considers how costs can be classified and the various uses of classification in management accounting.

ASSESSMENT CRITERIA

Explain the characteristics of different types of cost classifications and their use in costing (1.4K)

Describe the behaviour of these costs (2.5K):

- Fixed
- Variable
- Semi-variable
- Stepped

Record cost information using these costing systems (2.6S):

- Unit

Explain the effect of changing activity levels on unit costs (5.2K)

Calculate the effect of changing activity levels on unit costs (5.3S)

CONTENTS

1 Cost classification
2 Classification by element
3 Classification by function
4 Classification by nature
5 Classification by behaviour
6 Changing activity levels
7 The high-low method

1 Cost classification

1.1 Purpose of cost classification

Costs can be **classified** (collected into logical groups) in many ways. The particular classification selected will depend upon the purpose for which the resulting analysed data will be used, for example:

Classification	Purpose
By element – materials, labour and expenses	Cost control
By function – production (cost of sales), and non-production (distribution costs, administrative expenses).	Financial accounts
By nature – direct and indirect	Cost accounts
By behaviour – fixed, variable, stepped fixed and semi-variable	Budgeting, decision making

Classification of costs will also be determined by the **type of business** that is being run. For example fuel for a taxi firm is required for the service they provide whereas fuel for a delivery vehicle for a manufacturing company is not part of the product they produce.

2 Classification by element

2.1 Cost classification by element

Classification by element involves stating costs according to what the cost is as follows:

- **Materials** – includes raw materials for a manufacturer or alternatively the cost of goods that are to be resold in a retail organisation

- **Labour** – consists of basic pay and also overtime, commissions and bonuses as well.

- **Expenses** – includes electricity, depreciation and rent.

Activity 1

Classify the following costs for a clothes retailer by element.

Cost	Materials	Labour	Expenses
Designer skirts			
Heating costs			
Depreciation of fixtures and fittings			
Cashier staff salaries			

3 Classification by function

3.1 Cost classification by function

For financial accounting purposes costs are split into the following categories:

Production

- **Cost of sales** – also known as **production** costs. This category could include production labour, materials, supervisor salaries and factory rent.

Non-production

- **Distribution** – this includes selling and distribution costs such as sales team commission and delivery costs.

- **Administrative costs** – this includes head office costs, IT support and HR support.

Note that one cost you may meet in the exam is depreciation. This is a measure of how much a non-current asset is wearing out or being used up. The classification will depend on which asset is being depreciated. For example:

- Cost of sales – depreciation on a machine in the production line

- Distribution – depreciation of a delivery van

- Administration – depreciation of a computer in the accounts department

---

Activity 2

George plc makes stationery. Classify the following costs by function in the table below.

Cost	Production	Administration	Distribution
Purchases of plastic to make pens			
Managing director's bonus			
Depreciation of factory machinery			
Salaries of factory workers			
Insurance of sales team cars			

---

4 Classification by nature

4.1 Cost classification by nature

To be able to account for costs incurred it is necessary to know which costs are associated with the final product/service and which are incurred whilst producing the product/service.

Classification by nature is how this is done:

- A **direct cost** is an item of cost that is traceable directly to a cost unit. An example of direct costs for a toy maker producing teddy bears might be:

  Direct material – fur fabric, stuffing

  Direct labour – employee stuffing the bear

  Direct expenses – patent for bear design

The **total** of all **direct** costs is known as the **prime cost** per unit.

- An **indirect** cost is a cost that cannot be identified with any one finished unit. An example of indirect costs for a toy maker producing a teddy bear might be:

  Indirect material – cleaning products

  Indirect labour – the production line supervisor

  Indirect expenses – rent, rates, electric etc

These costs are incurred as a result of running the business but cannot necessarily be identified to an individual teddy bear.

Indirect costs are often referred to as **overheads**.

 Activity 3

Camberwell runs a construction company. Classify the following costs by nature (direct or indirect) in the table below.

Cost	Direct	Indirect
Bricks		
Plant hire for long term contract		
Builders' wages		
Accountants' wages		

---

5 Classification by behaviour

5.1 Cost classification by behaviour

For **short term** budgeting purposes, management needs to be able to predict **how costs will vary with differing levels of activity** (i.e. the number of units being produced).

For example, if a furniture manufacturer expected to produce 1,000 chairs in a particular month, what should he budget for the costs of wood, labour, selling costs, factory heat and light, manager's salaries, etc? How would these costs differ (if at all) if he expected to produce 2,000 chairs?

To make short term budgeting and forecasting easier, costs are split into the following categories:

- Variable
- Fixed
- Stepped
- Semi-variable

5.2 Variable costs

Variable costs are costs that vary with changes in level of activity. Variable costs are **constant per unit** of output and increase in direct proportion to activity.

For example, if you make twice the number of units then the amount (and hence the cost) of raw material used would double.

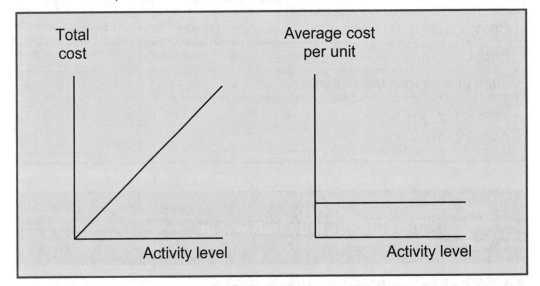

Example

If a business has total variable costs of £10,000 when it produces 1,000 units what is the variable cost per unit?

£10,000/1,000 = £10

What would be the total variable cost if the activity increased to 2,000 units?

£10 × 2,000 = £20,000

5.3   Fixed costs

Fixed costs are costs that, in the short term, are not affected by changes in activity level. The total cost stays constant as activity levels change. This leads to a decrease in the cost per unit of output as activity levels increase.

:Q: Example

If a business has total fixed costs of £15,000 when it produces 1,000 units what is the fixed cost per unit?

£15,000/1,000 = £15

If a business has total fixed costs of £15,000 when it produces 3,000 units what is the fixed cost per unit?

£15,000/3,000 = £5

What would be the total fixed cost if the activity increased to 5,000 units?

£15,000

5.4 Stepped costs

Stepped fixed costs are costs that remain fixed up to a particular level of activity, but which rise to a higher (fixed) level if activity goes beyond that range.

Example

A business has total fixed costs of £20,000 when it produces 1,000 units but if it goes above this level fixed costs increase by 50%. What would the fixed costs be if the business produced 2,000 units?

£20,000 × 1.5 = £30,000

5.5 Semi-variable costs

Semi-variable costs are those that have a fixed element and a variable element:

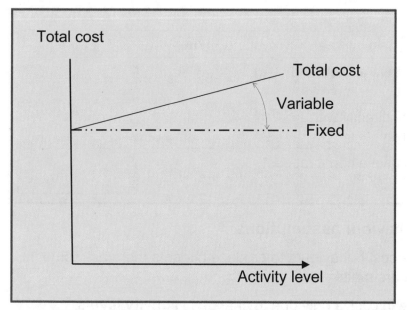

Activity 4

Gilbert plc is a furniture manufacturer. Classify the following costs by their behaviour in the table below.

Cost	Fixed	Variable	Semi-variable
Director's salary			
Wood			
Rent of factory			
Phone bill – includes a line rental			
Factory workers wage			

Activity 5

Identify the following statements as either true or false in the table below.

	True	False
Stepped costs have a fixed and variable element		
Fixed costs vary directly with changes in activity		
Variable costs have a constant cost per unit.		

5.6   Cost behaviour assumptions

To be able to use cost behaviours to produce budgets there are some assumptions that are made:

- Any **change** in cost is only due to change in **activity levels**

- Costs are assumed to be either **fixed** or **variable**, or at least **separable into these elements**.

- Total fixed costs remain fixed throughout the activity range charted (unless told otherwise).

- Total variable costs change in direct proportion to volume.

- Economies or diseconomies of scale are ignored; this ensures that **the variable cost per unit is constant**.

- Efficiency and productivity do not change with volume.

- If a cost is **direct** it will have a **variable** cost behaviour

Note: The use of cost behaviour to classify costs only holds in the short term, **in the long term** (by definition) **all costs are variable**.

6 Changing activity levels

6.1 Introduction

The **behavioural characteristics** of costs are used when planning or forecasting costs at different levels of production or activity.

When producing a forecast it may be necessary to identify the type of behaviour a cost is exhibiting. It is useful to remember the following:

* Fixed costs are constant in total

* Variable costs are constant per unit

* Semi-variable costs are neither constant in total nor constant per unit.

 Example

A company has a mix of variable, semi variable and fixed costs. Identify the behaviour for each of the costs shown below:

Cost	1,000 units £	3,000 units £
1	4,500	7,500
2	1,830	5,490
3	5,000	5,000
4	12,250	36,750

* **Cost 1** must be a **semi-variable cost** as the total cost changes when activity level change and the cost per unit also changes at the different activity levels

* **Cost 2** is a **variable cost** as the cost per unit is constant at each activity level

* **Cost 3** is a **fixed cost** as the total cost does not change as activity level changes

* **Cost 4** is a **variable cost** as the cost per unit is constant at each activity level

Workings:

Cost	1,000 units		3,000 units	
	Total	Per unit	Total	Per unit
	£	£	£	£
1	4,500	4.50	7,500	2.50
2	1,830	1.83	5,490	1.83
3	5,000	5.00	5,000	1.67
4	12,250	12.25	36,750	12.25

Activity 6

Identify if the following costs are variable, fixed or semi-variable.

	1,500 units	2,500 units
Material	£7,500	£12,500
Labour	£12,000	£20,000
Rent	£17,000	£17,000
Electricity	£16,750	£21,250

6.2 Stepped fixed costs

If a forecast has a stepped fixed cost included then information will have to be provided as to when the step up in cost would occur and by how much.

Example

A manufacturing business has variable production costs of £3 per unit and fixed costs of £60,000. A further cost is the salary of the factory supervisor of £18,000 per annum. If more than 100,000 units of the product are made then an additional factory supervisor must be employed at the same salary.

What is the total cost of production and the cost per unit at the following production levels:

(i)   60,000 units

(ii)   90,000 units

(iii) 120,000 units

	Production level		
	60,000 unit £	**90,000 units** £	**120,000 units** £
Variable production costs			
60,000 × £3	180,000		
90,000 × £3		270,000	
120,000 × £3			360,000
Fixed costs	60,000	60,000	60,000
Supervisor's salary (stepped)	18,000	18,000	36,000
Total production cost	258,000	348,000	456,000
Cost per unit	£4.30	£3.87	£3.80

The total costs are made up of both fixed and variable costs but the cost per unit falls as the production quantity increases. This is because the fixed costs are spread over a higher number of units of production

6.3 Semi-variable costs

Changes in activity level may also require the separation of the fixed and variable element of a semi-variable cost. The total fixed cost will remain constant as activity changes but the total variable cost will change in proportion to the activity changes.

The splitting or separating of a semi-variable cost is done by using the high-low method.

7 The high-low method

7.1 High-low method

If a semi-variable cost is incurred, it is often necessary to estimate the fixed element and the variable element of the cost for the purposes of budgeting. This can be done using the high-low method.

Remember:

Total cost = Fixed cost + (Variable cost per unit × Activity level)

Example

A factory has incurred the following power costs in the last six months with different levels of production in each month:

	Production units	Power costs £
January	20,000	18,000
February	16,000	16,500
March	18,000	17,200
April	24,000	20,500
May	22,000	19,400
June	19,000	17,600

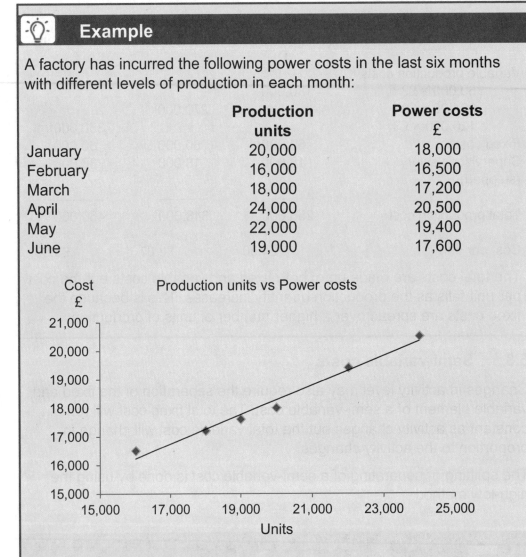

What are the fixed and variable elements of the power cost?

Step 1

Find the highest and lowest levels of production (activity) and their related costs.

		Units	Cost £
High	April	24,000	20,500
Low	February	16,000	16,500

Step 2

Find the variable cost element by determining the increased power cost per unit between highest and lowest production levels.

		Units	Cost £
High	April	24,000	20,500
Low	February	16,000	16,500
	Difference	8,000	4,000

The power cost has increased by £4,000 for an increase in 8,000 units of production. The variable power cost is therefore:

$$\frac{£4,000}{8,000} = £0.50 \text{ per unit}$$

Step 3

Using either the highest or the lowest production level (from step 1) find the fixed cost element by deducting the total variable cost from the total cost.

		£
April	Total cost	20,500
	Total variable cost 24,000 × 0.5	(12,000)
		8,500

		£
February	Total cost	16,500
	Total variable cost 16,000 × 0.5	(8,000)
		8,500

If production levels of 30,000 units are anticipated next month, what is the expected power cost?

The semi-variable power cost consists of the fixed cost (£8,500) and a variable cost per unit (£0.50). Therefore for an activity level of 30,000 units the total cost is predicted to be:

	£
Variable cost 30,000 × 0.50	15,000
Fixed cost	8,500
Total cost	23,500

Activity 7

The electricity used in a factory has a semi-variable cost behaviour. The manager wants to know how much electricity to budget for if he was to make 75 units.

Units	Total cost £
10	120
50	200
100	300

A £150

B £100

C £250

D £137.50

Activity 8

Charlie Ltd is preparing its budget for the next quarter and it needs to consider different production levels.

The semi-variable costs should be calculated using the high-low method. If 3,000 batches are produced then the semi-variable cost will be £8,500.

Complete the table below and calculate the estimated profit per batch at the different activity levels.

Units sold and produced	1,000	1,500	2,000
Sales revenue	25,000		
Variable cost			
Direct materials	5,000		
Direct labour	2,400		
Overheads	3,600		
Semi-variable costs	4,500		
Variable element			
Fixed element			
Fixed cost	3,500		
Total cost	19,000		
Total profit	6,000		
Profit per batch (to 2 decimal places)	6.00		

Activity 9

A manufacturing business has variable production costs of £3 per unit and fixed costs of £50,000. These include rent of £18,000 per annum. If more than 50,000 units of the product are made, then additional floor space must be rented at a cost of £20,000 per annum.

What is the total cost of production and the cost per unit at the 60,000 units:

	Total	Per unit
A	£230,000	£3.83
B	£250,000	£4.17
C	£268,000	£4.47
D	£88,000	£1.47

8 Summary

Costs can be classified in a variety of different ways for different purposes. The basic classification is into **materials, labour and expenses**, each of which will be dealt with in detail in the following chapters. A further method of classification of costs is between **direct and indirect** costs.

For decision-making and budgeting purposes, it is useful to distinguish costs according to their **behaviour** as production levels change. The basic classifications according to behaviour are **fixed** and **variable** costs although there are also **stepped** costs and **semi-variable** costs. The fixed and variable elements of semi-variable costs can be isolated using the **high/low method**.

Answers to chapter activities

Activity 1

Cost	Materials	Labour	Expenses
Designer skirts	☑		
Heating costs			☑
Depreciation of fixtures and fittings			☑
Cashier staff salaries		☑	

Activity 2

Cost	Production	Admin.	Distribution
Purchases of plastic to make pens	☑		
Managing director's bonus		☑	
Depreciation of factory machinery	☑		
Salaries of factory workers	☑		
Insurance of sales team cars			☑

Activity 3

Cost	Direct	Indirect
Bricks	☑	
Plant hire for long term contract	☑	
Builders wages	☑	
Accountants wages		☑

Activity 4

Cost	Fixed	Variable	Semi-variable
Director's salary	☑		
Wood		☑	
Rent of factory	☑		
Phone bill – includes a line rental			☑
Factory workers wage		☑	

Activity 5

	True	False
Stepped costs have a fixed and variable element		☑
Fixed costs vary directly with changes in activity		☑
Variable costs have a constant cost per unit.	☑	

Activity 6

To identify cost behaviours it is necessary to look at the total costs and the cost per unit.

A **fixed cost** will be constant in total as activity changes – **Rent** is a fixed cost

A **variable cost** will be constant per unit as activity changes – **Material** (£5 per unit) and **Labour** (£8 per unit) are variable costs

A **semi-variable cost** will be neither constant in total nor constant per unit as activity changes – **Electricity** is a semi-variable cost. The total cost changes and so does the cost per unit (£11.17 per unit for 1,500 units and £8.50 per unit for 2,500 units).

Activity 7

The cost for the electricity for 75 units is:

C   £250

Variable cost

$$\frac{300-120}{100-10} = £2$$

Fixed cost

$300 - (100 \times 2) = £100$

Cost for 75 units

$100 + (75 \times 2) = £250$

Activity 8

Batches sold and produced	1,000	1,500	2,000
Sales revenue	25,000	37,500	50,000
Variable cost			
Direct materials	5,000	7,500	10,000
Direct labour	2,400	3,600	4,800
Overheads	3,600	5,400	7,200
Semi-variable costs	4,500		
Variable element		3,000	4,000
Fixed element		2,500	2,500
Fixed cost	3,500	3,500	3,500
Total cost	19,000	25,500	32,000
Total profit	6,000	12,000	18,000
Profit per batch (to 2 decimal places)	6.00	8.00	9.00

Splitting the semi-variable cost:

$$\frac{8,500 - 4,500}{3,000 - 1,000} = £2 \text{ per unit}$$

Variable cost (at 3,000 units) = 3,000 × £2 = £6,000

Fixed cost = £8,500 – £6,000 = £2,500

Activity 9

B

	60,000 units £
Variable production costs 60,000 × £3	180,000
Fixed costs	50,000
Additional rentals	20,000
Total production cost	250,000
Cost per unit	£4.17

9 Test your knowledge

Workbook Activity 10

Direct costs are:

A   A unit of product or service for which costs are accumulated

B   A production or service location, function, activity or item of equipment for which costs are accumulated

C   Costs that relate directly to a unit

D   Costs that contain both a fixed and a variable element

Workbook Activity 11

P Harrington is a golf ball manufacturer. Classify the following costs by nature (direct or indirect) in the table below.

Cost	Direct	Indirect
Machine operators wages		
Supervisors wages		
Resin for golf balls		
Salesmen's salaries		

Workbook Activity 12

A semi-variable cost is:

A   A unit of product or service for which costs are accumulated

B   A production or service location, function, activity or item of equipment for which costs are accumulated

C   A cost that relate directly to a unit

D   A cost that contains both a fixed and a variable element

Workbook Activity 13

Which of the following best describes a 'pure' fixed cost?

A cost which:

A   represents a fixed proportion of total costs

B   remains at the same level up to a particular level of output

C   has a direct relationship with output

D   remains at the same level whenever output changes

Workbook Activity 14

The total production cost for making 10,000 units was £12,000 and the total production cost for making 25,000 was £21,000. What is the full production cost for making 40,000 units?

A cost which:

A   6,000

B   24,000

C   30,000

D   72,667

Workbook Activity 15

C Ling has a contract with a customer to produce 4,000, 5,000 or 6,000 units of product.

Revenues and costs for 4,000 units are shown below. Fixed overheads remain constant for the range charted but indirect labour will increase by £2,000 when production reaches 5,500 units.

Possible production level	4,000 units
	£
Sales revenue	50,000
Variable costs:	
Material	2,000
Labour	4,000
Overheads	6,000
Fixed costs:	
Indirect labour	12,000
Overheads	8,000
Total cost	32,000
Total profit	18,000
Profit per unit	4.50

Calculate:

- The sales revenue per unit if the contract is for 4,000 units.

- The variable cost per unit if the contract is for 4,000 units.

- The fixed cost per unit if the contract is for 4,000 units.

- The total cost if the contract is for 6,000 units.

- The total profit if the contract is for 6,000 units.

Workbook Activity 16

Biscuit Making Company

The general manager has given you the task of supplying cost data for the manufacture of a specific brand of chocolate biscuit for 20X9 on the basis of projected costs. A cost clerk has given you data on variable and fixed costs, which is relevant over the range of production.

Complete the budgeted cost schedule for the different levels of production.

BUDGETED COST SCHEDULE		YEAR 20X9		
		ACTIVITY (Packets)		
	150,000	175,000	200,000	225,000
Description	£	£	£	£
Variable costs				
Direct material	£12,000			
Direct labour	£9,000			
Packing costs	£1,500			
Fixed costs:				
Depreciation costs	£12,000			
Rent and rates	£26,000			
Supervisory costs	£12,000			
Administration costs	£8,000			
Total costs	£80,500			
Cost per packet (2 decimal places)	£0.54			

The cost per packet has *increased/decreased** because the fixed cost per unit has *increased/decreased**

*delete as appropriate

Workbook Activity 17

Wendy Sheds is preparing its budget for the next quarter and it needs to consider different production levels.

The semi-variable costs should be calculated using the high-low method. If 300 batches are produced then the semi-variable cost will be £600.

Complete the table below and calculate the estimated profit per shed at the different activity levels.

Sheds sold and produced	500	750	1,000
Sales revenue	8,000		
Variable cost			
Direct materials	800		
Direct labour	760		
Overheads	1,440		
Semi-variable costs	900		
Variable element			
Fixed element			
Fixed cost	700		
Total cost	4,600		
Total profit	3,400		
Profit per batch (to 2 decimal places)	6.80		

Inventory

3

Introduction

This chapter looks at the procedures that a business should have in place to ensure that records of inventory are kept accurate and up to date. In particular it looks at the purchasing of inventory, the valuation of inventory and inventory control.

ASSESSMENT CRITERIA	CONTENTS
Record cost information for material in accordance with the organisation's costing procedures (2.1S)	1 Inventory control cycle
	2 Materials documentation
Analyse cost information for materials in accordance with the organisation's costing procedures (2.2K)	3 Cost of having inventory
	4 The stores department
Define the various stages of inventory (2.3K)	5 Systems of inventory control
Value inventory using these methods (2.4S):	6 Pricing issues of raw materials
– First in first out (FIFO) – Last in first out (LIFO) – Weighted average (AVCO)	7 Integrated bookkeeping – inventory

1 Inventory control cycle

1.1 Introduction

Inventory often forms the **largest single item of cost** for a business so it is essential that the inventory purchased is the most suitable for the intended purpose.

Inventory includes:

* raw materials or components to be used in the manufacture of products

* items bought to be sold on (retailer or wholesaler)

* items that will be used for general day to day running of the business

1.2 Control of purchasing

When goods are purchased they must be ordered, received by the stores department, recorded, issued to the manufacturing department that requires them and eventually paid for. This process needs a great deal of paperwork and strict internal controls.

Internal control consists of full documentation and appropriate authorisation of all transactions, movements of inventory and of all requisitions, orders, receipts and payments.

If control is to be maintained over purchasing, it is necessary to ensure that:

* only necessary items are purchased

* orders are placed with the most appropriate supplier after considering price and delivery details

* the goods that are actually received are the goods that were ordered and in the correct quantity/quality

* the price paid for the goods is correct (i.e. what was agreed when the order was placed).

To ensure that all of this takes place requires a reliable system of checking and control.

KAPLAN PUBLISHING

1.3 Overview of procedures

It is useful to have an overview of the purchasing process.

There are many variations of the above system in practice, but it is a fairly typical system and does provide good control over the purchasing and issuing process. Details about the documentation mentioned in the diagram above follows.

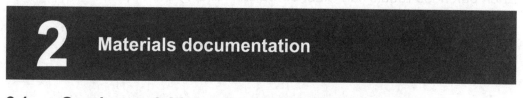

2 Materials documentation

2.1 Goods requisition note (also called 'materials requisition')

The user department (e.g. a production department) will notify the stores department that it requires certain goods using a 'goods requisition note'. This note will be authorised by the departmental manager.

> ### Example
>
> The production department requires 400 litres of a particular oil coded L04 from the stores department for product A.
>
> | GOODS REQUISITION NOTE | | |
> |---|---|---|
> | Requiring department: _Production_ | Number: _4027_ | |
> | Required for: _Product A_ | Date: _14 April 20X4_ | |
> | Code | Description | Quantity |
> | _L04_ | _Oil_ | _400 litres_ |
> | Authorised by: _Factory Manager_ | Received by: .... | |

2.2   Purchase requisition

It is important that an organisation **controls** the goods that are ordered from suppliers. Only goods that are genuinely necessary should be ordered. Therefore, before any order for goods is placed, a purchase requisition must be completed.

Each purchase requisition must be **authorised** by the appropriate person. This will usually be the storekeeper or store manager.

When the purchase requisition has been completed it is sent to the purchasing department so that the purchase order is prepared.

Example

The storekeeper completes the requisition to order the 400 litres of oil for production. The code for the type of oil that is to be purchased is L04. Delivery is to be made directly to the stores department by 2 May.

PURCHASE REQUISITION					
Date: 15 April 20X4				**Number:** 6843	
Purpose: General machinery maintenance					
Goods requisition note (if any): 4027					
Quantity	Material code	Job code	Delivery details		Purchase order details
			Date	Place	
400 litres	L04	–	2 May 20X4	Stores	
Origination department: Stores					
Authorisation: Storekeeper					

Note that the purchase requisition must have the following elements:

- Be dated.

- Be consecutively numbered.

- Include the purpose for which the materials are required, showing any relevant job code where necessary.

- Include a detailed description of the precise materials required.

- Show when and where the goods are required.

- Include space to record the eventual purchase order details.

- Be authorised by the appropriate person in the department placing the purchase requisition.

2.3 Purchase order

Purchase orders will be placed with suppliers by the purchasing department. The choice of supplier will depend upon the price, delivery promise, quality of goods and past performance.

The person placing the order must first check that the purchase requisition has been authorised by the appropriate person in the organisation.

Once the supplier of the goods has been chosen, the purchase price of the goods must be determined. This will either be from the price list of the supplier or from a special quotation of the price by that supplier. The price agreed will be entered on the purchase order together with details of the goods being ordered.

The purchase order must then be authorised by the appropriate person in the organisation before being dispatched to the supplier.

A copy of the purchase order is sent to the stores department as confirmation of expected delivery. The stores department therefore know that goods are due and can alert appropriate management if they are not received. A copy is also sent to the accounts department to be matched to the supplier's invoice. An example purchase order is shown below.

Example

Rowson Supplies Ltd has been chosen to supply the oil required by production. They agree to deliver the oil at a price of £1.50 per litre.

PURCHASE ORDER					
To: Rowson Supplies Ltd		Number: 81742			
		Date: 15 April 20X4			
		Purchase requisition number: 6843			
Please supply in accordance with attached conditions of purchase.					
Quantity	Description/code		Delivery date	Price £	Per
400 litres	L04		2 May 20X4	1.50	Litre
Your quotation:	£600 (400 litres × £1.50)				
Authorisation:	Purchasing Manager				

2.4 Delivery note

A delivery note is sent by the supplier to the stores with the goods being delivered. This will include a description of the goods being delivered along with the quantity. The contents and quality of the items delivered should be checked against the delivery note and this is then signed by the person receiving the goods as evidence that the goods arrived.

Any concerns about the goods (for example, too few, too many, the wrong colour, or the wrong size) should be referred immediately to the appropriate manager before accepting the goods.

Example

400 litres of oil is delivered buy Rowson Supplies

ROWSON SUPPLIES LTD – DELIVERY NOTE		
Delivery to: French Productions Ltd		Date: 2 May 20X4
Purchase order no: 81742		
Delivery note no: D6582		
Please supply in accordance with attached conditions of purchase.		
Quantity	Description	Code
400 litres	Oil	L04
Signed: Storeman		

2.5 Goods received note

When goods are received by the organisation they will be taken to the stores department rather than being delivered directly to the department that will use the goods. This enables the receipt of goods to be controlled. When the goods are received, the stores department will check:

(a) that the goods that arrive agree in **all** detail to those ordered on the purchase order

(b) that the details of the delivery note agree with the actual goods delivered.

When the stores department are satisfied with all of the details of the delivery, the details are recorded on a goods received note (GRN).

The GRN is evidence that the goods that were ordered have been received and therefore should be, and can be, paid for. The GRN will, therefore, be sent to the accounts department to be matched with the supplier's invoice.

As evidence of the actual receipt of the goods the GRN is also used for entering receipts of materials in the stores records.

Example

FRENCH PRODUCTIONS LTD
GOODS RECEIVED NOTE

No: GRN 272

SUPPLIER: Rowson Supplies Ltd   DATE: 2 May 20X4

PURCHASE ORDER NO: 81742

Description	Code	Qty	No of packages
Oil	LO4	400 litres	1

Received by: STORES – FINISHING AREA
Required by: PRODUCTION
Accepted by: STORES SUPERVISOR

QUALITY ASSURANCE
Inspected by: SIG: ....Storeman...
Qty passed: 400   **Qty rejected:** Nil

2.6 Issues to the user department (production department)

The circle is completed when the stores department issues the goods to the production department. The goods must agree with the original goods requisition note.

2.7 Purchase invoice

The purchase invoice for goods details the amount that the receiver of the goods must pay for them and the date that payment is due. The purchase invoice might be included when the goods themselves are delivered, or might be sent after delivery.

The person responsible for payment must check that the details of the purchase invoice agree to the goods received note, the delivery note and the purchase order. This is to ensure that:

- what was ordered was received
- what was received is what is being paid for
- the price charged is that agreed.

Once it is certain that the purchase invoice agrees with the goods that were actually received then the invoice can be authorised for payment by the appropriate person in the organisation.

Example

ROWSON SUPPLIES LTD – PURCHASE INVOICE		
To: *Ronson Supplies Ltd*	Date:	*2 May 20X4*
Purchase order no: 81742		
Invoice no: 16582		
		£
For supply and delivery of: 400 litres of oil L04 @ £1.50 per litre Payment due in 30 days		600.00

2.8 Goods returned note

If goods are damaged or are not as ordered, they will be returned to the supplier. A goods returned note will be used, authorised by the stores department's manager.

When unused materials are returned from user departments to the stores, the transaction will be recorded on a document similar to the materials requisition but usually printed in a different colour. This will be a goods returned note. It will be completed by the user department that is returning the goods and signed by the storekeeper as evidence that the goods were returned to stores.

When the goods are returned the details on the goods returned note must be checked to the actual goods themselves.

2.9 Credit note

If goods have been returned to the supplier, or there is some fault with the invoice (e.g. incorrect price or discount), a credit note will be requested from the supplier.

Activity 1

Which of the following documents would be completed in each situation?

	Material Requisition	Purchase Requisition	Goods received note	Goods returned note
Material returned to stores from production				
Form completed by the stores department detailing inventory requirements				
Materials returned to supplier				
Form completed by stores on receipt of goods				
Form completed by production detailing inventory requirements.				

3   Cost of having inventory

3.1   Introduction

Most businesses, whatever their size, will be concerned with the problem of which items to have in inventory and how much of each item should be kept.

There are three forms that inventory can exist in:

- **Raw material** – items that are to be used in the manufacture of products

- **Work in progress** – items that are part way through the manufacturing process

- **Finished goods** – items that have completed the manufacturing process and are ready to be sold

KAPLAN PUBLISHING

3.2 Functions of inventory

The principal reasons why a business needs to hold inventory are as follows:

(a) It acts as a buffer in times when there is an unusually high rate of consumption.

(b) It enables the business to take advantage of quantity discounts by buying in bulk.

(c) The business can take advantage of seasonal and other price fluctuations (e.g. buying coal in the summer when it is cheaper).

(d) To prevent any delay in production caused by a lack of raw material so production processes will flow smoothly and efficiently.

(e) It may be necessary to hold inventory for a technical reason: for example, whisky must be matured.

3.3 Costs of having inventory

Irrespective of the nature of the business, a certain amount of inventory will need to be held.

However, **holding inventory costs money** and the principal 'trade-off' in an inventory holding situation is between the costs of acquiring and storing inventories on the one hand and the level of service that the company wishes to provide on the other.

The **total cost of having inventory** consists of the following:

(a) **Purchase price**

(b) **Holding costs**:

   (i)   the opportunity cost of capital tied up

   (ii)   insurance

   (iii) deterioration

   (iv)   obsolescence

   (v)   damage and pilferage

   (vi)   warehouse upkeep

   (vii) stores labour and administration costs.

(c) **Ordering costs**:

   (i)   clerical and administrative expenses

   (ii)   transport costs.

   Note, if goods are produced internally, the set-up costs for each production run are equivalent to the re-order costs.

(d) **Stock-out costs** (items of required inventory are not available):

   (i)   loss of sales, therefore lost contribution

   (ii)   long-term damage to the business through loss of goodwill

   (iii) production stoppages caused by a shortage of raw materials

   (iv)   extra costs caused by the need for emergency orders.

(e) **Inventory recording systems costs**:

   (i)   maintaining the stores record card

3.4   Disadvantages of low inventory levels

To keep the holding costs low it may be possible to reduce the volume of inventory that is kept but this can cause some problems:

- Customer demand cannot always be satisfied; this may lead to loss of business if customers become dissatisfied.

- In order to fulfil commitments to important customers, costly emergency procedures (e.g. special production runs) may become necessary in an attempt to maintain customer goodwill.

- It will be necessary to place replenishment orders more frequently than if higher inventories were held, in order to maintain a reasonable service. This will result in higher ordering costs being incurred.

3.5   Disadvantages of high inventory levels

To reduce the problems mentioned above management may consider holding high levels of inventory but again this can have issues:

- Storage or holding costs are very high; such costs will usually include rates, rent, labour, heating, deterioration, etc.

- The cost of the capital tied up in inventories, i.e. the cash spent to buy the inventory, is not available to pay other bills.

- If the stored product becomes obsolete, a large inventory holding of that item could, at worst, represent a large capital investment in an unsaleable product whose cash value is only that of scrap.

- If a great deal of capital is invested in inventories, there will be proportionately less money available for other requirements such as improvement of existing production facilities, or the introduction of new products.

- If there is a sudden drop in the price of a raw material after a high level of inventory has already been purchased, then the extra spent over the new lower price represents the opportunity cost of purchasing in advance. It follows that it would seem sensible to hold higher inventories during an inflationary period and lower inventories during a period of deflation.

4 The stores department

4.1 Function of the stores department

The stores or inventory department is responsible for the receipt, storage, issue and recording of the raw materials used in the production process.

4.2 Receipt of goods

When raw materials are received from suppliers they will normally be delivered to the stores department. The stores personnel must check that the goods delivered are the ones that have been ordered, in the correct quantity, of the correct quality and in good condition using the goods received note and the purchase requisition or purchase order.

4.3 Storage of materials

Once the materials have been received they must be stored until required by the production departments.

Storage of materials must be appropriate to their type. For example, foodstuffs must be stored at the correct temperature and wood must be stored in dry conditions. Storage should also be laid out in such a manner that the correct materials can be accessed easily either manually or by machinery.

4.4 Issue of materials

When the production departments require raw materials for production, it is essential that the stores department can provide the correct quantity and quality of materials at the time they are required. This will require careful attention to inventory control policies to ensure that the most efficient levels of inventories of raw materials are kept. Inventory control policies are discussed in a later section.

4.5 Recording of receipts and issues

In many organisations the stores department is also responsible for the recording of the quantities of raw materials that are received from suppliers and issued to the production departments. This normally takes place on the bin cards or the stores/inventory record card.

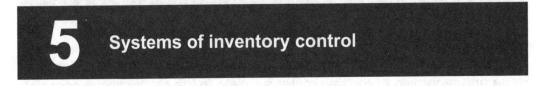

5 Systems of inventory control

5.1 Inventory control

Inventory control is 'the method of ensuring that the right **quantity** of the right **quality** of the relevant inventory is available at the right **time** and right **place**.

Inventory control is maintained through the use of the inventory record cards and by carrying out inventory checks on a regular basis.

5.2 Inventory control levels

Many inventory control systems will incorporate some or all of four inventory control levels that assist in keeping costs of inventory holding and ordering down, whilst minimising the chances of stock-outs. The four control levels are:

- re-order level – the level to which the inventory will be allowed to fall before an order is placed

- economic order quantity (EOQ) – the most economic quantity of inventory to be ordered to minimise the total of the cost having inventory.

- maximum inventory level – the highest quantity of inventory that should be held

- minimum inventory level – the lowest quantity of inventory that should be held (also known as buffer inventory).

5.3 Re-order level

This level will be determined with reference to the time it will take to receive the order (the lead time) and the possible inventory requirements during that time.

If it is possible to estimate the **maximum possible lead time** and the **maximum usage rate**, then a 'safe' re-order level, that will almost certainly avoid stock-outs, will be given by:

Re-order level = Maximum usage × Maximum lead time

If a company keeps some buffer inventory then the re-order level would be calculated as:

Re-order level = (Maximum usage × Maximum lead time) + buffer

5.4 Economic order quantity (EOQ)

Once the re-order level is reached, an order will be placed. The size of the order will affect:

(a) average inventory levels (the larger the order, the higher the inventory levels will be throughout the year)

(b) frequency of orders placed in the year (the larger the order, the longer it will take for inventories to fall to the re-order level, and thus the fewer the orders placed in the year).

Increasing the order size will have two conflicting effects on costs: increased holding costs through higher inventory levels and decreased re-ordering costs due to fewer orders placed in the year.

Under certain 'ideal' conditions (including constant rates of usage and constant lead times) a mathematical model can be used to determine the optimum (economic) order quantity (EOQ) that will minimise the total of these two costs – see graph.

The formula for the economic order quantity is:

$$EOQ = \sqrt{\frac{2 \times C_o \times D}{C_h}}$$

where: C_o =   cost of placing each order (note this is not the cost of the materials purchased but the administrative cost of placing the order).

   D =   annual demand/usage in units

   C_h =   cost of holding **one** unit of inventory for **one** year

Assumptions of the economic order quantity:

- Demand and lead time are constant and known
- Purchase price is constant
- No buffer inventory is held

💡 Example

The demand for a particular product is expected be 25 units a day. Each time an order is placed, administrative costs of £15 are incurred and one unit of inventory held for one year incurs £0.10 of holding costs.

The company operates a 300-day year.

Calculate the economic order quantity.

Solution

EOQ $= \sqrt{\dfrac{2 \times C_o \times D}{C_h}}$

EOQ $= \sqrt{\dfrac{[2 \times £15 \times 7,500\,(W)]}{£0.10}} = 1,500$ units

Working:

Annual demand D = days in year × usage per day

   D = 300 × 25 = 7,500

5.5 Maximum and minimum inventory levels

Many inventory systems will also incorporate maximum and minimum inventory 'warning' levels, above or below which (respectively) inventory should not be allowed to rise/fall.

In practice, the maximum inventory level is fixed by taking into account:

(a) rate of consumption of the material

(b) time needed to obtain new supplies

(c) financial considerations due to high inventories tying up capital

(d) storage space with regard to the provision of space and maintenance costs

(e) extent to which price fluctuates

(f) risks of changing specifications

(g) possibility of loss by evaporation, deterioration, etc

(h) seasonal considerations as to both price and availability

(i) economic order quantities.

The minimum inventory level is fixed by taking into account:

(a) rate of consumption

(b) time needed to obtain delivery of supplies

(c) the costs and other consequences of stock-outs.

A simplified method of determining these control levels is by reference to the re-order level, re-order quantity (EOQ) and estimates of possible lead times and usage rates, as follows:

Minimum level = Re-order level – (Average usage × Average lead time)

Maximum level = Re-order level + Re-order quantity –
(Minimum usage × Minimum lead time)

If at any time inventories **fall below the minimum level**, this is a warning that **usage or lead time are above average**. Thus the storekeeper will need to keep an eye on inventory levels and be prepared to place an emergency order if inventories get too low.

If inventories **rise above the maximum level** then **usage or lead time have actually been lower** than the expected minimum. If it is usage, this may indicate a general decline in the demand for the inventory and the order quantity (and possibly the re-order level) should be reviewed to avoid holding excess inventory with associated holding costs.

Example

The demand for a particular product is expected to vary between 10 and 50 per day. Lead time is, on average, 5 days, although it has been as short as 3 days and as long as 10 days. The company orders 1,500 units at a time. The company operates a 300-day year.

Calculate the re-order, maximum and minimum inventory levels.

Solution

Re-order level	=	Maximum usage × Maximum lead time
	=	50 per day × 10 days = 500 units
Minimum level	=	Re-order level – (Average usage × Average lead time)
	=	500 – (30 per day (W1) ×5 days) = 350 units
Maximum level	=	Re-order level + re-order quantity – (Minimum usage × Minimum lead time)
	=	500 + 1,500 – (10 per day × 3 days)
	=	1,970 units

Working 1:

$$\text{Average usage} = \frac{\text{minimum usage} + \text{maximum usage}}{2}$$

$$= \frac{10 + 50}{2}$$

$$= 30 \text{ units per day}$$

Activity 2

Given below is information about one inventory line that a business holds:

Daily usage (units) 20

Lead time (days) 5

The business operates for 250 days a year and keeps 50 units of inventory as buffer inventory.

The cost of placing each order is £20 and it costs £0.20 to hold an item of inventory for one year.

KAPLAN PUBLISHING

Calculate:

(i) the re-order level

(ii) the economic order quantity

After further investigation of usage and delivery times it has been discovered that usage can vary from 15 units a day to 25 units a day and lead time can be as short as 2 days but at the most 8 days. Calculate the maximum and minimum inventory levels based on this information and your calculations above.

(iii) the minimum inventory level

(iv) the maximum inventory level

5.6   Inventory control systems

There are two main types of inventory control systems:

(a) the re-order level (two-bin) system

(b) the periodic (cyclical) review system

5.7   Re-order level system

In a **re-order level system**, a replenishment order of fixed size is placed when the inventory level falls to the fixed re-order level. Thus a **fixed quantity** is ordered at **variable intervals of time**. This is the most common system used.

The most common practical implementation of the basic re-order level system is the two-bin system. Here, two bins of the inventory item are used and a replenishment order is placed when the first bin becomes empty; inventory is then drawn from the second bin until the order is received. When the order arrives, the second bin is filled up to its original level and the remainder goes into the first (empty) bin. Thus the amount of inventory held in the second bin gives the re-order level.

5.8   Periodic review system

In a **periodic review system**, the inventory levels are reviewed at fixed points in time, when the quantity to be ordered is decided. By this method **variable quantities** are ordered at **fixed time intervals**.

Although this may increase the chances of a stock-out (between review times), it has the advantage of being easier to plan the scheduling of inventory counts and orders in advance.

6   Pricing issues of raw materials

6.1   Introduction

The cost of materials purchased will normally be derived from suppliers' invoices but, where many purchases have been made at differing prices, a decision has to be taken as to which cost is used when inventory is issued to the user department (cost centre).

6.2   Methods of pricing

Various methods exist including:

(a)   FIFO (first in, first out)

(b)   LIFO (last in, first out)

(c)   Weighted average (AVCO)

The choice of method will not only affect the charge to the user department for which the material is required, but also the value of the inventory left in stores.

6.3   FIFO, LIFO and AVCO methods

These systems attempt to reflect the movements of individual units in and out of inventory under different assumptions.

- **FIFO** – assumes that issues will be made from the oldest inventory available, leaving the latest purchases in inventory. This means that transfers from stores to production will be made at the oldest prices and the newest prices will be used to value the remaining inventory.

  FIFO could be used when products are perishable e.g. milk

KAPLAN PUBLISHING

- **LIFO** – assumes that issues will be made from the newest inventory available, leaving the earliest purchases in inventory. This means that transfers from stores to production will be made at the newest prices and the older prices will be used to value the remaining inventory.

  LIFO could be used when products are not perishable e.g. stationery

- **AVCO** – assumes that the issues into production will be made at an average price. This price is derived from taking the total value of the inventory and dividing it by the total units in inventory thus finding the average price per unit. A new average cost is calculated before each issue to production.

  AVCO could be used when individual units of material are indefinable e.g. sand at a builders merchants

6.4 The stores record card

It is usual to record quantities of an inventory item (and often inventory values as well) on a **stores record card**. One such card is maintained for each different inventory item, showing receipts of new inventory from suppliers, issues of inventory to production, and balance of inventory remaining on hand.

Example

Sid makes the following purchases of Component X.

		Quantity	Unit price	
			£	£
Purchases:	10 January	50	1.00	50
	20 January	60	1.10	66
	30 January	40	1.25	50

On 25 January Sid issues 70 units for use in production.

On 31 January Sid issues 60 units for use in production.

No inventory was held at the beginning of the month.

Calculate the value of closing inventory and the cost of inventory issued to production using:

(a) a FIFO basis

(b) a LIFO basis

(c) an AVCO basis (round the average price per unit to 2 decimal places)

Solution

(a) **FIFO basis**

Stores Record Card

Material description: Component X

Code: X100

Date	Receipts			Issues			Balance	
	Quantity	Unit price £	Total £	Quantity	Unit price £	Total £	Quantity	Total £
10 Jan	50	1.00	50				50	50
20 Jan	60	1.10	66				50	50
							60	66
							110	116
25 Jan				50	1	50		
				20	1.10	22	40	44
				70		77		
30 Jan	40	1.25	50				40	44
							40	50
							80	94
31 Jan				40	1.10	44		
				20	1.25	25	20	25
				60		69	20	25

(b) LIFO basis

Stores Record Card

Material description: Component X

Code: X100

	Receipts			Issues			Balance	
Date	Quantity	Unit price £	Total £	Quantity	Unit price £	Total £	Quantity	Total £
10 Jan	50	1.00	50				50	50
20 Jan	60	1.10	66				50	50
							60	66
							110	116
25 Jan				60	1.10	66		
				10	1.00	10	40	40
				70		76		
30 Jan	40	1.25	50				40	40
							40	50
							80	90
31 Jan				40	1.25	50		
				20	1.00	20	20	20
				60		70	20	20

(c)   AVCO basis

Stores Record Card

Material description: Component X

Code: X100

Date	Receipts			Issues			Balance	
	Quantity	Unit price £	Total £	Quantity	Unit price £	Total £	Quantity	Total £
10 Jan	50	1.00	50				50 ___	50 ___
20 Jan	60	1.10	66				50	50
							60	66
							110 ___	116 ___
25 Jan				70	1.05	74	40	42
30 Jan	40	1.25	50				40	42
							40	50
							80 ___	92 ___
31 Jan				60	1.15	69	20 ___	23 ___
							20 ___	25 ___

Note: The average cost per unit is calculated based on what is in stores before the issue occurs. For example:

25 Jan £42 ÷ 40 units = £1.05 therefore the valuation of the issue is 70 units × £1.05 = £74 (rounded to the nearest whole number)

In the exam you will be told how many decimal places the 'per unit' figure and total figure need to be.

Activity 3

Amp plc is a printing company specialising in producing accounting manuals. No formal stores accounting system is in operation at present.

Complete the following inventory entries using:

FIFO, LIFO and AVCO (weighted average cost per unit to two decimal places of a £)

Material:	Paper – Code 1564A	
Opening inventory:	10,000 sheets – value £3,000	

Purchases			Issues	
3 May	4,000 sheets	£1,600	6 May	7,000 sheets
12 May	10,000 sheets	£3,100	15 May	6,000 sheets
			22 May	7,200 sheets

Stores Record Card FIFO

Material: Paper

Code: 1564A

Date	Details	Receipts		Issues			Inventory	
		Sheets	£	Sheets	Price	£	Sheets	£
1.5	Opening inventory							
3.5	Receipt							
6.5	Issue							
12.5	Receipt							
15.5	Issue							
22.5	Issue							

Stores Record Card LIFO

Material: Paper

Code: 1564A

Date	Details	Receipts		Issues			Inventory	
		Sheets	£	Sheets	Price	£	Sheets	£
1.5	Opening inventory							
3.5	Receipt							
6.5	Issue							
12.5	Receipt							
15.5	Issue							
22.5	Issue							

Stores Record Card AVCO

Material: Paper

Code: 1564A

Date	Details	Receipts		Issues			Inventory	
		Sheets	£	Sheets	Price	£	Sheets	£
1.5	Opening inventory							
3.5	Receipt							
6.5	Issue							
12.5	Receipt							
15.5	Issue							
22.5	Issue							

Activity 4

Navneet Ltd

Identify the method of inventory valuation and complete the stores record card shown below for steel component Magic, for the month of May 20Y0.

Note: Figures in the total columns should be shown to the nearest £. The company's policy is to round prices per unit to two decimal places.

STORES RECORD CARD FOR STEEL COMPONENT MAGIC								
Inventory valuation method:								
	Receipts			Issues			Balance	
Date 20Y0	Quantity kg	Cost per kg (£)	Total cost (£)	Quantity kg	Cost per kg (£)	Total cost (£)	Quantity kg	£
Balance as at 1 May							25,000	50,000
9 May	30,000	2.30	69,000				55,000	119,000
12 May				40,000		84,500		
18 May	20,000	2.50	50,000					
27 May				10,000				

6.5 Features of the different methods

FIFO has the following features:

- In times of rapidly increasing prices, material may be **issued** at an early and unrealistically low price, resulting in the particular job showing an unusually large profit.

- Two jobs started on the same day may show a different cost for the same quantity of the same material.

- In times of rapidly increasing prices FIFO will give a higher profit figure than LIFO or AVCO.

- FIFO can be used in the production of financial accounts as it is **acceptable to HMRC and adheres to IAS2 Inventories**

LIFO has the following features:

- **Closing inventories** will be shown at the earliest prices which mean that in times of rapidly increasing or decreasing prices the inventory figure bears little resemblance to the current cost of replacement therefore **does not adhere to IAS2** and should not be used for financial reporting of inventory values. LIFO should only be **used within an organisation**.

- As with FIFO, two jobs started on the same day may show a different cost for the same quantity of the same material.

- The LIFO method uses the latest prices for issues to production and therefore the cost obtained is more likely to be in line with other costs and selling prices.

- In times of rapidly increasing prices LIFO will give a lower profit figure than FIFO and AVCO.

AVCO is a compromise on valuation of inventory and issues and the average price rarely reflects the actual purchase price of the material.

6.6 Inventory valuation method and profit

As stated above FIFO will return a higher profit than LIFO if prices are increasing over a time period. If prices are declining LIFO then returns a higher profit. This is due to the valuation of closing inventory and its application in a statement of profit or loss.

Example

Charlie has the following extract from their inventory card and was wondering which method of inventory valuation would give him the highest profit.

- 1 July Received 100 units at £10 per unit

- 2 July Received 100 units at £11 per unit

- 3 July Issued 150 units to production.

There is no opening inventory.

Date	Receipts			Issues			Balance	
	Qty	Per unit	Total	Qty	Per unit	Total	Qty	Total
1 July	100	10	1,000				100	1,000
2 July	100	11	1,100				100	1,000
							100	1,100
							___	___
							200	2,100
3 July (FIFO)				100	10	1,000		
				50	11	550	50	550
				___		___		
				150		1,550		

OR

3 July (LIFO)				100	11	1,100	50	500	
				50	10	500			
				___		___			
				150		1,600			

If we now use the above data to produce a statement of profit or loss for the first few days in July:

FIFO

The closing inventory is valued at the most recent prices therefore the higher prices.

		£
Sales (illustrative figure)		2,000
Less: Cost of sales		
Opening inventory	0	
Purchases (from receipts)	2,100	
Less: closing inventory	(550)	
	___	
		(1,550)
		___
Gross profit		450

LIFO

The closing inventory is valued at the oldest prices therefore the lower prices

		£
Sales (illustrative figure)		2,000
Less: Cost of sales		
Opening inventory	0	
Purchases (from receipts)	2,100	
Less: closing inventory	(500)	
	___	
		(1,600)
		___
Gross profit		400

We can see that FIFO has a higher value of closing inventory (£550) therefore a lower cost of sales (£1,550) which leads to a higher profit. AVCO would return a profit in between FIFO and LIFO.

Activity 5

If raw material prices are subject to inflation, which method of valuing inventories will give the lowest profit?

A   FIFO

B   LIFO

C   AVCO

7 Integrated bookkeeping – inventory

7.1 Introduction

The costs of a business have to be recorded in a bookkeeping system. Many businesses use an **integrated bookkeeping system** where the ledger accounts kept provide the necessary **information for both costing and financial accounting**.

7.2 Stores record card (bin card)

Every line of inventory, e.g. component X and material Y, will have a record card showing precisely how much of this item is in inventory. Therefore each time a receipt of a material arrives from a supplier then the stores record card must be updated.

7.3 Stores department entries

In many management accounting systems only the quantity of the materials is entered by the stores department as that is the only information that they have.

7.4 Accounts department entries

Once the stores record card reaches the accounts department then the correct price of the materials, taken from the purchase invoice will be entered.

The stores record card is an important document that helps to control the movement of materials and assess inventory levels.

7.5 Inventory ledger account

The accounting for material is dealt with through a stores ledger account (or the material cost account). This is maintained by the accounting department, the physical inventory shown on these accounts is reconciled with the stores record card. The materials cost account is where the movement of the costs associated with the materials are recorded.

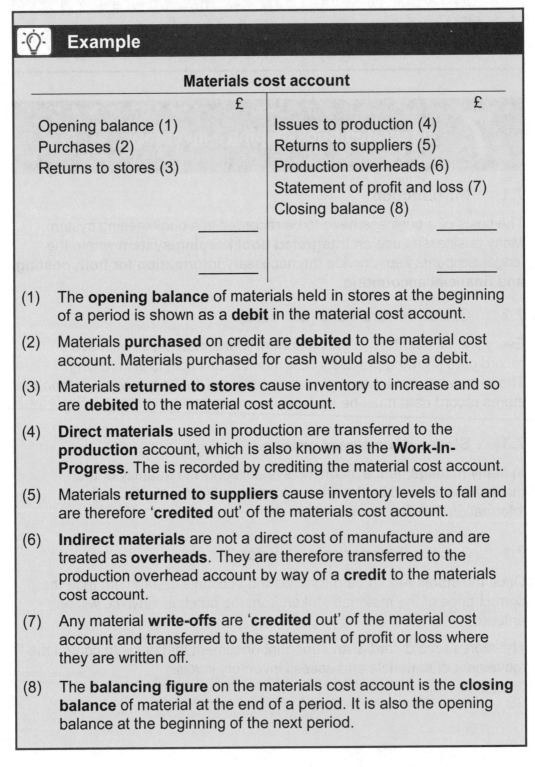

Example

Materials cost account

	£		£
Opening balance (1)		Issues to production (4)	
Purchases (2)		Returns to suppliers (5)	
Returns to stores (3)		Production overheads (6)	
		Statement of profit and loss (7)	
		Closing balance (8)	

(1) The **opening balance** of materials held in stores at the beginning of a period is shown as a **debit** in the material cost account.

(2) Materials **purchased** on credit are **debited** to the material cost account. Materials purchased for cash would also be a debit.

(3) Materials **returned to stores** cause inventory to increase and so are **debited** to the material cost account.

(4) **Direct materials** used in production are transferred to the **production** account, which is also known as the **Work-In-Progress**. The is recorded by crediting the material cost account.

(5) Materials **returned to suppliers** cause inventory levels to fall and are therefore '**credited** out' of the materials cost account.

(6) **Indirect materials** are not a direct cost of manufacture and are treated as **overheads**. They are therefore transferred to the production overhead account by way of a **credit** to the materials cost account.

(7) Any material **write-offs** are 'credited out' of the material cost account and transferred to the statement of profit or loss where they are written off.

(8) The **balancing figure** on the materials cost account is the **closing balance** of material at the end of a period. It is also the opening balance at the beginning of the next period.

KAPLAN PUBLISHING

Activity 6

What are the correct journal entries the following accounting transactions:

1   Receipt of material into stores paying on credit:

   A   Dr Bank, Cr Materials

   B   Dr Trade Payables Control, Cr Materials

   C   Dr Materials, Cr Bank

   D   Dr Materials, Cr Trade Payables Control

2   Issue of material from inventory to production.

   A   Dr Bank, Cr Materials

   B   Dr Materials, Cr Bank

   C   Dr Materials, Cr Production

   D   Dr Production, Cr Materials

3   Receipt of material into stores paying immediately by BACS.

   A   Dr Bank, Cr Materials

   B   Dr Trade Payables Control, Cr Materials

   C   Dr Materials, Cr Bank

   D   Dr Materials, Cr Trade Payables Control

4   Return of material from production to stores.

   A   Dr Materials, Cr Bank

   B   Dr Materials, Cr Trade Payables Control

   C   Dr Materials, Cr Production

   D   Dr Production, Cr Materials

8 Summary

Pricing issues of raw materials and valuing inventories are two of the most important techniques that you need to know about in the topic of materials. We have looked at three main methods of pricing issues and valuing inventories: FIFO, LIFO, and Weighted Average Cost. A common examination task is to ask you to record receipts and issues of materials onto a stores ledger card using one of these methods.

We have also looked at the **documents** involved in the process of purchasing materials and the different inventory control systems (re-order level (two-bin) system and the periodic review system.

Another important part of the topic of materials is that of **inventory control** levels – these assist in keeping the costs of inventory holding and inventory ordering at a minimum, whilst minimising stock-outs at the same time. Make sure that you can calculate the re-order level, the EOQ, the maximum inventory level and the minimum inventory level.

Answers to chapter activities

Activity 1

Which of the following documents would be completed in each situation?

	Materials Requisition	Purchase Requisition	Goods received note	Goods returned note
Material returned to stores from production				☑
Form completed by the stores department detailing inventory requirements		☑		
Materials returned to supplier				☑
Form completed by stores on receipt of goods			☑	
Form completed by production detailing inventory requirements.	☑			

Activity 2

(i)	Re-order level	=	(20 units × 5 days) + 50
		=	150 units

(ii) EOQ $= \sqrt{\dfrac{2 \times £20 \times 20 \times 250)}{0.2}}$

= 1,000 units

(iii) Minimum inventory level = Re-order level –
(Average usage × Average lead time)
= 150 – (20 × 5)
= 50 units

(iv) Maximum inventory level = Re-order level + EOQ –
(Minimum usage × Minimum lead time)
= 150 + 1,000 – (15 × 2)
= 1,120 units

Activity 3

Stores Record Card FIFO

Material: Paper

Code: 1564A

Date	Details	Receipts		Issues			Inventory	
		Sheets	£	Sheets	Price	£	Sheets	£
1.5	Opening inventory						10,000	3,000
3.5	Receipt	4,000	1,600				10,000	3,000
							4,000	1,600
							14,000	4,600
6.5	Issue						3,000	900
				7,000	0.30	2,100	4,000	1,600
				7,000		2,100	7,000	2,500
12.5	Receipt	10,000	3,100				3,000	900
							4,000	1,600
							10,000	3,100
							17,000	5600
15.5	Issue			3,000	0.30	900	1,000	400
				3,000	0.40	1,200	10,000	3,100
				6,000		2,100	11,000	3,500
22.5	Issue			1,000	0.40	400		
				6,200	0.31	1,922	3,800	1,178
				7,200		2,322	3,800	1,178

Stores Record Card LIFO

Material: Paper

Code: 1564A

Date	Details	Receipts		Issues			Inventory	
		Sheets	£	Sheets	Price	£	Sheets	£
1.5	Opening inventory						10,000	3,000
3.5	Receipt	4,000	1,600				10,000	3,000
							4,000	1,600
							14,000	4,600
6.5	Issue			4,000	0.40	1,600		
				3,000	0.30	900	7,000	2,100
				7,000		2,500	7,000	2,100
12.5	Receipt	10,000	3,100				7,000	2,100
							10,000	3,100
							17,000	5,200
15.5	Issue						7,000	2,100
				6,000	0.31	1,860	4,000	1240
				6,000		1,860	11,000	3340
22.5	Issue			4,000	0.31	1,240		
				3,200	0.30	960	3,800	1,140
				7,200		2,200	3,800	1,140

Stores Record Card AVCO

Material: Paper

Code: 1564A

Date	Details	Receipts		Issues			Inventory	
		Sheets	£	Sheets	Price	£	Sheets	£
1.5	Opening inventory						10,000	3,000
3.5	Receipt	4,000	1,600				14,000	4,600
6.5	Issue			7,000	0.33	2,310*	7,000	2,290*
12.5	Receipt	10,000	3,100				17,000	5,390
15.5	Issue			6,000	0.32	1,920	11,000	3,470
22.5	Issue			7,200	0.32	2,304	3,800	1,166

* The difference in these two values is the result of rounding the price p/unit to 33p. A more accurate unit price of 32.86p would have valued them both at £2,300.

Activity 4

INVENTORY RECORD CARD FOR STEEL COMPONENT MAGIC
Inventory valuation method: FIFO

Date 20Y0	Receipts Quantity kg	Cost per kg (£)	Total cost (£)	Issues Quantity kg	Cost per kg (£)	Total cost (£)	Balance Quantity kg	£
Balance as at 1 May							25,000	50,000
9 May	30,000	2.30	69,000				55,000	119,000
12 May				40,000	25,000 @ 2 15,000 @ 2.30	84,500	15,000	34,500
18 May	20,000	2.50	50,000				15,000 20,000 35,000	34,500 50,000 84,500
27 May				10,000	2.30	23,000	5,000 20,000 25,000	11,500 50,000 61,500

Activity 5

B   LIFO

Activity 6

What are the correct journal entries the following accounting transactions:

1   **D**   Dr Materials, Cr Trade Payables Control

2   **D**   Dr Production, Cr Materials

3   **C**   Dr Materials, Cr Bank

4   **C**   Dr Materials, Cr Production

9 Test your knowledge

Workbook Activity 7

Match the document with the correct situation.

Goods received note	Form completed by the purchasing department to order supplies
Purchase order	Form completed by the stores department detailing inventory requirements
Purchase requisition	Details the amount due to be paid and the date payment is due by
Stores record card	Form received with goods on delivery
Delivery note	Document completed to show the movement of inventory
Purchase invoice	Document completed by stores on receipt of goods

Workbook Activity 8

Cavernelli runs a pizza house. The inventory and usage of pizza bases for December was:

		Units	Value (£)
Opening inventory	1 Dec	200	180
Purchases	3 Dec	800	800
Purchases	20 Dec	1,200	1,140
Usage	w/e 7 Dec	400	
	w/e 14 Dec	350	
	w/e 21 Dec	410	
	w/e 28 Dec	475	

Calculate the value of issues and the closing inventory using the FIFO method of pricing (show figures to the nearest £).

The issues are priced at the end of each week.

Stores Record Card FIFO

Material: Pizza

Code: 1626

Date	Details	Receipts		Issues			Inventory	
		Units	£	Units	Price	£	Units	£

Workbook Activity 9

Crescent Engineering use a standard component AB3 and the inventory, receipts and issues for the month of September were:

Opening inventory 75 units @ £40 = £3,000.

Date	Receipts (units)	Unit cost £	Issues to production (units)
1 Sept	100	40	
10 Sept	75	42	
15 Sept			60
20 Sept			55
23 Sept	45	42	
30 Sept			50

The company uses the weighted average cost method for pricing issues and valuing inventory. Calculate the total usage for the month and the value of closing inventory (round per unit figures to 2 decimal places and total figures to the nearest £1).

Stores Record Card AVCO

Material: Component AB3

Code: 010203

Date	Receipts			Issues			Inventory	
	Units	Cost	£	Units	Cost	£	Units	£

Workbook Activity 10

Ravenscar Engineering uses a standard component XZ7.

It estimates the following information regarding this unit:

Weekly usage   50 units

Delivery period   5 weeks

The working year is 50 weeks

Ordering costs are £50.63 per order

It costs £5 per unit per year to store the component.

Ravenscar Engineering always keeps a buffer inventory of 20 units.

Calculate:

- Reorder level

- Economic order quantity

After further investigation of usage and delivery times it has been discovered that usage can vary from 30 units a week to 70 units a week and lead time can be as short as 3 weeks but at the most 7 weeks. Calculate the maximum and minimum inventory levels based on this information and your calculations above.

- Maximum inventory level

- Minimum inventory level

Workbook Activity 11

Kiveton Cleaning Services supplies its employees with protective clothing. One such item is protective gloves.

Records from the stores department for January showed:

1 Jan	Opening inventory 150 pairs @ £2 each
7 Jan	Purchases 40 pairs @ £1.90
15 Jan	Issues 30 pairs
29 Jan	Issues 35 pairs

Calculate the value of the issues and the closing inventory if the FIFO method is used to price the usage.

Stores Record Card FIFO

Material: Protective gloves

Code: 1607

Date	Details	Receipts		Issues			Inventory	
		Pairs	£	Pairs	Price	£	Pairs	£

What is the double entry for the receipt on the 7th January?

A   Dr Bank, Cr Materials

B   Dr Production, Cr Materials

C   Dr Materials, Cr Bank

D   Dr Materials, Cr Production

✏️ Workbook Activity 12

Retail Store Company

Issues are costed from the warehouse and transport department using the weighted average method.

Complete the stores ledger card below for an item of inventory in the clothing department for the month of May 20X8 using the weighted average method for costing issues and valuing inventory.

Note: Figures in the total columns should be shown to the nearest £. The company's policy is to round prices per unit to three decimal places.

Stores Record Card

Department: Month:

Date	Receipts			Issues			Balance	
	Quantity	Price £	Total £	Quantity	Price £	Total £	Quantity	Total £
1/5 Balance							2,420	12,584
7/5	2,950	5.500	16,226					
11/5	3,200	5.700	18,239					
14/5				4,105				
21/5	1,535	5.400	8,289					
27/5				1,800				
30/5				2,600				

What is the double entry for the issue on the 27th May?

A   Dr Bank, Cr Materials

B   Dr Materials, Cr Bank

C   Dr Materials, Cr Production

D   Dr Production, Cr Materials

Workbook Activity 13

Dennis plc has the following kg of raw material in inventory:

Date purchased	Quantity	Cost per kg (£)	Total cost (£)
April 24	500	1.20	600
April 26	450	1.30	585
April 30	600	1.50	900

Calculate the cost of issuing 1,000kg on 1 May and the value of the closing inventory (to the nearest £) using:

- FIFO
- LIFO
- AVCO

Labour

4

Introduction

Labour is a large cost for many organisations. The cost of labour will depend on the remuneration (payment) system used by an organisation for example: annual salary, hourly rates and overtime or piecework payments.

ASSESSMENT CRITERIA

Record cost information for labour in accordance with the organisation's costing procedures (2.1S)

Analyse cost information for labour in accordance with the organisation's costing procedures (2.2S)

CONTENTS

1   Employee records
2   Remuneration systems
3   Direct and indirect labour costs
4   Integrated bookkeeping – labour

1 Employee records

1.1 Personnel record details

When an employee joins an organisation it is necessary to record a number of details about him and the details of his job and pay. The personnel department completes this in the individual employee's personnel record.

The type of details that might be kept about an employee are as follows:

- Full name, address and date of birth.
- Personal details such as marital status and emergency contact name and address.
- National Insurance number.
- Previous employment history.
- Educational details.
- Professional qualifications.
- Date of joining organisation.
- Employee number or code.
- Clock number issued.
- Job title and department.
- Rate of pay agreed.
- Holiday details agreed.
- Bank details if salary is to be paid directly into bank account.
- Amendments to any of the details above (such as increases in agreed rates of pay).
- Date of termination of employment (when this takes place) and reasons for leaving.

Example

Jonathan Minor started to be employed by your organisation on 1 July 2001 as an engineer in the maintenance department of the organisation. He was born on 22 January 1983. His employee code and clock number are M36084 and his agreed rate of pay is £375.60 per week. He is to be paid in cash.

Complete the employee personnel record for Jonathan.

Solution

PERSONNEL RECORD CARD

PERSONAL DETAILS			EMPLOYMENT DETAILS
Surname: MINOR Other names: JONATHAN	Address: 24 Hill St Reading	Emergency contact: Jane MINOR 24 Hill St Reading	**Previous Employment History**
Date of birth: 22/1/83	Nationality: British	Sex: M	Employer: Date:
Marital status: Single		Dependents: None	(1)
National Insurance Number: WE 22 41 79 J9			(2)
EDUCATIONAL DETAILS			(3) (4)
Degree: –		Btec/HND: Engineering	**TRAINING DETAILS**
A Levels: 2	O Levels: 0	GCSE: 7 CSEs: 0	Course Date: attended:
University attended: – College attended: Reading Schools attended (with dates): Reading High (1994 – 1999) Reading Junior (1987 – 1994)			
JOB DETAILS			**OTHER DETAILS**
Date of joining: 1/7/01	Clock number: M36084		Bank account:
Job title: Engineer	Department: Maintenance		
Rate of pay: Date £ 1/7/01 375.60 pw	Overtime: 1½ times basic		Date of termination:
	Holiday: 15 days		
	Pension Scheme: Joined: 1/7/01		Reason for leaving:

1.2 Attendance records

In most businesses, **records** are needed of the time spent by each employee in the workplace (attendance time) and time spent on the operations, processes, products or services whilst there (job time). Such timekeeping provides basic data for statutory records, payroll preparation, ascertainment and control of labour costs of an operation or product, overhead distribution (when based on wages or labour hours) and statistical analysis of labour records for determining productivity.

Attendance may be recorded by using a **register**, in which employees note their times of arrival and departure, or by means of a **time recording clock** which stamps the times on a card inserted by each employee. Alternatively, employees may be required to submit periodic **timesheets** showing the amounts of normal and overtime work; these may also include job times.

1.3 Holiday records

An employee will usually have an agreed number of days holiday per year. This will usually be paid holiday for salaried employees but may well be unpaid for employees paid by results or on time rates.

It is important for the employer to keep a record of the number of holiday days taken by the employee to ensure that the agreed number per year is not exceeded.

1.4 Sickness records

The organisation will have its own policies regarding payment for sick leave as well as legal requirements for statutory sick pay. Therefore, it will be necessary to keep a record of the number of days of sick leave each year for each employee.

1.5 Other periods of absence

A record will need to be kept of any other periods of absence by an employee. These might be perfectly genuine such as jury service or training courses or alternatively unexplained periods of absence that must be investigated.

1.6 Source of information

Information about an employee's attendance will come from various sources such as clock cards, time sheets and cost cards.

1.7 Clock cards

A **clock card** is a document on which is recorded the starting and finishing time of an employee for ascertaining total actual attendance time.

A clock card is usually some form of electronic or computerised recording system whereby when the employee's clock card is entered into the machine the time is recorded. This will give the starting and finishing time for the day and also in some systems break times taken as well.

Clock cards are used as a source document in the calculation of the employee's earnings.

Example

Example of a clock card:

Works number:				Name:	
		Lunch			
Week ending	*In*	*Out*	*In*	*Out*	*Hours*
Monday					
Tuesday					
Wednesday					
Thursday					
Friday					
Saturday					
Sunday					
FOREMAN'S SIGNATURE:					

1.8 Daily timesheets

One of these sheets is filled in by each employee (to indicate the time spent by them on each job) and passed to the cost office each day. The total time on the timesheet should correspond to the time shown on the attendance record. Times are recorded daily meaning there is less risk of times being forgotten or manipulated, but these timesheets create a considerable volume of paperwork. Below is an illustration of a daily timesheet.

Example

Name:	Frank Smith				Date:	11/6/X5
Clock number:	3				Week number: 31	
Job order number	Description	Time		Hours worked	Rate	£
		Start	Finish			
349	Servicing Ford Ka Y625 AAB	9.00	11.05	2.05		
372	Repair to Range Rover TC03 XYZ	11.05	16.30	4.25		
Signed: F Smith	Certified: A Foreman				Office ref:	

1.9 Weekly timesheets

These are similar to daily timesheets but they are passed to the cost office at the end of the week instead of every day (although entries should be made daily in order to avoid error). Weekly timesheets are particularly suitable where there are few job changes in the course of a week.

2 Remuneration systems

2.1 Introduction

Employees in a business will be remunerated or paid for the work that they do. There are a variety of different ways in which this payment is calculated. The main systems of remuneration are:

- annual salaries
- hourly rates of pay and overtime payments
- piecework payments
- bonus schemes.

Different types of employees within a business may well be paid according to different systems depending upon which is the most appropriate for the type of work that they perform.

KAPLAN PUBLISHING

2.2 Annual salaries

Annual salaries tend to be paid to management and non-production staff such as administrators, secretaries, accounts staff, etc. The annual salary is simply divided by the 12 months in the year and that is the amount of gross pay for that employee for the month.

> ### :'Ọ́': Example
>
> The sales manager of a business has an annual salary of £30,000. What is the gross amount of his pay each month?
>
> **Solution**
>
> | Monthly gross pay | = | £30,000/12 |
> |---|---|---|
> | | = | £2,500 |

2.3 Hourly rates and overtime payments

Many production and manual workers will be paid for every hour that they work. Normally hourly paid workers will have a standard number of hours that they work each week. If they work for more than this number of hours then they will have worked overtime, which will usually be paid at more than the basic hourly rate.

Overtime has two terms that you need to be aware of – overtime payment and overtime premium.

- The **overtime payment** is the **total** amount paid for hours worked above the normal number of hours.

- The **overtime premium** is the **extra** paid above the normal rate for those overtime hours. For example, if an employee is paid time and a half for any hours above his/her basic, then the 'half' is the premium.

Overtime

Overtime payment
i.e. time and a half

Overtime premium
i.e. the 'half'

This distinction is often necessary for costing purposes, as the premium part of the overtime may be classified separately from the overtime hours at basic rate.

Overtime can be worked for a couple of reasons – **general pressures** in the workplace or to meet the demands of a **specific customer request**. This has an impact on how the overtime is treated in the accounts of a business.

Whether the **overtime premium** is treated as a direct or indirect labour cost will depend upon the reason the overtime was worked:

Premium

General pressure

Specific customer request

Indirect labour cost

Direct labour cost

Be careful when answering questions on labour costs – make sure to check what information you are being asked for. Do you need to show the overtime payment or premium? If an exam question asks for the payment then you would split your answer based on normal hours at basic rate and overtime hours at the basic rate plus the premium. If the question asks for premium you would record all the hours worked at a basic rate and then show the premium for the overtime hours separately.

Example

An employee works for a standard week of 40 hours at an hourly rate of pay of £8.20. Any overtime hours are paid at time and a half.

In one week he works for 45 hours.

(i) What is his gross pay, showing the overtime payment?

(ii) What is his gross pay, showing the overtime premium?

Solution

(i)

	£
Basic hours 40 × £8.20	328.00
Overtime payment 5 × (£8.20 × 1.5)	61.50
Gross pay	389.50

(ii)

	£
Basic hours 45 × £8.20	369.00
Overtime premium 5 × (£8.20 × 0.5)	20.50
Gross pay	389.50

Activity 1

Below is the weekly timesheet for Thomas Yung (employee number Y4791), who is paid as follows:

- For a basic six-hour shift every day from Monday to Friday – basic pay.

- For any overtime in excess of the basic six hours, on any day from Monday to Friday – the extra hours are paid at time-and-a-half.

- For three contracted hours each Saturday morning – basic pay.

- For any hours in excess of three hours on Saturday – the extra hours are paid at double time.

- For any hours worked on Sunday – paid at double time

Complete the columns headed Basic pay, Overtime premium and Total pay. Zero figures should be entered in cells where appropriate.

Employee's weekly timesheet for week ending 12 December

Name:		Thomas Yung	Cost centre:		Machining
Employee number:		Y4791	Basic Pay per hour:		£12

	Hours spent on:		Notes	Basic pay £	Overtime premium £	Total pay £
	Production	Indirect work				
Monday	6	2	1 – 3 pm cleaning machinery			
Tuesday	2	4	9 am – 1 pm training course			
Wednesday	8					
Thursday	6					
Friday	6	1	2 – 3 pm health and safety training			
Saturday	6					
Sunday	3					
Total	37	7				

Activity 2

An employee's basic week is 40 hours at a rate of pay of £5 per hour. Overtime is paid at 'time and a half'. What is the wage cost of this employee if he works for 45 hours in a week?

A £225.00

B £237.50

C £300.00

D £337.50

2.4 Piecework payments

Piecework rates are where the employee is paid per unit of output. The rate will often be based upon the standard (expected) time per unit. This method is an example of 'payment by results'.

Example

Graeme MacHue works in the Scottish Highlands producing carved wooden animals for a small company supplying the tourist market. In week 26 he worked 45 hours and his production was:

	Standard time allowed/unit
6 Stags	2.0 hours
5 Otters	1.5 hours
12 Owls	1.0 hour
6 Golden Eagles	2.0 hours

He is paid £5 per standard hour of production (irrespective of actual time worked).

What are his earnings for week 26?

Solution

		£
Stags	6 × 2 × £5	60.00
Otters	5 × 1.5 × £5	37.50
Owls	12 × 1 × £5	60.00
Golden Eagles	6 × 2 × £5	60.00
		217.50

Activity 3

A company operates a piecework system of remuneration. Employees must work for a minimum of 40 hours per week. Joe produces the following output for a particular week:

Product	Quantity	Standard time per item (hours)	Total actual time (hours)
Gaskets	50	0.2	9
Drive belts	200	0.06	14
Sprockets	100	0.1	12
Gears	10	0.7	6
			41

He is paid £6.20 per standard hour worked. What are his earnings for the week?

A   £129.60

B   £254.20

C   £241.80

D   £498.48

Advantages of the piecework system:

- It produces a constant labour cost per unit.

- It **encourages efficient work** – an employee taking more than the standard time per unit will only be paid for the standard time. In order for this to motivate, the employee must accept the standard as fair.

To increase motivation, a **differential piecework system** may be implemented, whereby the piece rate is increased for higher output levels.

Disadvantages of the piecework system

- Employees **lack security of income**, so may become demotivated.

- The employee can be **penalised** for low levels of production due to factors that are outside his/her control (e.g. machine breakdown)

2.5   Guaranteed minimum payment

To overcome these disadvantages, the **straight piecework rate** may be accompanied by a **guaranteed minimum payment** (weekly or daily).

Example

Standard rate per hour   =   £4.50
Guaranteed minimum per week   =   35 hours

Actual production: 10 units @ 3 hours per unit. Calculate the weekly pay.

Solution

Standard hours   =   10 × 3 = 30 hours
Pay   =   30 × £4.50 = £135
Subject to guaranteed minimum pay   =   35 × £4.50 = £157.50

Therefore weekly pay   =   £157.50

The employee is paid whichever is the highest value

Activity 4

Jones is paid £3.00 for every unit that he produces but he has a guaranteed wage of £28.00 per eight-hour day. In a particular week he produces the following number of units:

Monday	12 units
Tuesday	14 units
Wednesday	9 units
Thursday	14 units
Friday	8 units

Jones's wages for the week are:

A £176

B £175

C £172

D £171

Activity 5

Continuing with the example of Jones above, what would be his weekly wage if the guarantee were for £140 per week rather than £28 per day?

A £176

B £175

C £172

D £171

2.6 Bonus schemes

Bonus schemes are a compromise between a day rate and a piecework system. Earnings will comprise:

(a) a day rate amount, based on hours worked, and

(b) a bonus based on quantity produced (usually above a certain standard) or on time saved in relation to standard time allowance for the output achieved.

Example

On a particular day, Fred worked for 8.5 hours, producing 15 units. The standard time allowance for each unit is 40 minutes. Fred's basic hourly rate is £4.50 and he is paid a bonus for time saved from standard at 60% of his basic hourly rate.

Calculate Fred's pay for the day.

Solution

		£
Day rate = 8.5 × £4.50		38.25
Bonus		
Standard time 15 × 40/60	10 hours	
Actual time	8.5 hours	
	———	
Time saved	1.5 hours	
	———	
Bonus = 1.5 × £4.50 × 60%		4.05
		———
Total		42.30
		———

2.7 Group bonus schemes

In the case of, for example, an assembly line, where it is impossible for an individual worker on the line to increase productivity without the others also doing so, a group bonus scheme may be used. The bonus is calculated by reference to the output of the group and split between the members of the group (often equally).

Example

Ten employees work as a group. The standard output for the group is 200 units per hour and when this is exceeded each employee in the group is paid a bonus in addition to the hourly wage.

The bonus percentage is calculated as follows:

$$50\% \times \frac{\text{Excess units}}{\text{Standard units}}$$

The percentage is then applied to the standard hourly wage rate of £7.20 to calculate the bonus per hour for each employee:

The following is one week's record of production by the group:

	Hours worked	Production units
Monday	90	24,500
Tuesday	88	20,600
Wednesday	90	24,200
Thursday	84	20,100
Friday	88	20,400
Saturday	40	10,200
	480	120,000

Solution

The standard number of units for the time worked

480 × 200 = 96,000 units

The number of excess units produced

120,000 – 96,000 = 24,000 units

The bonus calculation

24,000/96,000 × 50% = 0.125 = 12.5%

Individual hourly bonus

£7.20 × 0.125 = £0.90

Group bonus

480 × £0.90 = £432

If Jones worked for 42 hours and was paid £6.00 per hour as a basic rate what would be his total pay for this week?

Basic	=	42 × £6.00	=	£252
Bonus	=	42 × £0.90	=	£37.80
Total			=	£289.80

2.8 Holiday pay

As well as the normal payments of wages and salaries, there are other labour costs which include holiday pay and training time.

Holiday pay is non-productive, but it is nevertheless charged to the cost of production by allocating the full year's holiday pay to overhead and charging it to production for the whole year.

Alternatively, wages may be allocated at **labour rates inflated to include holiday pay** and other non-productive time costs.

2.9 Training time and supervisors' wages

Wages paid during a period of **training** may be charged partly to the job and partly to production overhead. The fact that learners work more slowly than trained employees is offset by the learners' lower rate of pay. Apprentices' remuneration will be charged to a separate account.

Normally, **supervisors' wages** are treated as part of department overhead unless only a particular job is concerned. Where instruction is being given, the remuneration of instructors and supervisors may be included in training time.

2.10 Summary

Different types of employee in an organisation will be paid in different ways. For example, management are normally paid by salary, production workers will be either hourly paid or paid on a piecework basis and the sales team may well be paid according to a bonus scheme.

---

3 Direct and indirect labour costs

3.1 Recap on direct and indirect costs

- A **direct** cost is an item of cost that is traceable directly to a cost unit.

- An **indirect** cost is a cost that either cannot be identified with any one finished unit. Such costs are often referred to as 'overheads'.

We have seen that there are a variety of different methods of remunerating employees and a number of different elements to this remuneration. For costing purposes the total labour costs must be split between the **direct labour costs**, which can be charged to the units of **production** and any **indirect labour costs**, which are charged as **overheads** to the relevant cost centre.

3.2 Production workers

The wages that are paid to the production workers will **on the whole be direct labour costs** so long as they **relate directly** to the production of output, known as basic rate. The direct labour cost will also include the basic rate for any overtime hours but the **overtime premium** may be treated as an indirect cost.

3.3 Overtime premium

Whether the overtime premium is treated as a direct or indirect labour cost will depend upon the reasons for the overtime:

- If the overtime is worked due to a customer's specific instruction, then the overtime premium will be treated as a direct labour cost.

- If the overtime is due to general pressure of work, then the premium is treated as an indirect labour cost.

3.4 Holiday pay

Holiday pay is normally treated as an **indirect** labour cost as **no production** is occurring.

3.5 Training time

The hours paid for the labour force to train are treated as an **indirect** labour cost as **no production** is occurring.

3.6 Idle time

Controllable idle time is treated as an indirect labour cost. Uncontrollable idle time is treated as an expense in the costing income statement.

It should obviously be prevented as far as possible. It is important to analyse the causes of idle time so that necessary corrective action can be taken. There are three groups of causes of idle time:

(a) Productive causes (e.g. machine breakdown, power failure or time spent waiting for work, tools, materials or instructions).

(b) Administrative causes (e.g. surplus capacity, policy changes, unforeseen drop in demand).

(c) Economic causes (e.g. seasonal fluctuations in demand, cyclical fluctuations in demand, changes in demand because of tax changes).

3.7 Management and supervisors' salaries

Management salaries and supervisors' salaries are all labour costs that are **not related to actual production** of the cost units, therefore they are all treated as **indirect labour costs**.

Activity 6

G Dickson is a football manufacturer. Classify the following costs by nature (direct or indirect) in the table below.

Cost	Direct	Indirect
Basic pay for production workers		
Supervisors wages		
Bonus for salesman		
Production workers overtime premium due to general pressures.		
Holiday pay for production workers		
Sick pay for supervisors		
Time spent by production workers cleaning the machinery		

---

4 Integrated bookkeeping – labour

4.1 Introduction

The costs of a business have to be recorded in a bookkeeping system. Many businesses use an **integrated bookkeeping system** where the ledger accounts kept provide the necessary **information for both costing and financial accounting**.

4.2 Wages control account

Accounting for wages and salaries is based upon two fundamental principles:

- The accounts must reflect the full cost to the employer of employing someone.

- The accounts must show the payable for PAYE and NIC that must be paid over to the HMRC.

There are three accounts to record transactions:

- The wages expense account, which shows the total expense to business i.e. Gross Pay and Employer's NIC.

- The PAYE/NIC account /Trade Union account/Pension account which is used to record the liability owed to HMRC/due to Trade Union/Pension Company.

- The wages and salaries control account which is used as a control. One side of each double entry is put through the control account. This account is cleared out each payroll run and there is never a balance brought down.

The **wages and salaries control account** can also be called the **labour cost account** in a management accounting system.

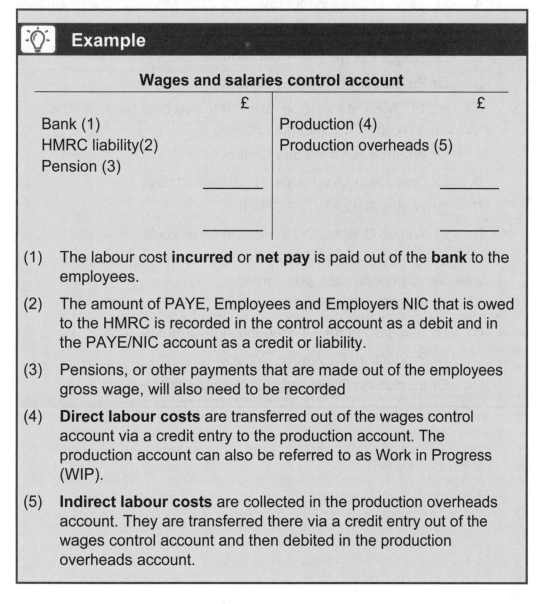

Example

Wages and salaries control account

	£		£
Bank (1)		Production (4)	
HMRC liability(2)		Production overheads (5)	
Pension (3)			

(1) The labour cost **incurred** or **net pay** is paid out of the **bank** to the employees.

(2) The amount of PAYE, Employees and Employers NIC that is owed to the HMRC is recorded in the control account as a debit and in the PAYE/NIC account as a credit or liability.

(3) Pensions, or other payments that are made out of the employees gross wage, will also need to be recorded

(4) **Direct labour costs** are transferred out of the wages control account via a credit entry to the production account. The production account can also be referred to as Work in Progress (WIP).

(5) **Indirect labour costs** are collected in the production overheads account. They are transferred there via a credit entry out of the wages control account and then debited in the production overheads account.

Activity 7

What are the correct journal entries the following accounting transactions:

1   Payment for labour:

   A   Dr Bank, Cr Wages Control

   B   Dr Trade Payables Control, Cr Wages Control

   C   Dr Wages Control, Cr Bank

   D   Dr Wages Control, Cr Trade Payables Control

2   Analysis of direct labour:

   A   Dr Bank, Cr Wages Control

   B   Dr Wages Control, Cr Bank

   C   Dr Wages Control, Cr Production

   D   Dr Production, Cr Wages Control

3   Analysis of payment for labour relating to overtime premium that was due to a specific customer request:

   A   Dr Production, Cr Wages Control

   B   Dr Production Overheads, Cr Wages Control

   C   Dr Wages Control, Cr Production

   D   Dr Wages Control, Cr Production Overheads

4   Analysis of payment for labour relating to overtime premium that was due to general work pressures.

   A   Dr Wages Control, Cr Production

   B   Dr Wages Control, Cr Production Overheads

   C   Dr Production, Cr Wages Control

   D   Dr Production Overheads, Cr Wages Control

Activity 8

Below is the weekly timesheet for Ekta Plasm (employee number EP0516), who is paid as follows:

- For a basic six-hour shift every day from Monday to Friday – basic pay.

- For any overtime in excess of the basic six hours, on any day from Monday to Friday – the extra hours are paid at time-and-a-third.

- For three contracted hours each Saturday morning – basic pay.

- For any hours in excess of three hours on Saturday – the extra hours are paid at double time.

- For any hours worked on Sunday – paid at double time

- Any overtime worked is due to general work pressures

Complete the columns headed Basic pay, Overtime premium and Total pay. Zero figures should be entered in cells where appropriate.

Employee's weekly timesheet for week ending 24 April						
Name:		Ekta Plasm		Cost centre:		Sewing
Employee number:		EP0516		Basic Pay per hour: £9		
	Hours spent on:		Notes	Basic pay £	Overtime premium £	Total pay £
	Production	Indirect work				
Monday	6					
Tuesday	3	3	10am – 1pm training course			
Wednesday	8					
Thursday	7					
Friday	6	1	2-3pm health and safety training			
Saturday	5					
Sunday	3					
Total	38	4				

Complete the Wages Control account below from the timesheet above.

Wages Control account

	£		£
Bank		Production	
		Production overheads	
	_____		_____
	_____		_____

5 Summary

This chapter has considered the **methods of payment** of labour that may be used by organisations. These may be annual salaries, hourly rates of pay, performance related pay (piecework) and profit related pay (bonus schemes). In order to pay the correct amount to employees there must be detailed recording of the time spent at work by each employee on time sheets or by a time clock and clock cards.

The distribution between **direct and indirect labour** costs is an important one.

Direct labour costs including the following:

- production workers' wages (excluding overtime premiums)
- bonus payments for production workers
- overtime premiums where overtime was worked at the specific request of the customer.

Indirect labour costs include the following:

- holiday pay
- training time
- idle time
- supervisors' salaries
- management salaries
- overtime premiums where overtime was due to the general pressure of work.
- production supervisors' wages that cannot be allocated to specific cost units.

Answers to chapter activities

📝 Activity 1

Employee's weekly timesheet for week ending 12 December

Name:		Thomas Yung	Cost centre:		Machining
Employee number:		Y4791	**Basic Pay per hour: £12**		

	Hours spent on:		Notes	Basic pay £	Overtime premium £	Total pay £
	Production	Indirect work				
Monday	6	2	1 – 3pm cleaning machinery	96	12	108
Tuesday	2	4	9am – 1pm training course	72	0	72
Wednesday	8			96	12	108
Thursday	6			72	0	72
Friday	6	1	2 – 3pm health and safety training	84	6	90
Saturday	6			72	36	108
Sunday	3			36	36	72
Total	37	7		528	102	630

📝 Activity 2

B

Basic	= 40 × 5	= £200
Overtime	= 5 × 5 × 1.5	= £37.50
Total pay		= £237.50

Activity 3

C   £241.80

Answer: Multiply the quantity by the standard time per item for each item to give a standard time of 39 hours. This is multiplied by the rate per standard hour. 39 × £6.20 = £241.80.

Activity 4

A

Total weekly wage:

	£
Monday (12 × £3)	36
Tuesday (14 × £3)	42
Wednesday (guaranteed)	28
Thursday (14 × £3)	42
Friday (guaranteed)	28
	176

Activity 5

D

	£
Monday (12 × £3)	36
Tuesday (14 × £3)	42
Wednesday (9 × £3)	27
Thursday (14 × £3)	42
Friday (8 × £3)	24
	171

As the weekly earnings are above £140, the guaranteed amount is not relevant to the calculations in this instance.

Activity 6

Cost	Direct	Indirect
Basic pay for production workers	☑	
Supervisors wages		☑
Bonus for salesman		☑
Production workers overtime premium due to general pressures.		☑
Holiday pay for production workers		☑
Sick pay for supervisors		☑
Time spent by production workers cleaning the machinery		☑

Activity 7

1   Payment for labour:

    C   Dr Wages control, Cr Bank

2   Analysis of direct labour:

    D   Dr Production, Cr Wages control

3   Analysis of payment for labour relating to overtime premium that was due to a specific customer request:

    A   Dr Production, Cr Wages control

4   Analysis of payment for labour relating to overtime premium that was due to general work pressures.

    D   Dr Production Overheads, Cr Wages control

Activity 8

Employee's weekly timesheet for week ending 24 April						
Name: Ekta Plasm				**Cost centre:** Sewing		
Employee number: EP0516				**Basic Pay per hour:** £9		
	Hours spent on:		Notes	Basic pay £	Overtime premium £	Total pay £
	Production	Indirect work				
Monday	6			54	0	54
Tuesday	3	3	10am – 1pm training course	54	0	54
Wednesday	8			72	6	78
Thursday	7			63	3	66
Friday	6	1	2 – 3pm health and safety training	63	3	66
Saturday	5			45	18	63
Sunday	3			27	27	54
Total	38	4		378	57	435

Wages control account

	£		£
Bank	435	Production	342
		Production overheads	93
	_____		_____
	435		435
	_____		_____

Production is **direct** labour cost **only** therefore the cost is:

Basic hours less the time spent on non-production activities

£378 – (4 × 9) = £342

Production overheads are the **indirect costs** (the overtime is worked due to general work pressure so is classed as indirect) therefore the cost is:

57 + (4 × 9) = £93

6 Test your knowledge

Workbook Activity 9

Brown and Jones is a firm of joiners. They have a workshop and employ six craftsmen. One of the employees is engaged on the production of standard doors for a local firm of builders.

This employee is paid a bonus based on time saved. The time saved is paid at a rate of 50% of the basic hourly rate.

In addition to the bonus, hours worked over the basic 40 per week are paid at time and a half.

In the week ended 13 February 20X1 the following details were available.

Basic hourly rate	£6.00
Time allowed per standard door	2 hours
Doors produced	25
Time worked	45 hours

The employee's gross pay for the week ended 13 February 20X1 is:

A   £270

B   £285

C   £300

D   £315

Workbook Activity 10

The following information relates to direct labour costs incurred during July 20Y0:

Normal time hours worked	8,000 hours
Overtime at time and a half worked	1,500 hours
Overtime at double time worked	1,000 hours
Total hours worked	10,500 hours
Normal time hourly rate	£7 per hour

Overtime premiums paid are included as part of direct labour costs.

The total cost of direct labour for the month of July 20Y0.

A   £91,000

B   £85,750

C   £70,000

D   £73,500

Expenses

5

Introduction

All other costs that are not material or labour related are known as expenses. This chapter looks at the distinction between different types of expense, how expenses are recorded and the difference between capital and revenue expenditure.

KNOWLEDGE
Record cost information for expenses in accordance with the organisation's costing procedures (2.1S)
Analyse cost information for expenses in accordance with the organisation's costing procedures (2.2S)

CONTENTS

1 Expenses
2 Direct and indirect expenses
3 Recording expenses
4 Capital and revenue expenditure

1 Expenses

1.1 Introduction

Costs incurred by a business, other than material and labour costs, are known as expenses.

Expenses of a business can cover a wide variety of areas. They might include:

- rent and rates
- electricity and power costs
- hire of machinery
- royalties
- patent costs
- sub-contractors costs
- insurance
- petrol for the delivery vans
- depreciation (depreciation provides a way of spreading the cost of a non-current asset over the life of the asset)

The list could go on and we will consider many of these later in this chapter and in the next chapters.

2 Direct and indirect expenses

2.1 Introduction

Remember that direct costs are those that can be related directly to a **cost unit,** whilst indirect costs (overheads) cannot be specifically traced to individual units.

2.2 Direct expenses

Expenses are far more likely to be indirect; however, some examples of direct expenses are given below.

Note that direct expenses are production costs.

- **Royalty or patent costs** payable for use of a particular component, technique, trade name, etc. in the production or service.

- **Sub-contracted charges**: if the business hires another company or a self-employed person to perform a particular function directly related to the product or service provided, this will be treated as a direct expense.

- Expenses associated with **machinery or equipment** used for a particular job: hire charges, maintenance, power, etc.

Note that payments to a sub-contractor are not treated as labour costs but as a direct expense.

For example, a building contractor will very often use sub-contractors to carry out electrical and plumbing work on a particular contract. The charge invoiced to the builder for this work (which will include both labour and materials) will be analysed as a direct expense of the contract.

2.3 Indirect expenses (overheads)

Indirect expenses are far more common and can be categorised in various ways, depending upon the organisational structure of the business and the level of detail required in the cost accounts.

Depending upon their nature, indirect expenses may be:

- production costs (production overheads); or

- non-production costs (non-production overheads).

3   Recording expenses

3.1 Allocation to cost centres

For control purposes, all costs eventually need to be **allocated to cost centres and/or cost units**. For materials and labour costs, this may be achieved by use of coded materials requisitions or analysed timesheets. The same principle will apply to expenses, although the allocation of indirect expenses may be done in stages.

The general approach to expense recording and allocation will be as follows.

3.2 Direct expenses

When the invoice arrives (e.g. from a sub-contractor), the relevant product/job/client will be identified and the invoice **coded** accordingly before being passed to the data processing department for recording in the ledgers.

3.3   Indirect expenses

These, by definition, will not be directly identifiable with a particular cost unit and will therefore initially be charged to an **appropriate cost centre**.

Some expenses will relate solely to **one cost centre**.

For example, advertising invoices will be allocated to the marketing/selling department and petrol bills for delivery vehicles will be charged to distribution. The invoices can therefore be coded to the appropriate centre.

Many expenses will, however, relate to **more than one cost centre** – for example, rent, rates and other buildings costs, where the building is shared by several cost centres.

Ultimately, these costs will need to be **shared between the appropriate cost** centres using some agreed basis (e.g. floor area occupied). This is known as overhead apportionment and is covered in detail in Chapter 7.

Initially, however, the invoiced expense will generally be coded to a '**collecting**' cost centre for such costs – for example, building costs may be defined as a cost centre in itself. The subsequent apportionment will then be made as a set of transfers from this centre to the appropriate organisational cost centres.

3.4   Documentation

Most expenses will be documented by way of a **supplier's invoice or bill**. The authorisation for payment, codings for posting to the appropriate ledger accounts/cost centres and other internally added information may be attached by way of a standard **ink stamp** with appropriate boxes for manual completion.

As with materials and labour, expense invoices will also be coded to indicate whether they are direct expenses or to which cost centre they are to be allocated if they are indirect expenses.

4 Capital and revenue expenditure

4.1 Introduction

One particular distinction in expenditure classification is between capital expenditure and revenue expenditure.

4.2 Capital expenditure

> **Definition**
>
> **Capital expenditure** is expenditure incurred in:
>
> (a) the acquisition of non-current assets required for use in the business and not for resale
>
> (b) the alteration or improvement of non-current assets for the purpose of increasing their revenue-earning capacity.

4.3 Revenue expenditure

> **Definition**
>
> **Revenue expenditure** is expenditure incurred in:
>
> (a) the acquisition of assets acquired for conversion into cash (e.g. goods for resale)
>
> (b) the manufacturing, selling and distribution of goods and the day-to-day administration of the business
>
> (c) the **maintenance** of the revenue-earning capacity of the non-current assets (i.e. repairs, etc).

In practice, there can be some **difficulty** in clearly distinguishing between alteration/improvement of non-current assets (capital) and their maintenance (revenue). For example, is the installation of a modern heating system to replace an old inefficient system an improvement or maintenance? However, you will not need to make such decisions in your assessment.

4.4   The accounting treatments

Capital expenditure is initially shown in the statement of financial position as non-current assets. It is then charged to the statement of profit or loss over a number of periods, via the depreciation charge.

Revenue expenditure is generally charged to the statement of profit or loss for the period in which the expenditure was incurred.

Activity 1

RFB plc makes wheels for a variety of uses: wheelbarrows, carts, toys, etc.

Complete the following form by putting a tick for each of the cost items into the appropriate column.

	Capital expenditure	Revenue expenditure
Purchase of a lorry		
Electricity and power costs		
Purchase of a chair for the office		
Road tax for the lorry		
Purchase of premises		
Repair of a broken window		

4.5   The relevance of the distinction to cost accounting

Cost accounting is mainly directed towards gathering and analysing cost information to assist management in planning, control and decision-making. In particular:

(a)   the determination of **actual and budgeted costs** and profits for a period and for individual cost centres and cost units

(b)   the valuation of **inventories** (raw materials, finished goods, etc).

Thus **revenue expenditure** is of far greater relevance than capital expenditure. The main impact of capital expenditure on the above will be the depreciation charges that arise and that may be charged as a direct product/service cost (as in the depreciation of machinery or equipment used in production or provision of a service) or as an overhead (depreciation of buildings, motor vehicles, etc).

5 Summary

We have now seen how expenses cover all expenditure that is not related to materials or labour. It is important that you are able to distinguish between **direct and indirect expenses**. Direct expenses are any expenses that can be related specifically to a cost unit. Indirect expenses are far more common and are known as overheads.

The distinction between **capital and revenue expenditure** is also important. You must be able to decide whether an expense is capital or revenue in nature. Revenue expenditure is written off to the statement of profit or loss in the period in which it is incurred, whilst capital expenditure is written off to the statement of profit or loss over a number of accounting periods, via a depreciation charge.

Answers to chapter activities

📝 Activity 1

RFB plc makes wheels for a variety of uses: wheelbarrows, carts, toys, etc.

Complete the following form by putting a tick for each of the cost items into the appropriate column.

	Capital expenditure	Revenue expenditure
Purchase of a lorry	☑	
Electricity and power costs		☑
Purchase of a chair for the office		☑
Road tax for the lorry		☑
Purchase of premises	☑	
Repair of a broken window		☑

6 Test your knowledge

✎ Workbook Activity 2

RFB plc makes wheels for a variety of uses: wheelbarrows, carts, toys, etc.

Complete the following form by putting a tick for each of the cost items into the appropriate column.

	Capital expenditure	Revenue expenditure
Repairs to machinery		
Purchase of new delivery vehicle		
Depreciation of delivery vehicle		
Vehicle tax for new vehicle		
Installation of air conditioning unit		
Redecoration of office		

Basic variance analysis

6

Introduction

In this chapter we are going to look at how to produce basic budgets, why budgets differ from actual results and the variances that arise.

ASSESSMENT CRITERIA
Compare budget costs with actual costs, noting any variances (4.1S)
Analyse variances for management reports (4.2S)
Provide information for budget holders of any significant variances, making valid suggestions for remedial action (4.3S)
Prepare management reports in an appropriate format, presenting these within the required timescales (4.4S)

CONTENTS

1 Fixed and flexed budgets
2 Causes of variances
3 Possible solutions for variances

1 Fixed and flexed budgets

1.1 Budgets

Budgets are prepared for number of reasons:

- To forecast future activity levels
- To communicate goals and objectives
- To plan for the use of resources – materials, labour, money
- To control the different departments
- To motivate by setting achievable targets

These are the same as the aims of management accounting.

1.2 Fixed budgets

> **Definition**
>
> A **fixed budget** is a budget produced for a **single** activity level.

A fixed budget is produced at the beginning of the period and is used to provide information as to the aims and objectives that the organisation is working towards in that particular period.

The simplest form of a budget report compares the original budget against actual results.

> **Example**
>
> | | Fixed budget | Actual |
> |---|---|---|
> | Units produced and sold | 1,000 | 1,200 |
> | | £ | £ |
> | Sales revenue | 10,000 | 11,500 |
> | Material costs | 1,300 | 1,040 |
> | Labour costs | 2,600 | 2,125 |
> | Fixed overheads | 1,950 | 2,200 |
> | Profit | 4,150 | 6,135 |

1.3 Analysis of a fixed budget and the actual results

The essential feature of any budgetary control system is the process of comparing budget with actual results. The difference between these figures is usually referred to as a variance.

> ### 🔍 Definition
>
> An **adverse variance** occurs when the actual costs exceed the budgeted costs or when the actual revenue is less than the budgeted revenue.
>
> A **favourable variance** occurs when the actual cost is less than the budgeted cost or when the actual revenue exceeds the budgeted revenue.

Using the information in 1.2 we are able to calculate the variances that have occurred:

> ### 💡 Example
>
> | | Fixed budget | Actual | Variance |
> | --- | --- | --- | --- |
> | Units produced and sold | 1,000 | 1,200 | 200F |
> | | £ | £ | £ |
> | Sales revenue | 10,000 | 11,500 | 1,500 A |
> | Material costs | 1,300 | 1,040 | 260 F |
> | Labour costs | 2,600 | 2,125 | 475 F |
> | Fixed overheads | 1,950 | 2,200 | 250 A |
> | Profit | 4,150 | 6,135 | 1,985 F |

Problems can happen if actual production and/or sales levels differ from the budgeted production levels. If we consider the variances above:

- Actual revenue is greater than budgeted but is this purely because we sold more units or is it because we sold them at a higher price?

- Actual material and labour costs are lower than budget but more units were produced so is this because we were more efficient with the usage of the material or use of the employee's time?

- Actual overheads are more than expected. Is this related to production levels or the actual cost itself?

If this control process is to be valid and effective, it is important that the variances are calculated in a meaningful way. One of the major concerns here is to ensure that the budgeted and actual figures reflect the same activity level. To overcome this issue budgets are flexed to match the actual production level.

1.4 Flexed budgets

> **Definition**
>
> A **flexed or flexible budget** is one which, by recognising cost behaviour patterns, is designed to change as volume of activity changes.

Flexed budgets are produced using cost behaviour and nature principles:

- **Variable costs** increase in direct proportion to activity, i.e. as activity increases so do the costs. Variable costs are constant per unit.

- **Direct costs** are assumed to be variable costs.

- **Fixed costs** are constant as activity increases. Fixed costs per unit decrease as activity increases.

- **Stepped costs** are fixed to a certain level of activity and then the cost steps up to a new fixed level.

- **Semi-variable costs** are costs that have a fixed and a variable element. The cost therefore increases as activity increases (the variable element) but will not have a zero cost at zero activity (the fixed element). The elements of the cost can be separated by using the high-low method.

- **Sales revenue** is assumed to have a variable behaviour unless stated otherwise i.e. the more units that are sold the more revenue there is and there is a constant selling price per unit.

If we flex the budget in 1.2

Example

	Fixed budget	Working	Flexed budget	Actual
Units produced and sold	1,000		1,200	1,200
	£	Working	£	£
Sales revenue	10,000	10,000/1,000 ×1,200	12,000	11,500
Material cost	1,300	1,300/1,000 × 1,200	1,560	1,040
Labour cost	2,600	2,600/1,000 × 1,200	3,120	2,125
Fixed overheads	1,950	N/A	1,950	2,200
Profit	4,150		5,370	6,135

Activity 1

Victor Ltd is preparing its budget for the next quarter and it needs to consider different production levels.

Complete the table below to calculate the flexed budgets for 1,500 batches and 2,000 batches.

Batches sold and produced	1,000	1,500	2,000
Sales revenue	40,000		
Variable costs:			
Direct materials	4,000		
Direct labour	3,800		
Fixed overhead	10,700		
Total cost	18,500		
Total profit	21,500		
Profit per batch (to 2 decimal places)	21.50		

1.5 Variance analysis using flexed budgets

When completing a budgetary control report using flexed budgets the flexed budget is prepared based on the actual activity level. This ensures that any variance discovered is not due to a change in activity level i.e. the number of units produced. Any variances identified will be due to the price charged or the amount used per unit of product. For example:

- If a material variance was discovered it would be due to the number of kg used per unit or the price paid per kg.

- If a labour variance was discovered it would be due to the number of hours worked per unit or the rate paid per hour.

The sub-division of variances into price/rate and usage/efficiency are covered at Level 4 but you need to be aware that the sub-division exists. This will be covered in more detail in a later section of this chapter.

Continuing with the figures from 1.2 – the **like for like** variances are:

	Flexed budget	Actual	Variance
Example			
Units produced and sold	1,200	1,200	0
	£	£	£
Sales revenue	12,000	11,500	500 A
Material cost	1,560	1,040	520 F
Labour cost	3,120	2,125	995 F
Fixed overheads	1,950	2,200	250 A
Profit	5,370	6,135	765 F

It is now possible to see:

- Actual revenue is adverse so we must have been selling at a lower price as we are now comparing using the same volume of sales.

- Actual material costs are still favourable so the usage of material or the price paid per kg of material was better than budgeted.

- Actual labour costs are still favourable so the efficiency of the staff or the rate paid per hour was better than budgeted.

- Actual fixed overheads were more than budget. Since they should not change when activity levels change this must be due an inaccurate budget or an unexpected expense occurring.

- Overall profit is more than budget – this we can be reasonably sure is because we have kept better control of the material and labour costs than planned.

Activity 2

Victor Ltd is now comparing its budget for the quarter with the actual revenue and costs incurred.

	Budget	Actual
Volume sold and produced	1,000	1,400
	£	£
Sales revenue	40,000	60,000
Less costs:		
Direct materials	4,000	6,000
Direct labour	3,800	5,300
Fixed overheads	10,700	13,600
Profit for the period	21,500	35,100

Complete the table below to show a flexed budget and the resulting variances, indicating if it is a favourable (F) or adverse (A) in the final column.

	Flexed budget	Actual	Variance value	Favourable or Adverse
Volume sold		1,400		
	£	£	£	
Sales revenue		60,000		
Less costs:				
Direct materials		6,000		
Direct labour		5,300		
Fixed overhead		13,600		
Profit for the period		35,100		

1.6 Reconciliation of actual with budget

Once the variances have been calculated it should be possible to reconcile the actual profit with the budgeted profit.

- An adverse variance will decrease the budgeted profit so this is subtracted from budgeted profit.

- A favourable variance will increase the budgeted profit so this is added to the budgeted profit.

Example

		Variance	
Flexed budget profit			5,370
		£	
Sales revenue	Subtract	500 A	
Material costs	Add	520 F	
Labour costs	Add	995 F	
Fixed overheads	Subtract	250 A	
Actual profit			6,135

2 Causes of variances

2.1 Investigation of variances

To be able to control aspects of the business, management will need to investigate why the variances have happened. To decide which variances to investigate management will consider:

- The size of the variance – is it significant compared to the cost incurred?

- The cost of investigating the variance – will it cost less to investigate and put it right than the variance itself?

- Whether it is adverse or favourable – some companies will only investigate the adverse variances?

- Ability to correct the variance – is the variance controllable in house (hours worked by staff) or uncontrollable (price charged by suppliers)?

2.2 Causes of variances

Differences between actual values and budgeted values can occur for a number of reasons.

One of the main reasons is that when producing a budget we are trying to predict the future. Prediction of the future is not an exact science and it is therefore extremely difficult to get it 100% correct.

This leads to the budgeted figures not being as accurate as they could be and therefore actual values are different from these.

2.3 Sales variances

A sales variance could occur for a number of reasons:

- **Price changes** – selling the product at a higher or lower price. This could happen if **discounts** are offered to the customer or discounts are removed or reduced, a price drop is required to remain **competitive** and/or an enforced price change due to **legislation**

- **Volume changes** – higher or lower volumes are sold than expected. This could be due to a successful or unsuccessful **advertising** campaign; changes in buyers' **habits**; a problem with production may reduce availability and/or changes in **market** conditions.

When comparing a flexed budget with actual results the volume changes are already accounted for by changing the volume in the budget to match actual sales volume

2.4 Material variances

When comparing a flexed budget with actual results we are looking at the material cost per unit of product. This can be broken down into the quantity of raw material that is used per unit and the price paid for the raw material.

Flexed versus actual comparisons remove the effect on cost that is due to the number of units manufactured.

A material variance can have a number of causes when we consider the raw material used to produce the product:

- **Price changes** – an increase or decrease in the price per unit of **material** purchased. This could be due to suppliers changing prices, loss or introduction of a **bulk discount**, higher delivery charges and/or a change in the **quality** of the material.

- **Usage changes** – an increase or decrease in the amount of material used. This could be due to more **efficient** or less efficient working conditions and/or a change in the **quality** of the materials purchased.

- **Quality** – if production uses a **higher quality** material then it will **cost more** to purchase. If a **lower quality** material is used it will be **cheaper** to purchase.

- **Combination of quality and quantity**. Higher quality costs more but may well lead to less wastage so use less. Lower quality costs less but may lead to more wastage so use more.

2.5 Labour variances

When comparing a flexed budget with actual results we are looking at the labour cost per unit of product. This can be broken down into the hours of labour worked and the rate paid per hour.

Flexed versus actual comparisons remove the effect on cost that is due to the number of units manufactured.

Variances in labour costs can be caused by:

- **Rate changes** – a higher or lower hourly rate is paid to the employees than expected. If a **higher grade** of labour is used then they will require **higher remuneration**. If a **lower grade** of labour is used then they will require as **lower remuneration**. There could be an increase in the basic rate of pay (minimum wage) or a bonus may have been paid.

- **Efficiency** of staff or the **hours worked** to produce output. If the actual time taken is **longer** than budgeted then this will **cost more** but if actual time taken is **shorter** than budgeted then it will **cost less**. This could be due to change in the grade of labour as the more experience the staff the more efficient they are assumed to be.

- **Overtime**. If there is extra time needed to complete the production then this may have to lead to having to pay some staff overtime. This is often paid at a **higher rate** than normal hours. This will **increase** the labour costs due to both increased hours and increased rates of pay

2.6 Fixed overheads variances

Fixed overheads should not change when activity levels change so the cause of any variance when comparing the flexed and actual figures is due to the budgeted **expenditure** being different from actual expenditure.

2.7 Interdependence between variances

In many cases the explanation for one variance might also explain why other variances occur. For example:

- Using cheaper materials would result in a drop in the price paid for materials (a favourable variance in the purchasing department) but using cheaper materials in production might increase the wastage rate (an adverse variance in the production department).

- An increase in wastage due to using cheaper material may reduce the productivity of the labour force leading to increased working hours to meet production demands (an adverse labour variance)

- Employees trying to improve productivity (work less hours) in order to win a bonus (increase in cost) might use materials wastefully in order to save time (an adverse material variance)

Activity 3

Victor Ltd has calculated the following variances. Discuss the possible causes for the variances.

	Flexed budget	Actual	Variance value	Favourable or Adverse
Volume sold	1,400	1,400		
	£	£	£	
Sales revenue	56,000	60,000	4,000	F
Less costs:				
Direct materials	5,600	6,000	400	A
Direct labour	5,320	5,300	20	F
Fixed overhead	10,700	13,600	2,900	A
Profit for the period	34,380	35,100	720	F

2.8 Sub-division of variances

Variances can be sub-divided to provide more detail:

- Sales variances can be sub-divided into the variance due to the quantity sold (volume variance) and the variance due to the sales prices charged (price variance).

- Material variances can be sub-divided into the variance due to quantity of the materials used (usage variance) and the variance due to the price paid for the materials (price variance).

- Labour variance can be sub-divided into the variance due to the hours worked (efficiency variance) and the variance due to the rate paid per hour (rate variance).

Activity 4

A company has a higher than expected staff turnover and as a result staff are less experienced than expected. As an indirect result of this, are the labour rate variances and material variances likely to be adverse or favourable?

	Labour rate	Material usage
A	Favourable	Favourable
B	Adverse	Favourable
C	Favourable	Adverse
D	Adverse	Adverse

Activity 5

A company is obliged to buy sub-standard materials at lower than standard price because nothing else is available, As an indirect result of this purchase, are the materials usage variance and labour efficiency variance likely to be adverse or favourable.

	Material usage	Labour efficiency
A	Favourable	Favourable
B	Adverse	Favourable
C	Favourable	Adverse
D	Adverse	Adverse

Note: You will not be asked to calculate the subdivisions, but you will be expected to answer discursive tasks that require knowledge of their subdivision.

Activity 6

Which of the following could be the cause of an adverse sales volume variance for garden furniture

(i)   The company offers discounts on sales prices in order to maintain business

(ii)   Poor weather leads to a reduction in sales

(iii)   A strike in the factory causes a shortage of finished goods

A   (i) and (ii) only

B   (i) and (iii) only

C   (ii) and (iii) only

D   All of them

3   Possible solutions for variances

3.1   Possible solutions for variances

Each variance should be considered in turn and any interdependence should be considered before solutions can be arrived at. Following are a number of possible solutions for variances that arise:

- Lower the price of the finished goods to increase volume of sales.

- Increase advertising to improve volume of sales without impacting on price.

- A change of supplier may be an option for improving prices for materials.

- Negotiation of bulk or trade discounts for materials purchased

- Updating machinery may make the usage of materials better and may also improve the efficiency of the labour force.

- Better quality control over the materials that are used in production may reduce wastage.

- Better supervision of staff may reduce idle time and errors in production.

- Increased training may reduce errors and make the staff more efficient.
- Closer monitoring of budgets may make the budgets more accurate.

This list is not exhaustive and it would be necessary to take each variance in turn and investigate the best way to improve the situation.

4 Summary

This chapter has demonstrated how **cost behaviours** are used to predict costs at activity levels different to budget and to produce **flexed** budgets. It will be necessary to be able to identify cost behaviours and use them to produce a flexed budget to then compare with actual results or **calculate variances**.

Another important aspect of this chapter is **analysis of variances** including possible causes and solutions to these variances.

Answers to chapter activities

Activity 1

Batches sold and produced	1,000	1,500	2,000
Sales revenue	40,000	60,000	80,000
Variable costs:			
Direct materials	4,000	6,000	8,000
Direct labour	3,800	5,700	7,600
Fixed overhead	10,700	10,700	10,700
Total cost	18,500	22,400	26,300
Total profit	21,500	37,600	53,700
Profit per batch (to 2 decimal places)	21.50	25.07	26.85

Activity 2

	Flexed budget	Actual	Variance value	Favourable or Adverse
Volume sold	1,400	1,400		
	£	£	£	
Sales revenue	56,000	60,000	4,000	F
Less costs:				
Direct materials	5,600	6,000	400	A
Direct labour	5,320	5,300	20	F
Fixed overhead	10,700	13,600	2,900	A
Profit for the period	34,380	35,100	720	F

Activity 3

	Flexed budget	Actual	Variance value	Favourable or Adverse
Volume sold	1,400	1,400		
	£	£	£	
Sales revenue	56,000	60,000	4,000	F
Less costs:				
Direct materials	5,600	6,000	400	A
Direct labour	5,320	5,300	20	F
Fixed overhead	10,700	13,600	2,900	A
Profit for the period	34,380	35,100	720	F

Sales revenue

As the budget has been flexed to match actual sales volume the variance can only be due to price. Victor must have been able to sell at a higher price than budgeted.

Direct materials

An adverse variance could be due to an increase in the price paid per unit of raw material or an increase in the volume used in production.

Direct labour

A favourable variance could be due to a decrease in the hours worked to produce the output or a decrease in the hourly rate of pay

Fixed overhead

An adverse variance could be due to understating the budget or an unknown expense occurring.

Activity 4

C

Less experienced staff are likely to be paid at a lower rate and therefore the labour rate variance will be favourable

Usage of materials is likely to be adverse as the staff are less experienced, thus there will be more wastage and a higher level of rejects

Activity 5

D

Usage of materials is likely to be adverse as the materials are sub-standard, thus there will be more wastage and a higher level of rejects

Time spent by the labour force on rejected items that will not become output leads to higher than standard time being spent per unit of output, therefore efficiency will decline.

Activity 6

C

Option (i) will cause an adverse sales price variance but would hopefully lead to a favourable volume variance.

Options (ii) and (iii) will both impact on the volume of garden furniture to be sold.

5 Test your knowledge

Workbook Activity 7

Youssef Ltd is preparing its budget for the next quarter and it needs to consider different production levels.

Complete the table below and calculate the estimated profit per batch at the different activity levels.

Batches sold and produced	1,000	1,500	2,000
Sales revenue	80,000		
Variable cost			
Direct materials	8,000		
Direct labour	7,600		
Overheads	14,400		
Fixed cost	7,000		
Total cost	37,000		
Total profit	43,000		
Profit per batch (to 2 decimal places)	43.00		

Youssef Ltd is now comparing its budget for the quarter with the actual revenue and costs incurred.

	Budget	Actual
Volume sold	1,000	1,200
	£	£
Sales revenue	80,000	100,000
Less costs:		
Direct materials	8,000	9,000
Direct labour	7,600	9,300
Overheads	14,400	17,500
Fixed cost	7,000	7,100
Profit for the period	43,000	57,100

Complete the table below to show a flexed budget and the resulting variances, indicating if it is a favourable (F) or adverse (A) in the final column.

	Flexed budget	Actual	Variance value	Favourable or Adverse
Volume sold		1,200		
	£	£	£	
Sales revenue		100,000		
Less costs:				
Direct materials		9,000		
Direct labour		9,300		
Overheads		17,500		
Fixed cost		7,100		
Profit for the period		57,100		

Overheads

7

Introduction

This chapter looks at how **overheads** (indirect expenses) are **allocated** or **apportioned** to cost centres and how overheads are then **absorbed** into the cost of a product via an **overhead absorption rate**. This chapter applies **absorption costing principles.**

ASSESSMENT CRITERIA

Attribute overhead costs to production and service cost centres in accordance with agreed bases of allocation and apportionment (3.1S):

– Direct
– Step down

Calculate overhead absorption rates in accordance with suitable bases of absorption (3.2S):

– Machine hours
– Labour hours

Make adjustments for under and over recovered overhead costs in accordance with established procedures (3.3S)

Review methods of allocation, apportionment and absorption at regular intervals and implement agreed changes to methods (3.4S)

Communicate with relevant staff to resolve any queries in overhead cost data (3.5S)

CONTENTS

1 Overheads
2 Production overheads
3 Allocation and apportionment
4 Reapportionment
5 Absorption
6 Under/over absorption of overheads
7 Integrated bookkeeping – overheads
8 Absorption costing
9 Non-production overheads

1 Overheads

1.1 Introduction

There are three categories of indirect costs (making up total overheads):

- indirect materials
- indirect labour
- indirect expenses.

1.2 Production and non-production overheads

Production overheads are included in the total production cost of a product. They could include factory rent, rates, insurance, light, heat, power and other factory running cost.

For a **service business**, it is more difficult to make a clear distinction between production and non-production overheads. For example, there is rarely a building that is devoted entirely to the provision of the service itself (i.e. equivalent to a factory) that does not also house the administrative, financial, selling and other functions of the business. Thus it is common to include most, if not all, of a service business's expenses under the other functional headings described below.

Non-production overheads can be split into different categories determined by why or how the cost is incurred:

(a) **Administrative costs**

These are usually: non-production buildings' running costs; staff and other expenses for the accounts, secretarial, data processing, general maintenance and other support service departments; management salaries and motor vehicle expenses; training costs.

(b) **Selling and distribution costs**

These are usually: sales persons' salaries, commissions, etc; running costs of sales showrooms and offices; delivery vehicle expenses; packaging costs; advertising and promotional costs.

(c) **Finance costs**

These are usually: loan and overdraft interest payable; bank charges; lease interest element; cost of irrecoverable debts.

(d) **Legal and professional charges**

These are usually: auditors', accountants', solicitors', financial advisors' fees; professional subscriptions; professional indemnity insurance; licence costs.

2 Production overheads

2.1 Allocation, apportionment and absorption

The purpose of **allocation** and **apportionment** is to attribute production overhead costs to production cost centres. The purpose of **absorption** is to include the production overheads of a cost centre in the costs of the units produced by the cost centre.

Where a business has a mix of production and service cost centres, it may be necessary to allocate and apportion production overheads to both types of centre and then **reapportion** the service centres' costs to the production centres.

There are 3 steps to achieving the process:

Step 1: Overheads are allocated or apportioned to cost centres using suitable bases.

Step 2: Any service centre costs are reapportioned to production centres using suitable bases.

Step 3: Overheads are absorbed into units of production again using suitable bases.

Overhead expenses Incurred

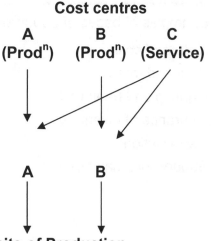

Step 1: Allocation or Apportionment

Cost centres

Step 2: Reapportion

Step 3: Absorb

Units of Production

Each stage of this process is detailed below.

3 Allocation and apportionment

3.1 Allocation

> **Definition**
>
> When an overhead relates entirely to one production or service centre it can be **wholly attributed** to that single production or service centre. This is allocation.

Examples of costs that relate to one specific cost centre are given below:

Cost centre	Allocated cost
Accounts	Accounting overhead
Machining department	Insurance of machines
Stores	Stores wages
Canteen	Maintenance of kitchen equipment
Packing department	Depreciation of fork lift trucks

3.2 Apportionment

> **Definition**
>
> When an overhead relates to **more than one** production and/or service centre it is shared over these centres on a fair or suitable basis. This is apportionment.

Examples of bases of apportioning overheads are as follows:

Nature of cost	Possible bases of apportionment
Rent and rates	Floor space (m^2)
Lighting and heating	Usage of electricity (KwH)
Insurance of inventory	Value of inventory
Depreciation	Carrying amount of asset
Supervisors' salaries	Time spent supervising

Example

Example of cost allocation and apportionment

A Ltd has three departments: assembly, machining and administration. It incurs the following indirect costs in the year to December 20X4:

	£
Oil for machining department	2,000
Salary of assembly department supervisor	20,000
Insurance of machines in machining department	4,000
Rent of factory	16,000
Maintenance salaries	40,000
Canteen costs for factory	15,000
	97,000

You are required to:

(a) Allocate the costs that can be allocated to the relevant department.

(b) Apportion the costs that cannot be allocated using the information below:

	Assembly	Machining	Maintenance	Total
Area (sq ft)	3,000	3,000	2,000	8,000
No of employees	15	10	5	30

Solution

Looking at the indirect costs it is possible to identify 4 costs that are wholly attributable to one centre – Oil for **machining**, supervisors' salary for **assembly,** insurance for the machines in the **machining** department and salaries for the **maintenance** department. These costs are allocated to specific centres.

The remaining costs relate to more than one centre so need to be shared or apportioned across the centre they relate to.

To do this, the calculation is:

$$\frac{\text{Total overhead}}{\text{Total of basis}} \times \text{centre basis}$$

Rent

Assembly

$$\frac{16,000}{8,000} \times 3,000 = 6,000$$

Machining

$$\frac{16,000}{8,000} \times 3,000 = 6,000$$

Maintenance

$$\frac{16,000}{8,000} \times 2,000 = 4,000$$

Canteen costs

Assembly

$$\frac{15,000}{30} \times 15 = 7,500$$

Machining

$$\frac{15,000}{30} \times 10 = 5,000$$

Maintenance

$$\frac{15,000}{30} \times 5 = 2,500$$

It is also possible to use percentages or fractions to share the costs over the cost centres. With some information percentages or fractions will be a quicker and easier to use to perform the apportionment and may save you time in the exam.

	Assembly	Machining	Maintenance	Total
Area (sq ft)	3,000	3,000	2,000	8,000
Area as a %	$\frac{3,000}{8,000} \times$ 100 = 37.5%	$\frac{3,000}{8,000} \times$ 100 = 37.5%	$\frac{2,000}{8,000} \times 100 =$ 25%	$\frac{8,000}{8,000} \times 100$ = 100%
No of employees	15	10	5	30
Employees as fractions	$\frac{15}{30} = \frac{1}{2}$	$\frac{10}{30} = \frac{1}{3}$	$\frac{5}{30} = \frac{1}{6}$	$\frac{30}{30} = 1$

Rent

Assembly

$16,000 \times 37.5\% = 6,000$

Canteen costs

Assembly

$\frac{1}{2} \times 15,000 = 7,500$

KAPLAN PUBLISHING

Machining

$16,000 \times 37.5\% = 6,000$

Machining

$\dfrac{1}{3} \times 15,000 = 5,000$

Maintenance

$16,000 \times 25\% = 4,000$

Maintenance

$\dfrac{1}{6} \times 15,000 = 2,500$

Overhead cost	Basis of allocation/ apportionment	Total £	Assembly £	Machining £	Maintenance £
Oil	Allocate	2,000		2,000	
Salary (supervisor)	Allocate	20,000	20,000		
Insurance	Allocate	4,000		4,000	
Rent	Floor area	16,000	6,000	6,000	4,000
Salaries (maintenance)	Allocate	40,000			40,000
Canteen	No of employees	15,000	7,500	5,000	2,500
		97,000	33,500	17,000	46,500

Activity 1

An organisation has four departments Fixing, Mending, Stores and Canteen.

The overhead costs for the organisation in total are as follows:

	£
Rent	32,000
Building maintenance costs	5,000
Machinery insurance	2,400
Machinery depreciation	11,000
Machinery running expenses	6,000
Power	7,000

There are specific costs that have been allocated to each cost centre as follows:

	£
Fixing	5,000
Mending	4,000
Stores	1,000
Canteen	2,000

The following information about the various cost centres is also available:

	Fixing	Mending	Stores	Canteen	Total
Floor space (sq ft)	15,000	8,000	5,000	2,000	30,000
Power usage %	45	40	5	10	100
Value of machinery (£000)	140	110	–	–	250
Machinery hours (000)	50	30			80
Value of equipment (£000)	–	–	5	15	20
Number of employees	20	15	3	2	40
Value of stores requisitions (£000)	100	50	–	–	150

Task

Allocate and apportion the costs to the four departments.

Overhead cost	Basis	Total £	Fixing £	Mending £	Stores £	Canteen £
Specific overheads		12,000				
Rent		32,000				
Building maintenance		5,000				
Machinery insurance		2,400				
Machinery depreciation		11,000				
Machinery running cost		6,000				
Power		7,000				
		75,400				

4 Reapportionment

4.1 Introduction

The next stage in the process is to apportion the service cost centre total costs to the production cost centres that make use of the service cost centre. This process is known as **reapportionment** or secondary apportionment.

The reason for doing this is that we want all the production costs to be identified with a **production** cost centre so that we can then work out the **cost of the units** that the production cost centre produces.

4.2 A single service centre

⌁ Example

A business has one service centre, the canteen, which serves two production centres. The overhead costs for a period have been allocated and apportioned between the three departments as given below.

	Production A	Production B	Canteen
Overhead	£10,000	£15,000	£12,000
Number of employees	100	200	

Reapportion the canteen's overheads to the production departments on the basis of the number of employees.

Solution

Exactly the same technique is used to reapportion as is used to apportion.

	Department A £	Department B £	Canteen £
Overhead	10,000	15,000	12,000
Number of employees 1:2	4,000	8,000	(12,000)
Total overhead for production department	14,000	23,000	

✎ Activity 2

The cost of the stores department and the personnel department of RFB plc have to be apportioned across the other cost centres. What bases would you recommend?

Stores department

A   Number of employees

B   Floor space

C   Number of issues to production

D   Kilowatt hours

Personnel department	
A	Number of employees
B	Floor space
C	Number of issues to production
D	Kilowatt hours

4.3 Two service centres

Problems may arise when there are two or more service centres that need to re-apportion costs to production cost centres. There are two ways of doing this that are examinable in CSTR:

(a) The service centres only supply services to the production cost centres i.e. they do not provide services to each other.

(b) One of the service centres (number 2 in diagram) provides services to the production cost centres and to the other service centre. The remaining service centre (number 1 in the diagram) only provides services to the production cost centres.

4.4 The direct method

This is used in situation (a) above i.e., where the service centres do not supply services to each other.

You will typically be given the information about which centre provides services to whom as follows.

Example

A business has two production centres, departments A and B, and two service centres, a canteen and a maintenance department. The proportion of the service departments services supplied to each department is as follows.

	Production A	Production B
Usage of maintenance dept	40%	60%
Usage of canteen	45%	55%

This tells you that the maintenance department supplies 40% of its services to department A, 60% to department B and nothing to the canteen.

The canteen supplies 45% to department A, 55% to B and nothing to the maintenance department.

Example

If we now add some numbers to the above percentage usage, the calculations will become clear.

The costs allocated and apportioned to the four departments are as follows (before any of the service department costs have been apportioned to the production departments).

	£
Production A	50,000
Production B	60,000
Canteen	8,000
Maintenance	10,000

Apportion the service department's costs to the production departments.

Solution

	Dept A £	Dept B £	Canteen £	Maintenance £
	50,000	60,000	8,000	10,000
Reapportionment of maintenance	(40%) 4,000	(60%) 6,000	–	(10,000)
Reapportionment of canteen	(45%) 3,600	(55%) 4,400	(8,000)	–
Total	57,600	70,400	0	0

It does not matter which service cost centre you re-apportion first when using this method.

4.5 The step down method

This is used in situation (b) above i.e., where one of the service centres supplies services to the other.

Example

We shall modify the above example so that the proportion of the service departments services supplied to each department is as follows.

	Production A	Production B	Canteen
Usage of maintenance dept	40%	45%	15%
Usage of canteen	45%	55%	–

This tells you that the maintenance department supplies 40% of its services to department A, 45% to department B and 15% to the canteen.

The canteen supplies 45% to department A, 55% to B and nothing to the maintenance department.

Apportion the service departments costs to the production departments.

Solution

	Dept A £	Dept B £	Canteen £	Maintenance £
	50,000	60,000	8,000	10,000
Secondary apportionment of maintenance	(40%) 4,000	(45%) 4,500	(15%) 1,500	(10,000)
Secondary apportionment of canteen	(45%) 4,275	(55%) 5,225	(9,500)	–
Total	58,275	69,725	0	0

The method is as follows.

Step 1 Identify the service department whose services are used by the other service department and apportion its costs to all the departments. In this case the maintenance department services the canteen so the maintenance costs are apportioned first.

Step 2 Now apportion the new total costs of the canteen (i.e. its original costs (£8,000) plus its share of the maintenance costs (£1,500)) to the production departments.

This is referred to as the step down method.

Activity 3

Adam has a factory with two production departments, machining and painting, which are serviced by the maintenance and quality control departments.

Relevant information for a particular period is as follows:

	Machining	Painting	Maintenance	Quality Control
Apportioned overheads	£20,000	£40,000	£10,000	£15,000
Maintenance	30%	60%		10%
Quality Control	50%	50%		

Required:

Show the reapportionment necessary using the step down method and the resulting total overheads to be attributed to each production department.

	Machining £	Painting £	Maintenance £	Quality control £
Apportioned overheads	20,000	40,000	10,000	15,000
Reapportionment of maintenance				
Reapportionment of quality control				
Total				

5 Absorption

5.1 Introduction

Having collected all indirect production costs in the production cost centres via overhead allocation and apportionment/reapportionment, the total overhead of each production cost centre must be charged to the **output of the production cost centres.**

Q Definition

Overhead absorption is the charging of a production cost centre's overhead costs to the cost units produced by the cost centre.

The **absorption rate** is calculated at the start of the period and is therefore **based on budgeted activity** and on **budgeted overheads**. Various bases for absorption exist and the most suitable one should be chosen depending on the situation.

5.2 One product business

It is possible to calculate the overhead absorption rate (OAR) using the planned production in units if only one type of product is being produced. If this is the situation the procedure to assign the correct amount of overhead to each unit is to allocate and apportion the overheads and then calculate how much overhead should be absorbed by each unit of product using the following calculation:

$$\frac{\text{Budgeted overhead}}{\text{Budgeted units produced}}$$

Once we know how much overhead each unit is absorbing we can calculate the full production cost per unit.

💡 Example

Henry produces one product. Each unit of the product uses £20 worth of material and £10 of labour. Henry has two production centres, assembly and finishing. The following overheads are expected to be incurred:

Rent and rates	£12,000
Light and heat	£15,000

The assembly department occupies twice the floor area of the finishing department. Production is budgeted for 1,000 units.

Calculate the assembly overhead cost per unit, the finishing overhead cost per unit and hence the total cost per unit.

Solution

Step 1

Apportion the overheads to the cost centres, on the basis of size, therefore in the ratio of 2 to 1.

Overhead	Basis	Total £	Assembly £	Finishing £
Rent and rates	Area 2:1	12,000	8,000	4,000
Light and heat	Area 2:1	15,000	10,000	5,000
		———	———	———
		27,000	18,000	9,000

Step 2

Calculate an overhead absorption rate per unit for each department.

Overhead per unit

Assembly

$$\frac{\text{Budgeted overhead}}{\text{Budgeted units produced}} = \frac{£18,000}{1,000} = £18 \text{ per unit}$$

Finishing

$$\frac{\text{Budgeted overhead}}{\text{Budgeted units produced}} = \frac{£9,000}{1,000} = £9 \text{ per unit}$$

Step 3

Total production cost per unit:	£
Direct costs	
Materials	20
Labour	10
Overheads	
Assembly	18
Finishing	9
	57

5.3 Multi-product business

The use of an absorption rate per unit is fine for one-product businesses/cost centres, but **may be inappropriate for multi-product businesses.**

Example

Sam produces pocket calculators and has one production department, incurring £15,000 overheads. Sam has planned production of 5,000 units.

Overhead absorption rate per unit = $\dfrac{£15,000}{5,000}$ = £3/unit

Suppose Sam instead makes 3,000 pocket calculators and 2,000 scientific calculators. The scientific calculators take up twice as much time to produce as the pocket calculators. The total overhead is the same as before. The overhead absorption rate per unit produced will be the same as before:

Overhead absorption rate per unit = $\dfrac{£15,000}{3000 + 2,000}$ = $\dfrac{£15,000}{5,000}$ = £3/unit

Decide whether this is a reasonable basis to absorb overheads.

Solution

This is probably not a reasonable basis. The scientific calculator takes longer to make and would involve the use of more of the indirect costs (e.g. supervisor's time). It is therefore necessary to choose an absorption basis that best reflects the demand of that product on the production department through which it passes. It may be more appropriate to calculate an overhead absorption rate per hour.

Bases commonly used as an **alternative to the rate per unit**, when more than one product is involved, are as follows.

(a) rate per direct labour hour

(b) rate per machine hour.

The calculation is as before but rather than dividing by budgeted units, budgeted activity it used:

$$\frac{\text{Budgeted overhead}}{\text{Budgeted activity}}$$

Whichever method or combination of methods is used, the result will still only be a **rough estimate** of what each product costs.

Example

Sam makes 3,000 pocket calculators and 2,000 scientific calculators. The scientific calculators take up 2 hours to produce and the pocket calculators take only 1 hour to produce. The total overhead is the same as before. The overhead absorption rate per hour produced will be:

Overhead absorption rate per unit = $\dfrac{£15,000}{3000hr + 4,000hr}$ = $\dfrac{£15,000}{7,000}$

$= £2.14/hour$

This then needs to be assigned on a per unit basis.

The pocket calculators take one hour to produce so will be charged with one hour's worth of overhead = £2.14

The scientific calculators take two hours to produce so will be charged with two hours' worth of overhead = £2.14 × 2 = £4.18

The difference in unit overhead charges should reflect the effort that has been made in producing the units.

Activity 4

Bertram manufactures three products, the cost of each being:

	Apple	Banana	Carrot
Direct materials	£14.40	£25.60	£36.00
Direct labour			
Machining @ £4.80 per hour	2 hours	1.5 hours	2 hours
Assembling @ £3.20 per hour	2 hours	2.5 hours	1 hour

Planned production is:

Product A 10,000 units

Product B 20,000 units

Product C 40,000 units

KAPLAN PUBLISHING

Production overheads for the forthcoming year are estimated at £120,000.

What would be the budgeted overhead absorption rate per product using the direct labour hour rate?

	Apple £/hr	Banana £/hr	Carrot £/hr
A	1	0.75	1
B	2	2	1.5
C	1	1.25	0.5
D	4	4	3

5.4 Choosing an absorption rate

The choice of which rate to be used depends largely on the nature of the operations concerned.

There is no correct method but in order to produce useful information it will always be preferable to choose an absorption rate which is in some way related to the costs being incurred.

Thus, for example, if the overhead consisted mainly of depreciation of machinery then it would be sensible to use the machine hour rate. On the other hand, if the overhead consisted mainly of the salaries of supervisors who supervise the workforce then it would make sense to use the labour hour rate.

Example

A factory has two production departments, cutting and finishing. The budgeted overheads and production details are:

	Cutting	Finishing
Budgeted overhead	£100,000	£80,000
Budgeted direct labour hours	10,000	40,000
Budgeted machine hours	60,000	5,000

The cutting department is a machine intensive department whilst finishing is labour intensive.

The factory makes two products, the Pig and the Cow. The production details for these are:

	Pig	Cow
Direct labour hours		
Cutting	1	2
Finishing	4	6
Machine hours		
Cutting	8	6
Finishing	2	2

Calculate the overhead cost to be absorbed into each product using an appropriate absorption rate for each cost centre.

Solution

Step 1 Choose and calculate the absorption rates

It makes sense to use the machine hour rate for the machine intensive cutting department and the labour hour rate for the labour intensive finishing department.

$$\text{Cutting – machine hour rate} = \frac{£100,000}{60,000}$$

$$= £1.67 \text{ per machine hour}$$

$$\text{Finishing – labour hour rate} = \frac{£80,000}{40,000}$$

$$= £2 \text{ per direct labour hour}$$

Step 2 Absorption into unit costs

	£
Product Pig	
Cutting 8 hours × £1.67	13.36
Finishing 4 hours × £2	8.00
	21.36
Product Cow	
Cutting 6 hours × £1.67	10.02
Finishing 6 hours × £2	12.00
	22.02

As the cutting cost centre is machine intensive then a machine hour absorption rate will best reflect how the overhead is incurred and, as the finishing cost centre is labour intensive, a direct labour hour rate is most appropriate in this cost centre.

Which rate should be used? Possibly both – **it depends upon the nature of the overheads**.

Activity 5

Pears plc manufactures children's clothing. The General Manager is concerned about how the costs of the various garments it produces are calculated. The material cost varies from one garment to another and the rates of pay in the various departments also vary to reflect the different skills offered. Both these prime costs are charged direct to individual garments so that any variation is taken into account.

	Overhead cost £000	Numbers employed	Labour hours	Material issued £000	Machine hours
Production departments					
Cutting	187	10	400	180	12,000
Sewing	232	15	300	240	28,000
Finishing	106	8	12,000	90	
Service departments					
Stores	27	2		–	
Maintenance	50	3		90	
Totals	602	38	12,700	600	40,000

Using the overhead analysis sheet below, apportion:

(a) (i) stores department's costs to the production and maintenance departments

    (ii) maintenance department's costs to the cutting and sewing departments only.

Select the most suitable basis for each apportionment and state the bases used on the overhead analysis sheet. (Calculations to the nearest £000.)

Overhead analysis sheet

	TOTAL	PRODUCTION			SERVICE	
		Cutting	Sewing	Finishing	Stores	Maintenance
	£000	£000	£000	£000	£000	£000
Overheads	602	187	232	106	27	50
Apportion store Basis:						
Apportion maintenance Basis:						
Total						

(b)   What would be the overhead rate for the three production departments if cutting and sewing were highly mechanised and finishing required high human input:

	Cutting	Sewing	Finishing
A	17.58	10.04	9.17
B	5.55	7.39	2.89
C	5.28	7.03	2.75
D	21.10	18.73	9.17

6   Under/over absorption of overheads

6.1   Introduction

The **overhead absorption rates** that were calculated in the previous section are calculated at the start of the accounting period. Therefore they are based upon **budgeted figures**. This means that the calculation is based upon the budgeted overhead cost and the budgeted production details, be it units, labour hours, machine hours, etc.

The reason for this is that management will need to know the **budgeted cost of each unit of production** in order to be able to make decisions about the products and the sales and production. This requires not only budgeted figures for direct materials, direct labour and direct expenses, but also for overheads.

6.2 Absorption of overheads

During the accounting period the cost of each unit produced will include overheads based upon the budgeted overhead absorption rate.

But what happens if:

(a) the **actual production levels** are different from the budgeted levels and/or

(b) the **actual overheads** for the period are different from the budgeted overheads?

If either or both of these occur, the use of the predetermined absorption rate will result in an **over- or under-absorption of overheads** (sometimes referred to as over or under recovery of overheads.)

Example

A factory budgets to produce 10,000 units, its budgeted overhead is £30,000 and the budgeted direct labour hours are 4,000.

The factory actually produced only a total of 8,000 units in the coming year, due to a machine breakdown, in 3,200 labour hours. In addition, the cost of machine repairs resulted in actual factory overheads amounting to £34,000.

The factory absorbs the overhead based on labour hours.

What is the under- or over-absorbed overhead?

Solution

The over-/under-absorbed overheads can be determined by the comparison of the actual total overhead cost with the overheads that are absorbed during production at the budgeted overhead absorption rate. There is a 3 step calculation to calculate the under- or over-absorption.

Step 1 – calculate the budgeted overhead absorption rate

$$\text{OAR} = \frac{\text{Budgeted overhead cost}}{\text{Budgeted activity}}$$

$$= \frac{£30,000}{4,000}$$

$$= £7.50 \text{ per direct labour hour}$$

Step 2 – calculate the overhead absorbed by actual production

Absorbed	= OAR × Actual activity
	= £7.50 × 3,200 hours
	= £24,000

Step 3 – calculate the under- or over-absorption

Under- or over-absorption	= Actual overhead cost – Absorbed overhead cost
	= £34,000 – £24,000
	= £10,000

The absorbed overhead is less than the actual overhead so there has been an under-absorption of the overhead

---

Activity 6

The actual overheads for a department were £6,500 last period and the actual output was 540 machine hours. The budgeted overheads were £5,995 and the budgeted output was 550 machine hours.

What is the OAR?

A   £11.82

B   £10.90

C   £12.04

D   £11.10

How much overhead will be absorbed into production?

A   £6,622

B   £5,994

C   £5,886

D   £6,383

What is the under- or over-absorption of the overheads?

A   £122 over

B   £506 under

C   £614 under

D   £117 under

KAPLAN PUBLISHING

✎ Activity 7

R Noble and Sons are a firm of agricultural engineers based in North Yorkshire.

They have a large workshop from which they operate. The business is divided into cost centres which include:

- Machining
- Fabrication
- Canteen
- Stores

A summary of their budgeted overhead for the three months ended 31 March 20X1 showed:

	£
Depreciation of machinery	5,000
Insurance of machinery	2,100
Heat and light	800
Power	1,750
Rent and rates	2,250
	———
	11,900
	———

Other relevant costs and data for the period showed:

	Machining	Fabrication	Stores	Canteen
No of employees	2	2	1	0
Value of plant	£40,000	£19,000	£2,500	£1,000
Floor area (sq m)	300	350	100	50
Kilowatt hours	600	500	400	250
Material requisitions	195	99	–	–
Direct labour hours	1,600	1,067	–	–

(a) Complete the overhead analysis sheet below (round to the nearest £).

Overhead analysis sheet

	BASIS	TOTAL	PRODUCTION		SERVICE	
			Machining	Fabrication	Stores	Canteen
Dep'n of machinery						
Insurance of machinery						
Heat and light						
Power						
Rent and rates						
Sub-total						
Reapportion canteen						( )
Reapportion stores					( )	
TOTAL						

(b) What would be the overhead rate per kilowatt hour for the production departments is:

	Machining	Fabrication
A	£12.15	£9.22
B	£4.56	£4.32
C	£37.38	£46.57
D	£24.30	£13.17

(c) Based on the OAR calculated above what would be the under or over absorption in each department if the following occurred.

The actual Kilowatt hours for the period were: machining 614 hours and fabrication 495 hours.

The actual overhead for the period was: machining £7,960 and fabrication £3,800

	Machining	Fabrication
A	£500 over	£764 under
B	£764 over	£500 under
C	£500 under	£764 over
D	£764 under	£500 over

KAPLAN PUBLISHING

7 Integrated bookkeeping – overheads

7.1 Introduction

The costs of a business have to be recorded in a bookkeeping system. Many businesses use an **integrated bookkeeping system** where the ledger accounts kept provide the necessary **information for both costing and financial accounting**.

7.2 Production overheads account

The production overhead account is where the movement of the costs associated with the overheads (indirect costs) are recorded.

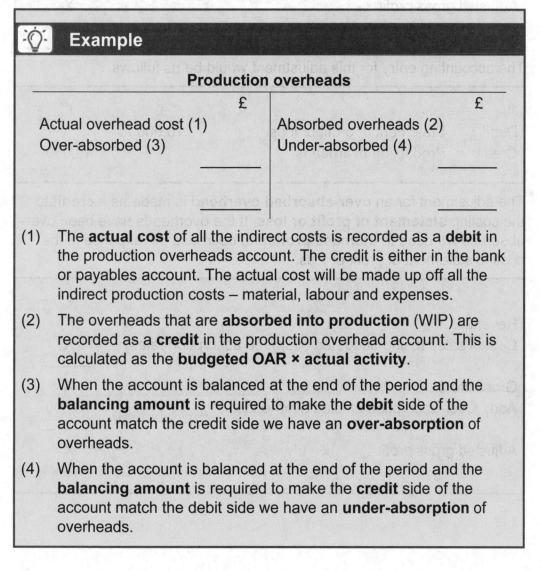

Example

Production overheads

	£		£
Actual overhead cost (1)		Absorbed overheads (2)	
Over-absorbed (3)		Under-absorbed (4)	
	————		————
	————		————

(1) The **actual cost** of all the indirect costs is recorded as a **debit** in the production overheads account. The credit is either in the bank or payables account. The actual cost will be made up off all the indirect production costs – material, labour and expenses.

(2) The overheads that are **absorbed into production** (WIP) are recorded as a **credit** in the production overhead account. This is calculated as the **budgeted OAR × actual activity**.

(3) When the account is balanced at the end of the period and the **balancing amount** is required to make the **debit** side of the account match the credit side we have an **over-absorption** of overheads.

(4) When the account is balanced at the end of the period and the **balancing amount** is required to make the **credit** side of the account match the debit side we have an **under-absorption** of overheads.

7.3 The adjustment for under-/over-absorption

The adjustment for an **under-absorbed overhead** is made as a **debit** to the costing **statement of profit or loss**. If the overheads have been under-absorbed we need to **decrease profit** and increase the expense in the costing statement of profit or loss.

	£
Revenue	X
Cost of sales (using budgeted overhead absorption rates)	X
Gross profit	X
Less: Under-absorption of fixed overheads	(10,000)
Adjusted gross profit	X

The accounting entry for this adjustment would be as follows.

		£	£
Debit:	Statement of profit or loss	10,000	
Credit:	Production overheads		10,000

The adjustment for an **over-absorbed overhead** is made as a **credit** to the costing **statement of profit or loss**. If the overheads have been over-absorbed we need to **increase profit** and decrease the expense in the costing statement of profit or loss.

	£
Revenue	X
Cost of sales (using budgeted overhead absorption rates)	X
Gross profit	X
Add: Over-absorption of fixed overheads	10,000
Adjusted gross profit	X

The accounting entry for this adjustment would be as follows.

		£	£
Debit:	Production overheads	10,000	
Credit:	Statement of profit or loss		10,000

Activity 8

What are the correct journal entries the following accounting transactions:

1   Indirect material issued from stores:

    A   Dr Bank, Cr Material

    B   Dr Production overheads, Cr Material

    C   Dr Material, Cr Bank

    D   Dr Material, Cr Production overheads

2   Indirect wages analysed in the wages control account:

    A   Dr Production, Cr Wages control

    B   Dr Wages control, Cr Production

    C   Dr Wages control, Cr Production overheads

    D   Dr Production overheads, Cr Wages control

3   Production overheads absorbed into the cost of production:

    A   Dr Production, Cr Production overheads

    B   Dr Production overheads, Cr Statement of profit or loss

    C   Dr Production overheads, Cr Production

    D   Dr Statement of profit or loss, Cr Production overheads

4   Over-absorption of overheads

    A   Dr Production, Cr Production overheads

    B   Dr Production overheads, Cr Statement of profit or loss

    C   Dr Production overheads, Cr Production

    D   Dr Statement of profit or loss, Cr Production overheads

8 Absorption costing

8.1 Absorption costing

Absorption costing values each unit of inventory at the total cost incurred to **produce** the unit. This includes direct materials, direct labour, direct expenses, variable production overheads and fixed production overheads. All these costs would be referred to as **product costs**. **Non-production** costs are considered **period costs** so are deducted in full from the gross profit.

🔍 Definition

Absorption costing is a method of building up a full product cost which adds direct costs and a proportion of production overhead cost by means of one or a number of overhead absorption rates.

This chapter has detailed the procedure for assigning production overheads to units of output.

The basic layout for calculating the budgeted profit or loss under absorption costing is as follows (with illustrative figures).

	£
Sales revenue (10,000 × £10)	100,000
Cost of sales (at full **production** cost, £8)	(80,000)
Gross profit	20,000
Less: **Non-production** costs	(12,000)
Profit for the period	8,000

Activity 9

XYZ plc

XYZ plc manufactures toy horses and has produced a budget for the quarter ended 30 June 20X5 (Quarter 1) as follows.

Sales	190 units @ selling price of £12
Production	200 units
Opening inventory	20 units
Variable production cost per unit	£8
Fixed production overhead	£400
Selling and distribution costs	£250

Required:

Draft the statement of profit or loss using absorption costing principles:

	£	£
Sales revenue		
Less: Cost of sales		
Opening inventory		
Production costs		
Closing inventory		
Gross profit		
Non-production costs		
Profit for the period		

8.2 Advantages of absorption costing

Absorption costing has a number of advantages:

- The costing technique adheres to the accounting standard for the valuation of inventory (IAS 2) so can be used for **statutory financial reporting**.

- When valuing inventory using absorption costing the total production cost is considered. This means that when deciding on a selling price all production costs should be covered.

- The analysis of under- or over-absorption of overheads is a useful exercise in controlling costs.

9 Non-production overheads

9.1 Introduction

So far, only production overheads have been considered. There are other, non-production overheads which can be divided into the broad categories listed below, all of which can be absorbed into each cost unit using similar methods as described, if desired.

But remember, if the **non-production overheads are absorbed into units**, the **cost per unit will not be the inventory value per unit**. The inventory value per unit comprises only the production costs, direct and indirect.

9.2 Administrative overheads

Expenditure attributable to the general office, data processing, finance charges and audit fees.

9.3 Selling overheads

Expenditure attributable to the selling of the product, e.g. sales personnel, costs of advertising, cash discounts allowed, rent and rates of show rooms and sales offices.

9.4 Distribution overheads

Expenditure incurred in packing and delivery.

10 Summary

This chapter has considered how the overheads of a business are gathered together and traced through to the cost units to which they relate. Under the **absorption costing** approach the budgeted overheads of the business are collected together in each of the cost centres, either by **allocation**, if the overhead relates to only one cost centre or by **apportionment** on a fair basis if the overhead relates to a number of cost centres.

Once the overheads have been allocated and apportioned, the next stage is to **reapportion** any **service** cost centre overheads into the production cost centres. Care must be taken here where the service cost centres provide their service to other service cost centres. In these cases the step down method is required to reapportion the service cost centre overheads.

When all of the budgeted overheads are included in the production cost centres, an **absorption rate** must be calculated. In many cases this will be either on a direct labour hour basis or on a machine hour basis. This will depend on the nature of the business and the nature of the cost centre.

The overhead absorption rate is based upon the budgeted overheads and the budgeted production level. This rate is then used to include the overheads in the production throughout the accounting period. If the activity levels and/or the amount of the overhead are different to the budgeted figures, then the overhead will be either **over- or under-absorbed**. An adjustment is made for this when the costing statement of profit or loss is prepared.

Answers to chapter activities

Activity 1

OVERHEAD ANALYSIS SHEET		PERIOD ENDING			
	Total	Production		Service	
		Fixing	Mending	Stores	Canteen
	£	£	£	£	£
Overheads allocated directly to cost centres	12,000	5,000	4,000	1,000	2,000
Overheads to be apportioned Rent Basis: floor space					
32/30 × 15,000	32,000	16,000			
32/30 × 8,000			8,534		
32/30 × 5,000				5,333	
32/30 × 2,000					2,133
Building maintenance Basis: floor space	5,000				
5/30 × 15,000		2,500			
5/30 × 8,000			1,333		
5/30 × 5,000				834	
5/30 × 2,000					333
Machinery insurance Basis: machine value	2,400				
2400/250 × 140		1,344			
2400/250 × 110			1,056	–	–
Machinery depreciation Basis: machine value	11,000				
11,000/250 × 140		6,160			
11,000/250 × 110			4,840	–	–
Machinery running expenses Basis: machine hours	6,000				
6,000/80 × 50		3,750			
6,000/80 × 30			2,250	–	–

	Total £	Production		Service	
		Fixing £	Mending £	Stores £	Canteen £
Power Basis: power usage percentages £7,000 × 45% £7,000 × 40% £7,000 × 5% £7,000 × 10%	7,000	3,150	2,800	350	700
Allocated and apportioned costs	75,400	37,904	24,813	7,517	5,166

Activity 2

Stores – **C**

Personnel – **A**

Activity 3

	Machining £	Painting £	Maintenance £	Quality control £
Apportioned overheads	20,000	40,000	10,000	15,000
Reapportionment of maintenance	3,000	6,000	(10,000)	1,000
				16,000
Reapportionment of quality control	8,000	8,000		(16,000)
	31,000	54,000		

Activity 4

B

	Apple	Banana	Carrot	Total
Production (units)	10,000	20,000	40,000	70,000
Production hours				
Machining	20,000	30,000	80,000	130,000
Assembly	20,000	50,000	40,000	110,000
Total hours	40,000	80,000	120,000	**240,000**

Fixed overhead per direct labour hour: $\dfrac{£120,000}{240,000} = £0.50$

	Apple £	Banana £	Carrot £
Overheads	(4 hr × £0.50) = 2.00/hr	(4 hr × £0.50) = 2.00/hr	(3 hr × £0.50) = 1.50/hr

Activity 5

(a)

Overhead analysis sheet	TOTAL	PRODUCTION			SERVICE	
		Cutting	Sewing	Finishing	Stores	Maint'nce
	£000	£000	£000	£000	£000	£000
Overheads	602	187	232	106	27	50
Apportion store Basis: Mat issued		8	11	4	(27)	4
Apportion maint'nce Basis: Mach hours		16	38			(54)
Total	602	211	281	110		

(b) **A**

	Cutting	Sewing	Finishing
Apportioned o/heads	£211,000	£281,000	£110,000
Machine hours	12,000	28,000	
Labour hours			12,000
Absorption rates	£17.58	£10.04	£9.17

Activity 6

(a) **B**

  £5,995/550 hours = £10.90

(b) **C**

  £10.90 × 540 = £5,886

(c) **C**

  £6,500 – £5,886 = £614 under-absorbed

Activity 7

(a) **Overhead analysis sheet**

	BASIS	TOTAL	PRODUCTION		SERVICE	
			Machining	Fabrication	Stores	Canteen
Dep'n of machinery	Value	5,000	3,200	1,520	200	80
Insurance of machinery	Value	2,100	1,344	638	84	34
Heat and light	Square metres	800	300	350	100	50
Power	Kw	1,750	600	500	400	250
Rent and rates	Square metres	2,250	844	984	281	141
Sub-total		11,900	6,288	3,992	1,065	555
Reapportion canteen	Staff		222	222	111	(555)
Reapportion stores	Requisitions		780	396	(1,176)	
TOTAL			7,290	4,610		

(b) What would be the overhead rate per kilowatt hour for the production departments is:

	Machining	Fabrication
A	£12.15	£9.22

(c)   *Machining*   *Fabrication*

    C   £500 under   £764 over

Machining actual = £7,960

Machining absorbed = £12.15 × 614 = £7,460

Under absorption   £500

Fabrication actual = £3,800

Fabrication absorbed = £9.22 × 495 = £4,564

Over absorption   £764

Activity 8

1   **B**

2   **D**

3   **A**

4   **B**

Activity 9

There will be closing inventory of 30 units.

Opening inventory + production – sales = closing inventory

The cost per unit will included the variable production cost and a proportion of fixed production overhead

The £400 fixed production costs will be absorbed into the 200 units of production, giving a fixed cost per unit of £2 and a total absorption cost of £10 per unit.

	£	£
Sales revenue (190 × £12)		2,280
Less: Cost of sales		
Opening inventory (20 × £10)	200	
Production costs (200 × £10)	2,000	
Closing inventory (30 × £10)	(300)	
		(1,900)
Gross profit		380
Non- production costs		(250)
Profit for the period		130

11 Test your knowledge

Workbook Activity 10

A company budgeted to spend fixed overheads of £5 per hour in a given month. The actual activity level for the month was 10,000 hours and the actual overhead expenditure was £48,000.

Calculate the over or under absorption of overheads for the month.

Workbook Activity 11

Ray Ltd has the following four production departments:

- Machining 1
- Machining 2
- Assembly
- Packaging

The budgeted fixed overheads relating to the four production departments for Quarter 3 2005 are:

	£	£
Depreciation		80,000
Rent and rates		120,000
Indirect labour costs:		
Machining 1	40,500	
Machining 2	18,300	
Assembly	12,400	
Packaging	26,700	
Total		97,900
Assembly costs		15,600
Total fixed overheads		313,500

Fixed overheads are allocated or apportioned to the production departments on the most appropriate basis.

The following information is also available:

Department	Carrying amount of non-current assets (£000)	Square metres occupied	Number of employees
Machining 1	1,280	625	8
Machining 2	320	250	4
Assembly	960	500	3
Packaging	640	1,125	7
Total	3,200	2,500	22

Complete the overhead analysis sheet below (round to the nearest £)

Overhead analysis sheet

	Basis	Total	Machining 1	Machining 2	Assembly	Packaging
Depreciation						
Rent and rates						
Indirect Labour cost						
Assembly costs						
TOTAL						

Workbook Activity 12

You have been asked to calculate the under- or over- absorption in a production division, this division is highly automated and operates with expensive machinery, which is run wherever possible on a 24-hour a day, seven days a week basis.

The following information relates to this division for July 20Y0:

Total budgeted departmental overheads	£400,000
Total actual departmental overheads	£450,000
Total budgeted direct labour hours	3,000
Total budgeted machine hours	10,000
Total actual direct labour hours	2,500
Total actual machine hours	9,000

What is the budgeted fixed overhead absorption rate for the division for July 20Y0, using the most appropriate basis of absorption?

A   £50.00

B   £40.00

C   £45.00

D   £44.44

What is the value of the overhead absorbed into production?

A   £500,000

B   £405,000

C   £360,000

D   £444,400

What is the under- or over absorption for the division?

A   £50,000 under

B   £50,000 over

C   £90,000 over

D   £90,000 under

What is the double entry for the above?

A   Dr Production overheads £90,000, Cr Statement of profit or loss £90,000

B   Dr Statement of profit or loss £90,000, Cr Production overheads £90,000

C   Dr Production overheads £50,000, Cr Statement of profit or loss £50,000

D   Dr Statement of profit or loss £50,000, Cr Production overheads £50,000

Workbook Activity 13

During period 5, the month of May 20X1, Lester Bird's under- and over-recovery of overhead per cost centre was:

Cost centre	Overhead absorbed	Actual overhead	(under)/over-absorbed
	£	£	£
Painting	3,950	4,250	(300)
Finishing	2,950	3,150	(200)
Trimming	1,640	1,600	40
Firing	2,750	2,600	150
	£11,290	£11,600	(310)

Post the total figures to the overhead account, showing the transfer of the under-absorption to the costing statement of profit or loss.

Production overhead control account

£		£
£		£

Workbook Activity 14

Biscuit Making Company

The general manager has asked you to monitor the absorption of overheads for the production departments for November 20X8.

Company policy is to absorb overheads on the following basis.

Department	Basis
Mixing	Per £ of labour cost
Baking	Machine hours
Packing	Labour hours

Budgeted and actual data for November 20X8 is:

	Mixing	Baking	Packing
Budgeted overheads	£164,000	£228,900	£215,000
Actual labour hours worked			16,000
Budgeted labour hours			17,200
Actual machine hours		16,100	
Budgeted machine hours		16,350	
Actual labour costs	£63,700		
Budgeted labour costs	£65,600		

Calculate the budgeted overhead absorption rate for each department.

	Mixing £	Baking £	Packing £
Budgeted overhead Absorption rate			

Complete the tables and production overhead account.

PRODUCTION OVERHEAD SCHEDULE			
Month:			
	Mixing £	Baking £	Packing £
Budgeted overheads			
Actual overheads	171,500	224,000	229,000
Overhead absorbed			

	Mixing £	Baking £	Packing £
Over-absorbed overheads			
Under-absorbed overheads			

Production overhead control account

	£		£
£		£	

Job, batch and service costing

8

Introduction

We are now going to turn our attention to three costing systems. **Job costing** involves individual jobs with different materials and labour requirements (for example, car repairs). **Batch costing**, on the other hand, is suitable for businesses that produce batches of identical items (for example, bars of soap) though batch costs may vary from product to product. **Service costing** is used when an organisation provides a service rather than a product.

ASSESSMENT CRITERIA	CONTENTS
Record cost information using these costing systems: (2.6S) – Job – Batch – Service	1 Different types of production 2 Job costing 3 Batch costing 4 Service costing

1 Different types of production

1.1 Costing systems

There are different types of costing system that are used depending on the type of production a business uses.

- **Specific order costing** is the costing system used when the work done by an organisation consists of **separately identifiable jobs** or **batches**.

- **Continuous operation costing** is the costing method used when goods or services are produced as a direct result of a **sequence of continuous operations or processes**.

2 Job costing

2.1 Job costing

Job costing is a form of **specific order costing** and it is used in a business where the production is made up of **individual jobs.** Each job is different and has different inputs of materials and labour. Each job is identified separately and the costs are identified for this specific job, coded to it and recorded as job costs. Effectively **the job is the cost unit**.

Typical examples of businesses that use job costing would be ship building, civil engineering, construction, aeroplane manufacture, and vehicle repairs.

2.2 Job card

Each job is given a separate identifying number and has its own job card. The job card is used to record all of the direct costs of the job and the overheads to be absorbed into the job.

KAPLAN PUBLISHING

A typical job card might look like this:

Example

JOB NO	217		
Materials requisitions	**Quantity**	**£**	**Total**
0254 G 3578	100 kg	4,200	
0261 K 3512	50 kg	3,150	
		――――	7,350

Wages – employees	**Hours**	**£**	
13343	80	656	
15651	30	300	
12965	40	360	
	――――	――――	
	150		1,316
	―――		

Overheads	**Hours**	**£**	
Absorption rate £12	150	1,800	1,800
		―――――	
Total cost			10,466
			―――――

Activity 1

Given below are the direct costs of job number 3,362.

	£
Materials requisitions:	
15,496	1,044
15,510	938
15,525	614
Wages analysis:	
Employee 13,249 40 hours	320
Employee 12,475 33 hours	231
Employee 26,895 53 hours	312

Overheads are apportioned to jobs at the rate of £3.50 per direct labour hour.

What is the total cost of Job 3,362?

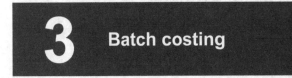

JOB NO 3,362		
Materials requisitions	**£**	**Total**
		_____
Wages – employees	**Hours**	**£**
	_____	_____
		_____
Overheads	**Hours**	**£**
		_____
		_____

The principles behind a job costing system are exactly the same as those in a unit costing system with the **job** being treated as the **cost unit**. A job costing system needs tight controls over the coding of all materials requisitions and hours worked to ensure that each job is charged with the correct direct costs and eventually overheads.

3 Batch costing

3.1 Introduction

Batch costing is also a form of **specific order costing**. It is suitable for a business that produces **batches of identical units**, but each batch is for different units.

For example, a clothing manufacturer may have a production run for a batch of men's white shirts of collar size 16 inches. It may then have a production run for a batch of men's trousers with a waist size of 34 inches.

Each batch of production will have different costs but each unit within the batch should have the same cost. Therefore the total cost of the batch of production is calculated and divided by the number of units in that batch to find the cost per unit for that batch of production.

3.2 Costs included

As with any costing system the costs to be included in the batch cost are the direct costs of material, labour and any direct expenses plus the overheads that are to be absorbed into the batch.

Each **batch** of production is treated, for cost accounting purposes, as a **cost unit**.

Example

A paint manufacturer is producing 1,000 litres of matt vinyl paint in 'sea blue'. The direct costs of the production run are:

	£
Materials	1,600
Labour 15 hours @ £10	150

Overheads are to be absorbed into the batch at a rate of £16 per direct labour hour.

What is the cost per litre of this batch of paint?

Solution

Batch cost	£
Materials	1,600
Labour	150
Overheads 15 hours @ £16	240
	———
Total batch cost	1,990
	———
Cost per litre	£1.99

Activity 2

A manufacturer of frozen meals produces a batch of 20,000 units of salmon tagliatelli. The direct costs of this batch are:

	£
Materials	15,000
Labour 1,000 hours	4,200

Overheads are to be absorbed at rate of £1.20 per direct labour hour. The cost of each portion of salmon tagliatelli is?

A £1.20

B £0.96

C £2.16

D £1.02

4   Service costing

4.1   Service costing

Service costing is a form of **continuous operation costing**. The output from a service industry differs from manufacturing for the following four reasons:

- **Intangibility** – the output is in the form of 'performance' rather than tangible or touchable goods or products

- **Heterogeneity** – the nature and standard of the service will be variable due to the high human input

- **Simultaneous production and consumption** – the service that you require cannot be inspected in advance of receiving it

- **Perishability** – the services that you require cannot be stored

4.2   Service cost units

One of the main difficulties in service costing is the establishment of a suitable cost unit. Examples for a hotel might include:

- **Meals served** for the restaurant

- **Rooms occupied** for the cleaning staff

- **Hours worked** for the reception staff

A **composite cost unit** may be more appropriate. For example a bus company might use passenger miles or how many passengers travel how many miles.

4.3 Cost per service unit

The total cost of providing a service will include the same costs as manufacturing but overheads may make up a larger proportion of the cost than direct costs. It is also possible that labour costs would be the only direct cost incurred by a service provider.

To calculate the cost per service unit the total cost of providing the service is divided by the number of service units used to provide the service.

$$\text{Cost per service unit} = \frac{\text{Total costs for providing the service}}{\text{Number of service units used to provide the service}}$$

Activity 3

The canteen of a company records the following income and expenditure for a month.

	£	£
Income		59,010
Food	17,000	
Drink	6,000	
Bottled water	750	
Fuel costs	800	
Maintenance of machinery	850	
Repairs	250	
Wages	15,500	
Depreciation	1,000	

During the month the canteen served 56,200 meals. The canteen's cost unit is one meal.

Calculate the average cost per meal served and the average income per meal served.

---

5 Summary

A business that produces **one-off products** for customers, each of which is different, will use a **job costing** system. This treats each individual job as a cost unit and therefore attributes the direct costs to that job, as well as the overheads according to the organisation's overhead absorption basis.

In a business which produces a number of different products in **batches of identical units** then a **batch costing** system is appropriate. Here the costs of each batch of production are gathered together as though the batch was a cost unit and the actual cost per unit is calculated by dividing the batch cost by the number of units produced in that batch.

Answers to chapter activities

Activity 1

JOB NO	3,362		
Materials requisitions		**£**	**Total**
15496		1,044	
15510		938	
15525		614	
		——	2,596

Wages – employees	**Hours**	**£**	
13249	40	320	
12475	33	231	
26895	53	312	
	126		863
	——		

Overheads	**Hours**	**£**	
Absorption rate £3.50	126	441	441
			——
Total cost			3,900
			——

Activity 2

D

	£
Materials	15,000
Labour	4,200
Overheads 1,000 hours @ £1.2	1,200
Total cost	20,400
Cost per unit £20,400 ÷ 20,000 =	£1.02

Activity 3

Total canteen expenditure = £42,150

Total meals served = 56,200

Average cost per meal served = £42,150 ÷ 56,200 = £0.75 per meal

Average income per meal served = 59,010 ÷ 56,200 = £1.05 per meal

6 Test your knowledge

Workbook Activity 4

Jetprint Limited

Jetprint Limited specialises in printing advertising leaflets and is in the process of preparing its price list. The most popular requirement is for a folded leaflet made from a single sheet of A4 paper. From past records and budgeted figures, the following data have been estimated for a typical batch of 10,000 leaflets:

Artwork (fixed cost)	£65
Machine setting (fixed cost)	4 hours @ £22 per hour
Paper	£12.50 per 1,000 sheets
Ink and consumables	£40 per 10,000 leaflets
Printers' wages	4 hours @ £8 per hour per 10,000 leaflets

General fixed overheads are £15,000 per period during which a total of 600 printers' labour hours are expected to be worked (not all, of course, on the leaflet). The overheads are recovered only on printers' hours.

Task

Calculate the cost (to the nearest pound) of the leaflets for batches of 10,000 and 20,000 leaflets.

	10,000 leaflets	20,000 leaflets
Artwork		
Machine setting		
Paper		
Ink and consumables		
Printers' wages		
General fixed overheads		
Total		

Process costing

9

Introduction

Process costing is used when goods or services result from a **sequence of continuous** or repetitive operations or processes, for example in the manufacture of paint.

ASSESSMENT CRITERIA	CONTENTS
Record cost information using these costing systems: (2.6S) – Process Define the various stages of inventory (2.3K)	1 Process costing 2 Losses in process 3 Scrap value of losses 4 Transferring losses and gains 5 Closing work in progress (CWIP) 6 Opening work in progress (OWIP)

1 Process costing

1.1 Introduction

Process costing is the costing method applicable where goods or services result from a **sequence of continuous** or repetitive operations or **processes**. Process costing is used when a company is **mass producing** the same item and the item goes through a number of different stages.

Process costing is an example of continuous operation costing.

Examples include the chemical, cement, oil refinery, paint and textile industries.

1.2 Illustration of process costing

Here is an example of a two-process manufacturing operation:

> ### Example
>
> HYRA has a manufacturing operation that involves two processes. The data for the first process during a particular period is as follows:
>
> - At the beginning of the period, 2,500 kg materials are introduced to the process at a cost of £3,500.
>
> - These materials are then worked upon, using £600 of labour and incurring/absorbing £450 of overheads.
>
> The resulting output is passed to the second process.

To keep track of the costs we could prepare a process account for each process. This resembles a **T account with extra columns**. The reason for the extra columns is that we have to keep track of how many material units we are working on as well as their value.

The costs appearing in such an account are those for **materials, labour and overheads**. (Labour and overheads are often combined under the heading 'conversion costs'.) In the case of **materials we record both units and monetary amount**; in the case of conversion costs we record the monetary amount only, because they do not add any units.

With process accounts the **inputs** into the process go on the **left** (debit) side of the account and **output** on the **right** (credit) side.

Example

The process account for the above example might thus appear as follows.

Process 1 account

	Kg	£		Kg	£
Materials	2,500	3,500	Output		
Labour		600	materials to		
Overheads		450	Process 2	2,500	4,550
	2,500	4,550		2,500	4,550

1.3 The basic process cost per unit

Process costing is very similar to batch costing, as we calculate the total costs for the process and divide by the number of units to get a cost per unit.

The main difference is that the process is ongoing so the costs and output for a particular time period are used.

Using the example above we can calculate the cost per kg of output that will be transferred to the second process:

The calculation that needs to be done is:

$$\text{Cost per unit} = \frac{\text{Net costs of input}}{\text{Expected output}}$$

Net costs of input = £3,500 + £600 + £450 = £4,550

Expected output = 2,500 kg

Thus, the output to process 2 would be costed at:

$$\frac{£4,550}{2,500\,\text{kg}} = £1.82 \text{ per kg output}$$

Example

Following on from the above example the Process 2 account might appear as follows.

Process 2 account

	Kg	£		Kg	£
Input Materials			Finished goods	2,500	6,350
from process 1	2,500	4,550			
Labour		800			
Overheads		1,000			
	2,500	6,350		2,500	6,350

The finished goods are then valued at:

Cost per unit $= \dfrac{\text{Net costs of input}}{\text{Expected output}}$

Net costs of input = £4,550 + £800 + £1,000 = £6,350

Expected output = 2,500 kg

Thus, the output from process 2 (i.e. the finished goods) would be costed at:

$\dfrac{£6,350}{2,500 \text{ kg}}$ = £2.54 per unit

2 Losses in process

2.1 Introduction

In many industrial processes, some input is lost (through evaporation, wastage, etc.) or damaged during the production process. This will give rise to losses in the process. We will look at the concepts of normal losses and abnormal losses or gains.

Normal loss represents items that you **expect** to lose during a process, and its cost is therefore treated as part of the cost of good production. **Abnormal losses or gains** are **not expected** so are valued at the same cost as **good production**.

2.2 Normal losses

Normal losses are usually stated as a percentage of input e.g. the normal loss is expected to be 5% of the input material. Unless the normal loss can be sold as scrap the cost of the loss is absorbed into the production cost i.e. it has a nil value.

☀ Example

At the start of a heating process 1,000 kg of material costing £16 per kg is input. During the process, conversion costs of £2,000 are incurred. Normal loss (through evaporation) is expected to be 10% of input. During March 1,000 kg were input and output was 900 kg.

Compute the unit and total cost of output in March.

Solution

First we need to sort out the units. We can do this using the flow of units equation:

Input	=	Output	+	Loss
1,000 kg	=	900 kg	+	100 kg (to balance)

The normal loss is 10% of input = 100 kg thus the loss was as expected.

We now need to compute the cost per unit of good output.

Total input costs:

Materials	£16 × 1,000 kg	£16,000
Conversion costs		£2,000
		————
		£18,000

These costs will be spread over the expected output units – thus the cost attributable to the normal loss units is absorbed into the good units. Cost per unit of output:

$$= \frac{\text{Net costs of input}}{\text{Expected output}}$$

Where the expected output is the input units less the normal loss units:

$$= \frac{£18,000}{(1,000 - 100)}$$

$$= £20 \text{ per kg}$$

Total cost of output = 900 kg × £20 = £18,000.

This can be represented in a process account as follows.

Process account – March

	Kg	£		Kg	£
Input	1,000	16,000	Output	900	18,000
Conversion			Normal loss	100	–
costs	–	2,000			
	1,000	18,000		1,000	18,000

Notice that the units and the monetary amounts balance. Normal loss is valued at zero as its cost has been absorbed into that of good output.

2.3 Abnormal loss

Any actual **loss in excess of the normal** (expected) loss is known as **abnormal loss**. This is not treated as part of normal production cost and is separately identified and costed throughout the process.

Example

In April, 1,000 kg were input (at £16 per kg) to the same process as above and actual output was 800 kg. Conversion costs were £2,000 as before.

Required:

Prepare the process account for the month of April.

Solution

Again look at the units only to start with.

Input	=	Output	+	Loss
1,000 kg	=	800 kg	+	200 kg (to balance)

The total loss is now 200 kg, when we only expected a (normal) loss of 100 kg.

Input	=	Output	+	Normal loss	+	Abnormal loss
1,000 kg	=	800 kg	+	100 kg	+	100 kg

The extra 100 kg is an abnormal loss. It represents items that we did not expect to lose. In this example it may have been that the temperature was set too high on the process, causing more of the input to evaporate.

To make the units balance we therefore need to include 100 units on the credit side of the process account to represent this abnormal loss:

Process account – April (units only)

	Kg	£		Kg	£
Input	1,000		Output	800	
Conversion			Normal loss	100	
costs	–		Abnormal loss	100	
	1,000			1,000	

Now we examine the costs:

Cost per unit of output

$$= \frac{\text{Net costs of input}}{\text{Expected output}}$$

Where the expected output is the input units less the normal loss units:

$$= \frac{£18,000}{(1,000 - 100)}$$

$$= £20 \text{ per kg}$$

Total cost of output = 800 kg × £20 = £16,000.

This can be represented in a process account as follows.

Input, normal loss and output are valued as before. The value for abnormal loss is the same as that of output, i.e. £20 per kg.

Process account – April

	Kg	£		Kg	£
Input	1,000	16,000	Output	800	16,000
Conversion			Normal loss	100	–
costs	–	2,000	Abnormal loss	100	2,000
	1,000	18,000		1,000	18,000

The units and values are now balanced. The £2,000 value of the abnormal loss represents lost output.

2.4 Abnormal gain

An **abnormal gain** occurs where **losses are less than expected**. Its treatment is the same as abnormal loss only the debits and credits are reversed i.e. the gain is a debit in the t-account.

·Ọ· Example

In May 1,000 kg at £16 per kg were input to the heating process and £2,000 conversion costs incurred. This month output was 950 kg.

Required:

Prepare the process account for the month of May.

Solution

We begin by looking at the units flow.

Input	=	Output	+	Loss
1,000 kg	=	950 kg	+	50 kg (to balance)

The total loss is now only 50 kg, when we expected a (normal) loss of 1,000 × 10% = 100 kg. We have therefore made an abnormal gain of 50 kg.

To balance the units on the process account then, we need to put the normal loss (100 kg) on the right and the abnormal gain (50 kg) on the left.

Abnormal gain	+	Input	=	Output	+	Normal loss
50 kg	+	1,000 kg	=	950 kg	+	100 kg

Now we examine the costs:

Cost per unit of output:

$$= \frac{\text{Net costs of input}}{\text{Expected output}}$$

Where the expected output is the input units less the normal loss units, we were not expecting the loss to be any different.

$$= \frac{£18,000}{(1,000 - 100)}$$

$$= £20 \text{ per kg}$$

Total cost of output = 950 kg × £20 = £19,000.

This can be represented in a process account as follows.

Input, normal loss and output are valued at the same cost per kg as before. The value for abnormal gain is the same as that of output, i.e. £20 per kg.

The completed process account is shown below.

Process account – May

	Kg	£		Kg	£
Input	1,000	16,000	Output	950	19,000
Conversion			Normal loss	100	–
costs	–	2,000			
Abnormal					
gain	50	1,000			
	1,050	19,000		1,050	19,000

The abnormal gain has to go on the debit side to avoid having negative numbers in the T account.

We have an additional 50 units to sell at £20 per unit.

Activity 1

You are given the following information about the 'mashing' process of Mushypeas Ltd during June:

Ingredients input	1,600 kg @ £2.80 per kg
Labour	100 hours @ £6 per hour
Overheads	100 hours @ £3.60 per hour

Actual Output from the process is 1,250 kg.

Water loss from the process is expected to result in a 15% loss in input volume.

Calculate the cost per kg of output and use it to complete the mashing process account overleaf.

Solution

Mashing process – June

	Kg	£		Kg	£
Ingredients	1,600		Normal loss		
Labour			Output	1,250	
Overheads					
	——	——		——	——
	——	——		——	——

Use the following phrases and numbers to complete the above T-account (some of them may be used twice, some of them will not be required at all):

Abnormal Loss	Abnormal Gain	9,600
5,760	5,000	4,480
600	440	360
240	110	4.35
4.00	5,440	0

3 Scrap value of losses

3.1 Introduction

It may be possible to **sell** the **normal** loss that occurs in a process as a by-product of the process for example wood shavings as a by-product of making wooden tables and chairs.

Example

Maine Ltd produces tables and chairs. When they are made wood shavings are produced. These wood shavings are saved and sold off for 90p/kg. Normal waste is 10% of input. Costs for batch 975D were as follows.

	£
Materials (10,000 kg @ £2 per kg)	20,000
Labour	2,000
Overheads	500
	——
Total	22,500
Actual output	8,500 kg

Required:

Prepare the process account.

Solution

First, the units:

Input	=	**Output**	+	**Loss**
10,000 kg	=	8,500 kg	+	1,500 kg (to balance)

The total loss is 1,500 kg, when we only expected a (normal) loss of 10% × 10,000 = 1,000 kg. Thus, we have an abnormal loss of 500 kg.

Input	=	**Output**	+	**Normal Loss**	+	**Abnormal Loss**
10,000 kg	=	8,500 kg	+	1,000 kg	+	500 kg

In this example we would sell the normal loss at £900 (1,000 kg @ £0.90 = £900). This is entered in the process account. The same amount is then subtracted from the process costs, reducing the cost of the inputs i.e. to the net cost of inputs.

$$\text{Cost per unit} = \frac{\text{Net costs of input}}{\text{Expected output}}$$

$$\text{Cost per unit} = \frac{£22,500 - £900}{10,000 - 1,000} = £2.40 \text{ per kg}$$

Although we actually have 1,500 loss units to sell (1,000 litres of normal loss plus 500 units of abnormal loss), we only include the sales value of the normal loss in this calculation as this is all we are **expecting** to sell.

Process account

	Kg	£		Kg	£
Input	10,000	20,000	Output @ £2.40	8,500	20,400
Material Labour	–	2,000	Normal loss		
Overheads	–	500	@ £0.90	1,000	900
			Abnormal loss		
			@ £2.40	500	1,200
	10,000	22,500		10,000	22,500

Activity 2

Maston Ltd produces special oil in a single process. The oil is made by introducing 10,000 litres of liquid into a process at a cost of £5 per litre.

The normal loss is 500 litres which can be sold for £1 per litre.

Each process requires £4,000 of labour. The overhead is recovered at 150% of labour.

If there are no abnormal losses or gains, produce the process account for the above.

Process 1

	litres	£		litres	£
Materials			Normal loss		
Labour			Output		
Overhead					

Activity 3

A chemical compound is made by raw material being passed through two processes. The output of Process A is passed to Process B where further material is added to the mix. The details of the process costs for the financial period number 10 were as shown below.

Process B
Input from process A	1,400 kg @ £19 per kg
Direct material	1,400 kg @ £12 per kg
Direct labour	£4,200
Process plant time	80 hours @ £72.50 per hour

The departmental overhead for period 10 was £2,460.

Process B
Normal loss	10% of input
Actual output	2,620 kg

Normal loss is identified as all material enters process B. This is sold as scrap for £1.50 per kg from Process B.

Required:

Prepare the process accounts below (show totals to the nearest whole £):

Process B

	kg	£		kg	£
Input from A			Normal loss		
Material added			Output		
Labour					
Process time					
Overhead					
	___	___		___	___
	___	___		___	___

Activity 4

Mike Everett Ltd produces animal feeds. 'Calfextra' is one of its products. The product is produced in a single process.

The following information relates to week ended 10 February 20X1.

Inputs:	Direct material	720 tonnes at £55 per tonne.
	Direct labour	40 labour hours at £7.20 per hour.
	Overhead	£3,240 for the period

Normal loss is based on an allowance of 5% of input and waste has a saleable value of £1 per tonne.

Output for the period was 675 tonnes.

Prepare the process account for the period:

Calfextra

	tonnes	£		tonnes	£
Materials			Normal loss		
Labour			Output		
Overhead					
	___	___		___	___
	___	___		___	___

Activity 5

Mike Everett Ltd produces animal feeds. A further product is 'Pigextra' and this is produced in a single process.

For the week ended 10 March 20X1 the following information was available and related to 'Pigextra' production.

Inputs:	Direct material	1,000 tonnes at £17.20 per tonne.
	Direct labour	280 hours at £10.50 per hour.
	Overhead	£32 per direct labour hour.

Normal loss allowance is 5% of input and waste is saleable at £12 per tonne.

Output for the period was 980 tonnes.

Prepare the process account.

Pigextra

	tonnes	£		tonnes	£
Materials			Normal loss		
Labour			Output		
Overhead					
	___	___		___	___
	___	___		___	___

Activity 6

X plc processes a chemical. Input to a batch was as follows.

	£
Materials (10,000 litres)	10,000
Labour and overheads	800
Total	10,800

Normal loss is 10% of input.

Actual output = 8,700 litres. The remaining liquid was skimmed off and sold for 36p per litre.

Required:

Complete the process account.

Process account

	Ltr	£		Ltr	£
Materials			Normal loss		
Conversion			Output		
	———	———		———	———
	———	———		———	———

---

4 Transferring losses and gains

4.1 Introduction

Any losses or gains need to be fully accounted for in the accounts of a business. To do this we need to introduce 2 new accounts – the scrap account and the abnormal loss/gain account.

4.2 Abnormal loss

Example

Abnormal loss

A business puts 1,000 units of material into a process at a cost of £30,000 and spends £10,000 converting it into output. Output from the process is expected to be 900 units but the business only gets 850 completed units out of the process. The units of normal loss can be sold for £17.50 each.

The business has completed the process account as below:

Process account

	Units	£		Units	£
Materials	1,000	30,000	Output	850	36,125
Conversion		10,00	Normal loss	100	1,750
			Abnormal loss	50	2,125
	———	———		———	———
	1,000	40,000		1,000	40,000

Complete the transfer of the normal loss and abnormal loss.

1   Normal loss is transferred to the scrap account at the value it is
     sold at: Cr Process account; Dr Scrap account

Process account

	Units	£		Units	£
Materials	1,000	30,000	Output	850	36,125
Conversion		10,000	*Normal loss*	100	*1,750*
			Abnormal loss	50	2,125
	1,000	40,000		1,000	40,000

Scrap account

	Units	£		Units	£
Process account	*100*	*1,750*			

2   Abnormal loss is transferred to the Abnormal loss/gain account at
     the average cost per unit (as per the valuation in the process
     account): Cr Process account; Dr Abnormal loss/gain account

Process account

	Units	£		Units	£
Materials	1,000	30,000	Output	850	36,125
Conversion		10,000	Normal loss	100	1,750
			Abnormal loss	50	*2,125*
	1,000	40,000		1,000	40,000

Abnormal loss/gain account

	Units	£		Units	£
Process account	*50*	*2,125*			

3   Abnormal loss is then transferred to the scrap account at the sales value of the normal loss. The normal loss in this example can be sold for £17.50 so the abnormal loss can also be sold at this price, giving it a value of £875.

Abnormal loss: Dr Scrap account; Cr Abnormal loss/gain account

Abnormal loss/gain account

	Units	£		Units	£
Process account	50	2,125	Scrap account	50	875

Scrap account

	Units	£		Units	£
Process account	100	1,750			
Abnormal loss	50	875			

4   The balancing figure in the abnormal loss/gain account is the true cost of the loss.

Abnormal loss/gain account

	Units	£		Units	£
Process account	50	2,125	Scrap account	50	875
			SOPL		1,250
	50	2,125		50	2,125

5   The balancing figure in the scrap account is the total amount of cash received from the total loss made.

Scrap account

	Units	£		Units	£
Process account	100	1,750	Cash	150	2,625
Abnormal loss	50	875			
	150	2,625		150	2,625

4.3　Abnormal gain

Example

Abnormal gain

A business puts 1,000 units of material into a process at a cost of £30,000 and spends £10,000 converting it into output. Output from the process is expected to be 900 units but the business gets 950 completed units out of the process. The units of normal loss can be sold for £17.50 each.

The business has completed the process account as below:

Process account

	Units	£		Units	£
Materials	1,000	30,000	Output	950	40,375
Conversion		10,000	Normal loss	100	1,750
Abnormal gain	50	2,125			
	1,050	42,125		1,050	42,125

Complete the transfer of the normal loss and abnormal gain.

1　Normal loss is transferred to the scrap account at the value it is sold at: Cr Process account; Dr Scrap account

Process account

	Units	£		Units	£
Materials	1,000	30,000	Output	950	40,375
Conversion		10,000	*Normal loss*	*100*	*1,750*
Abnormal gain	50	2,125			
	1,050	42,125		1,050	42,125

Scrap account

	Units	£		Units	£
Process account	*100*	*1,750*			

2   Abnormal gain is transferred to the Abnormal loss/gain account at the average cost per unit (as per the valuation in the process account): Dr Process account; Cr Abnormal loss/gain account

Process account

	Units	£		Units	£
Materials	1,000	30,000	Output	850	36,125
Conversion		10,000	Normal loss	100	1,750
Abnormal gain	*50*	*2,125*			
	1,050	40,000			
				1,050	40,000

Abnormal loss/gain account

	Units	£		Units	£
			Process account	*50*	*2,125*

3   Abnormal gain is then transferred to the scrap account at the sales value of the normal loss. The normal loss in this example can be sold for £17.50 so the abnormal gain should have been sold at this price, giving it a value of £875.

Abnormal gain is Cr Scrap account; Dr Abnormal loss/gain account

Abnormal loss/gain account

	Units	£		Units	£
Scrap account	*50*	*875*	Process account	*50*	*2,125*

Scrap account

	Units	£		Units	£
Process account	100	1,750	*Abnormal gain*	*50*	*875*

4   The balancing figure in the Abnormal loss/gain account is the true saving of the gain

Abnormal loss/gain account

	Units	£		Units	£
Scrap account	50	875	Process account	50	2,125
SOPL		1,250			
	50	2,125		50	2,125

5   The balancing figure in the scrap account is the total amount of cash received from the total remaining loss made.

Scrap account

	Units	£		Units	£
Process account	100	1,750	Abnormal gain	50	875
			Cash		875
	100	1,750		50	1,750

Activity 7

Gair Plc produces tin cans in a single process. The cans are made by introducing 1,000 kg of metal into a process at a cost of £5 per kg.

The normal loss is 50 kg which can be sold for £0.50 per kg.

Each process requires £400 of labour and £800 of overhead.

Output for process 1 was 900 kg of cans.

Complete the process account, scrap account, abnormal loss/gain account.

Process 1

	Kg	£		Kg	£
Materials			Normal loss		
Labour			Output		
Overhead					

Scrap account

	Kg	£		Kg	£
	——	——		——	——
	——	——		——	——

Abnormal loss/gain account

	Kg	£		Kg	£
	——	——		——	——
	——	——		——	——

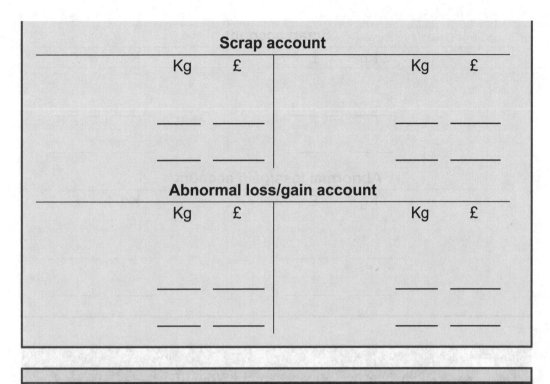

Activity 8

Stardust Ltd produces wooden ceiling decorations. When they are produced wood shavings are also produced. These wood shavings are saved and sold off for 60p/kg. Normal loss is 5% of input. Costs for batch 13 were as follows.

	£
Materials (20,000 kg @ £2 per kg)	40,000
Labour	4,600
Overheads	1,600
Actual output	19,500 kg

Complete the process account, scrap account and abnormal loss/gain account.

Process account

	Kg	£		Kg	£
Materials			Normal loss		
Labour			Output		
Overheads					
	——	——		——	——
	——	——		——	——

5 Closing work in progress (CWIP)

5.1 Introduction

Process costing is also used when products **are not all completed at the end of a time period** (e.g. manufacturing cars). This means that the process costs are shared between finished or complete units and **closing work in progress (CWIP) or partially completed units.**

We need to decide how the costs should be split over these different categories of production.

5.2 Equivalent units

To be able to assign the correct amount of cost to finished and partially completed units of product we use a concept called **Equivalent units** or EU. To demonstrate this concept:

If we had 1,000 units that are 50% complete at the end of a period. How many finished units is this equivalent to?

1,000 × 50% = 500 equivalent units (EU).

In other words, we assume we could have made 500 units and finished them instead of half finishing 1,000 units.

The calculation of equivalent units:

Equivalent units = Number of physical units × percentage completion.

🔆 Example

Situation A – completion levels are equal

DL Ltd is a manufacturer. In Period 1 the following production occurred.

Started = 1,400

Closing work-in-progress = 400 units

Degree of completion for the CWIP:

    Materials   25%

    Conversion   25%

Solution

Started = > Finished + CWIP

1,400 = > 1,000 (to balance) + 400

Finished units are 100% complete for both material and conversion.

			EUs
Finished	1,000	× 100%	1,000
WIP	400	× 25%	100
			———
Total			1,100
			———

5.3 Equivalent units for different degrees of completion

A process involves direct materials being processed by the addition of direct labour and overheads.

Usually, all the material is put in at the beginning of the process, whereas the conversion is 'added' as the product advances through the process. This means there may be a **different amount of equivalent units for conversion and materials.**

If completion levels in the closing work in progress are unequal we have to keep track of the equivalent units for materials and for conversion separately.

💡 Example

Situation B – completion levels are unequal

EM Ltd is a manufacturer. In Period 1 the following production occurred.

Started = 1,400

Closing work-in-progress = 400 units

Degree of completion:

Materials   100%

Conversion   50%

Solution

Started = > Finished + CWIP

1,400 = > 1,000 (to balance) + 400

Finished units are 100% complete for both material and conversion.

		EUs
Materials	– Finished 1,000 × 100%	1,000
	– CWIP 400 × 100%	400
		–––––
		1,400
		–––––
Conversion	– Finished 1,000 × 100%	1,000
	– CWIP 400 × 50%	200
		–––––
		1,200
		–––––

5.4 Cost per equivalent unit

We need to be able to calculate the cost of an equivalent unit to ultimately be able to value the cost of finished goods and CWIP. We will first look at this when completion levels of the CWIP are equal.

Note: You will only be required to calculate the cost per equivalent unit, not calculate the valuation of finished goods or CWIP. This is shown here for completion.

Example

Situation A continued – completion levels are equal

DL Ltd is a manufacturer. In Period 1 the following production occurred.

Started   =   1,400

Closing work-in-progress   =   400 units

Degree of completion for the CWIP:

    Materials   25%

    Conversion   25%

Costs incurred in Period 1 = £6,600

Solution

Started   =   Finished   +   CWIP

1,400   =   1,000 (to balance)   +   400

Finished units are 100% complete for both material and conversion.

		EUs
Finished	1,000 × 100%	1,000
WIP	400 × 25%	100
Total		1,100

The cost per equivalent unit is simply calculated as total cost divided by the number of EUs produced.

The cost per EU would be £6,600/1,100 = £6 per EU.

This can be used to calculate the value of the finished goods and closing WIP:

Value of finished units = 1,000 × £6 = £6,000

Value of closing WIP = 100 × £6 = £600

Activity 9

Process WIP

On 1 March 20X0 a process started work on 350 units and at the end of the month there were still 75 units in the process, each 60% complete.

The total cost of materials, labour, etc. input during March was £3,696.

Required:

What is the cost per equivalent unit:

A £8.70

B £9.36

C £11.55

D £12.45

Now we need to look at calculating the cost per equivalent unit when completion levels of the CWIP are unequal.

Example

Situation B continued – completion levels are unequal

EM Ltd is a manufacturer. In Period 1 the following production occurred.

Started   =   1,400

Closing work-in-progress   =   400 units

Degree of completion:

    Materials   100%

    Conversion   50%

Costs incurred in Period 1:

    Materials   £81,060

    Conversion   £71,940

Solution

Started	=	Finished	+	CWIP
1,400	=	1,000 (to balance)	+	400

Finished units are 100% complete for both material and conversion.

		EUs
Materials	– Finished 1,000 × 100%	1,000
	– CWIP 400 × 100%	400
		1,400
Conversion	– Finished 1,000 × 100%	1,000
	– CWIP 400 × 50%	200
		1,200

Total costs are then divided by the total EU to get a cost per EU for each type of input cost, and a total cost for each completed unit:

Material cost per equivalent unit = £81,060/1,400 = £57.90

Conversion cost per equivalent unit = £71,940/1,200 = £59.95

The costs may now be attributed to the categories of output as follows:

		£	£
Completed units:	1,000 × (£57.90 + £59.95)		117,850
Closing WIP:	Materials 400 × £57.90	23,160	
	Conversion 200 × £59.95	11,990	
			35,150
			153,000

Activity 10

Egton Farm Supplies Ltd produces fertilisers and chemicals. One of its products 'Eg3' is produced in a single process.

The following information relates to period 5, 20X1.

Inputs:	Direct material	1,000 tonnes of 'X' at £70/tonne.
	Direct labour	60 hours at £8/hour.
	Overhead recovery rate	£4/hour.

Completed output:	800 tonnes
Closing work-in-progress:	200 tonnes

There were no losses in the process.

Work-in-progress degree of completion

Material   100%

Labour   80%

Overhead   80%

Calculate the cost per EU for period 5.

Activity 11

NH Ltd

NH Ltd has two processes.

Process 1:

Material for 12,000 items was put into process 1. There were no opening inventory and no process losses. Other relevant information is:

Transfers to process 2	9,000 items
Direct material cost	£36,000
Direct labour cost	£32,000
Overheads	£8,530

The unfinished items were complete as to materials and 50% complete as to labour and overheads.

Process 2:

Transfers from process 1	9,000 items transferred at £61,740
Items completed	8,200 items
Labour cost	£34,596
Overheads	£15,300

There were no materials added in process 2 other than the units transferred from process 1. There were no process losses.

The unfinished items were deemed to be 25% complete in labour and overheads

Required:

Calculate the cost per equivalent unit for each process.

6 Opening work in progress (OWIP)

6.1 Introduction

At the start of a period there may be some work in progress from a previous period (closing work in progress) that is waiting to be finished. This is the known as the **opening work in progress (OWIP)** in the new period.

The OWIP needs to be considered to be able to calculate how much of the completed output at the end of the period was completed wholly in the period and how much only required partial effort to complete it within the period.

There are 2 different methods that can be applied to OWIP – Average cost (AVCO) and First in, first out (FIFO).

6.2 Average cost (AVCO)

The average cost method would be used where it is not possible to distinguish individual units present at the start of a process from those produced during the period e.g. liquids. In this case the **costs incurred so far to complete the OWIP are included with the period costs when calculating the cost per EU.**

> ### Example
>
> **Than Pele**
>
> Than Pele Ltd is a manufacturer. The details of the first process in Period 2 are as follows:
>
> | | |
> |---|---|
> | **OWIP** | = 400 units |
>
> Costs incurred so far
>
> | | |
> |---|---|
> | Materials | £19,850 |
> | Conversion | £4,100 |
>
> | | |
> |---|---|
> | **Completed output** | = 1,700 units |
>
> **Costs incurred in Period 2:**
>
> | | |
> |---|---|
> | Materials | £100,000 |
> | Conversion | £86,000 |
>
> **Solution**
>
> | OWIP | + | Started | = | | Finished |
> |---|---|---|---|---|---|
> | 400 | + | 1,300 (bal fig) | = | | 1,700 |
>
> | **Equivalent units** | **Material** | **Conversion** |
> |---|---|---|
> | Completed Output | 1,700 | 1,700 |
> | Total EU | 1,700 | 1,700 |
> | **Costs** | | |
> | OWIP | 19,850 | 4,100 |
> | Period | 100,000 | 86,000 |
> | Total cost | 119,850 | 90,100 |
> | **Cost per EU** | £70.50 | £53.00 |

Activity 12

Yeknom

Yeknom produces a diet drink on a production line. The details of the process in Period 7 are as follows:

OWIP	= 200 units
Costs incurred so far	
Materials	£22,000
Conversion	£9,960
Completed output	= 900 units

Costs incurred in Period 7:

Materials	£97,700
Conversion	£98,940

Required:

Calculate the cost per EU using the AVCO method of valuing OWIP

Equivalent units		Material	Conversion
	Completed Output		
	Total EU		
Costs			
	OWIP		
	Period		
	Total cost		
Cost per EU			

6.3 First in, first out (FIFO)

The first in, first out method would be used when it may be essential to complete the started goods from previous periods before new units can be started e.g. car production lines. In this case we need to consider **how much work is required to complete the OWIP in this period. The costs incurred in the previous period for the OWIP are not included in the cost per EU calculation but are instead included within the final valuation of the completed output.**

Example

Than Pele

Than Pele Ltd is a manufacturer. The details of the first process in Period 3 are as follows:

OWIP		= 400 units
Costs incurred so far		
Materials		£19,850
Conversion		£4,100
Degrees of completion		
Materials	100%	
Conversion	25%	
Completed output		= 1,700 units
Costs incurred in Period 3:		
Materials	£100,100	
Conversion	£86,000	

Solution

OWIP	+	Started	=	Completed
400	+	1,300 (bal fig)	=	1,700

The completed units consist of 400 OWIP that were completed this period and then a further 1,300 units that were started and finished in this period.

To complete the OWIP no more material is required but 75% more conversion is needed.

Equivalent units		Material	Conversion
	OWIP to complete	0 (400 – 400 × 100%)	300 (400 – 400 × 25%)
	Started and finished	1,300	1,300
	Total EU	1,300	1,600
Costs			
	Period	100,100	86,000
	Total cost	100,100	86,000
Cost per EU		£77.00	£53.75

Activity 13

Effarig

Effarig is makes safari hats on a production line. The details of the process in Period 3 are as follows:

OWIP		= 200 units
Costs incurred so far		
Materials		£1,800
Conversion		£4,000
Degrees of completion		
Materials	100%	
Conversion	75%	
Completed output		= 2,000 units

Costs incurred in Period 3:

Materials	£18,900
Conversion	£37,925

Required:

Calculate the cost per EU using the FIFO method of valuing OWIP

Equivalent units	Material	Conversion
OWIP to complete		
Started and finished		
Total EU		
Costs		
Period		
Total cost		
Cost per EU		

7 Summary

Process costing is used when a company is mass producing the same item and the item goes through a number of different stages. As the item goes through the different stages, **losses** may occur: normal losses, abnormal losses and abnormal gains. Losses may be scrapped or they may have a '**scrap value**' which means that they can be sold (and that the revenue generated is used to reduce the costs of the process concerned).

Sometimes, at the end of an accounting period, a process may not be finished and there may be incomplete (**work-in-progress**) units. When this happens, it is necessary to use the concept of **equivalent units** to decide how the process costs should be split over work-in-progress and finished goods.

Note: Process and job costing systems represent the extreme ends of a continuum, and many organisations need a combination of these two elements (as in batch costing).

Answers to chapter activities

Activity 1

Actual output = 1,250 kg

Flow of units:

Input	**=**	**Output**	**+**	**Loss**
1,600 kg	=	1,250 kg	+	350 kg (to balance)

Normal loss = 240 kg and we therefore have an abnormal loss of 110 kg.

Process costs = £5,440

$$\text{Cost per unit of output} = \frac{\text{Total process costs}}{\text{Input units} - \text{Normal loss units}}$$

$$= \frac{£5,440}{(1,600 - 240)}$$

$$= £4 \text{ per kg}$$

Mashing process – June

	kg	£		kg	£
Ingredients	1,600	4,480	Output	1,250	5,000
Labour		600	Normal loss	240	–
Overheads		360	Abnormal loss	110	440
	1,600	5,440		1,600	5,440

Activity 2

Process 1

	Litre	£		*Litre*	£
Direct material	10,000	50,000	Normal loss	500	500
Direct labour		4,000	Output	9,500	59,500
Overhead		6,000			
	10,000	60,000		10,000	60,000

Activity 3

Chemical compound

Process B

	kg	£		kg	£ per kg	£
From			Finished			
Process A	1,400	26,600	goods (W6)	2,620	22.00	57,640
Direct			Normal loss			
material	1,400	16,800	(W4)	280	1.50	420
Direct labour		4,200				
Overhead		2,460				
Processing time		5,800				
Abnormal						
gain (W5, W6)	100	2,200				
	2,900	58,060		2,900		58,060

(W4) Normal loss = 10% × (1,400 + 1,400) = 280

(W5) Expected output = 2,800 − 280 = 2,520 units; actual output 2,620; 100 units abnormal gain

(W6) Cost per unit = £(55,860 − 420)/(2,800 − 280) = £22.00

Activity 4

Mike Everett Ltd – 'Calfextra'

Determination of losses/gains:

	Tonnes
Input	720
Normal loss 5% of input	36
Normal output	684
Actual output	675
Difference = abnormal loss	9

Calfextra

	tonnes	£		tonnes	£
Material	720	39,600	Normal loss	36	36
Labour		288	Output	675	42,525
Overhead		3,240	Abnormal loss	9	567
	720	43,128		720	43,128

Normal cost of normal production:

$$\frac{£43,128 - £36}{720 - 36} = \frac{£43,092}{684}$$

$$= £63 \text{ per tonne}$$

Output	675 × £63	=	£42,525
Abnormal loss	9 × £63	=	£567

Activity 5

Mike Everett Ltd – 'Pigextra'

Determination of losses/gains:

	Tonnes
Input	1,000
Normal loss 5% of input	50
Normal output	950
Actual output	980
Difference = abnormal gain	30

Pigextra

	tonnes	£		tonnes	£
Material	1,000	17,200	Normal loss	50	600
Labour		2,940	Output	980	29,400
Overhead		8,960			
Abnormal gain	30	900			
	1,030	30,000		1,030	30,000

Normal cost of normal production:

$$\frac{£29,100 - £600}{1,000 - 50} = \frac{£28,500}{950}$$

$$= £30 \text{ per tonne}$$

Output	980 tonnes × £30	= £29,400
Abnormal gain	30 tonnes × £30	= £900

Activity 6

X plc

Process account

	Ltrs	£		Ltrs	£
Input material	10,000	10,000	Output	8,700	10,092
Labour and			Normal loss	1,000	360
overheads	–	800	Abnormal loss	300	348
	10,000	10,800		10,000	10,800

Output valued at (£10,800 – £360)/9,000 = £1.16 per litre

Activity 7

Gair plc

Process account

	Kg	£		Kg	£
Material	1,000	5,000	Normal loss	50	25
Labour		400	Output	900	5,850
Overheads		800	Abnormal loss	50	325
	1,000	6,200		1,000	6,200

Output valued at (£6,200 – £25)/950 = £6.50 per kg

Abnormal loss/gain account

	Kg	£		Kg	£
Process account	50	325	Scrap account	50	25
			SOPL		300
	50	325		50	325

Scrap account

	Kg	£		Kg	£
Process account	50	25	Cash	100	50
Abnormal loss	50	25			
	100	50		100	50

Activity 8

Stardust Ltd

Process account

	Kg	£		Kg	£
Material	20,000	40,000	Normal loss	1,000	600
Labour		4,600	Output	19,500	46,800
Overheads		1,600			
Abnormal gain	500	1,200			
	20,500	47,400		20,500	47,400

Output valued at (46,200 – 600/19,000 = £2.40 per kg.

Abnormal loss/gain account

	Kg	£		Kg	£
Scrap account	500	300	Process account	500	1,200
SOPL		900			
	500	1,200		500	1,200

Scrap account

	Kg	£		Kg	£
Process account	1,000	600	Abnormal gain	500	300
			Cash	500	300
	1,000	600		1,000	600

Activity 9

C

Physical flow of units

	Units started		Units completed		Closing WIP
	350	=	275 (bal fig)	+	75

Equivalent units of production

Units started and finished	275
Closing WIP (75 × 60%)	45
	320

Cost per equivalent unit $= \dfrac{£3,696}{320} =$ £11.55

Activity 10

Egton Farm Supplies Ltd

Statement of equivalent units and statement of cost

	Completed output	CWIP	Equivalent units	Cost £	Cost per unit £
Direct materials	800	200	1,000	70,000	70.00
Direct labour	800	160	960	480	0.50
Overhead	800	160	960	240	0.25

Activity 11

NH Ltd

Process 1

The physical flow of units:

Units started = Units completed + Closing WIP
12,000 = 9,000 + 3,000 (bal)

| Input | Equivalent units | | | Costs | Costs per EU (£) |
	Completed in period	CWIP	Total EU	Total costs (£)	
Materials	9,000	3,000 (100%)	12,000	36,000	3.00
Conversion	9,000	1,500 (50%)	10,500	40,530	3.86

Process 2

The physical flow of units:

Units started = Units completed + Closing WIP
9,000 = 8,200 + 800 (bal)

| Input | Equivalent units | | | Costs | Costs per EU (£) |
	Completed in period	CWIP	Total EU	Total costs (£)	
Material from Process 1	8,200	800 (100%)	9,000	61,740	6.86
Conversion	8,200	200 (25%)	8,400	49,896	5.94

Activity 12

Equivalent units		Material	Conversion
	Completed Output	900	900
	Total EU	900	900
Costs			
	OWIP	22,000	9,960
	Period	97,700	98,940
	Total cost	119,700	108,900
Cost per EU		£133	£121

Activity 13

OWIP + Started = Completed
200 + 1,800 = 2000

The completed units consist of 200 OWIP that were completed this period and then a further 1,800 units that were started and finished in this period.

To complete the OWIP no more material is required but 25% more conversion is needed.

Equivalent units		Material	Conversion
	OWIP to complete	0 (200 – 200 × 100%)	50 (200 – 200 × 75%)
	Started and finished	1,800	1,800
	Total EU	1,800	1,850
Costs			
	Period	18,900	37,925
	Total cost	18,900	37,925
Cost per EU		£10.50	£20.50

8 Test your knowledge

Workbook Activity 14

Blake Ltd produces a soft drink. The following information relates to period 1.

Direct material	1,000 kg at £90.30 per kg
Direct labour	320 hours at £15.50 per hour
Overhead	£1,914

Normal loss allowance is 3% of input, which can be sold for £64 per kg

Finished output 990 kg

There was no opening or closing work in progress

Prepare a process account for the above process.

Process soft drink

	kg	£		kg	£
Materials			Normal loss		
Labour			Output		
Overhead					
	___	___		___	___
	___	___		___	___

Workbook Activity 15

Maston Ltd produces special oil. The oil is made by introducing 10,000 litres of liquid into a process at a cost of £5 per litre.

The normal loss is 500 litres which can be sold for £1 per litre.

Each process requires £4,000 of labour. The overhead is recovered at 150% of labour.

The output of process 1 is 9,300 litres.

Produce the process account, scrap account and abnormal/loss gain account for process 1.

Process 1

	litres	£		litres	£
Materials			Normal loss		
Labour			Output		
Overhead					
	___	___		___	___
	___	___		___	___

Scrap account

	litres	£		litres	£
	___	___		___	___

Abnormal loss/gain account

	litres	£		litres	£
	___	___		___	___
	___	___		___	___

Workbook Activity 16

Taylor Ltd makes a product using a number of processes. Details for process 1 during a particular period are as follows:

Inputs	5,000 kilo at £2.47 per kilo
Labour	£1,225
Overheads	£1,862
Completed output:	4,750 kilo
Closing work-in-progress:	250 kilo

There were no losses in the process.

Work-in-progress degree of completion

Material	100%
Labour	60%
Overhead	60%

Calculate the cost per EU for period 1.

Workbook Activity 17

Ipako

Ipako produces perfume on a production line. The details of the process in Period 4 are as follows:

OWIP = 400 units

Costs incurred so far:

Materials	£48,000
Conversion	£34,800

Completed output = 1,200 units

Costs incurred in Period 4:

Materials	£120,000
Conversion	£78,000

Calculate the cost per EU using the AVCO method of valuing OWIP.

Workbook Activity 18

Noil

Noil makes electric cars on a production line. The details of the process in Period 2 are as follows:

OWIP = 250 units

Costs incurred so far:

Materials	£54,000
Conversion	£42,000

Degrees of completion:

Materials	100%
Conversion	60%

Completed output = 3,200 units

Costs incurred in Period 2:

Materials	£135,700
Conversion	£97,600

Calculate the cost per EU using the FIFO method of valuing OWIP.

Marginal costing

10

Introduction

Marginal costing is used within management accounting to aid decision making. The marginal cost of a product is the **total variable production costs**. In marginal costing **fixed overheads** are treated as **period costs** and are charged in full against the profit for the period. Absorption costing assigns fixed production overheads to the inventory: see Chapter 7.

This chapter describes marginal costing and how to reconcile absorption costing and marginal costing profits.

ASSESSMENT CRITERIA	CONTENTS
Explain the differences between marginal and absorption costing (1.5K)	1 Marginal costing 2 The concept of contribution 3 Marginal versus absorption costing 4 The impact of changing inventory levels 5 Advantages of marginal costing

1 Marginal costing

1.1 Marginal costing

Marginal costing values each unit of inventory at the **variable production cost** required to make each unit (the marginal cost). This includes direct materials, direct labour, direct expenses and variable overheads. Variable non-production costs do not form part of the product cost but are subtracted after the cost of sales to calculate **contribution**. No **fixed overheads** (production or non-production) are included in the product costs; they are treated as a **period cost** and deducted in full lower down the statement of profit and loss.

> ### Definition
>
> The **marginal production cost** is the cost of one unit of product or service which would be avoided if that unit were not produced, or the amount by which costs would increase if one extra unit were produced.

Marginal costing requires knowledge of cost behaviours as costs are split based on whether they are fixed or variable. Semi-variable costs would need to be separated into their fixed and variable elements by using the high-low method. See Chapter 2.

The basic layout for calculating budgeted profit or loss under marginal costing is as follows (with illustrative figures).

	£	£
Sales revenue (10,000 × £10)		100,000
Cost of sales (at **marginal/variable** cost, £6)		(60,000)
Variable non-production costs (£1)		(10,000)
Contribution		30,000
Less: **Fixed** production costs	20,000	
Fixed non-production costs	2,000	
		(22,000)
Profit for the period		8,000

Activity 1

XYZ plc

XYZ plc manufactures toy horses and has produced a budget for the quarter ended 30 June 20X5 (Quarter 1) as follows.

Sales	190 units @ selling price of £12
Production	200 units
Opening inventory	20 units
Variable production cost per unit	£8
Fixed production overhead	£400
Selling and distribution costs (fixed)	£250

Required:

Draft the statement of profit or loss using marginal costing principles:

	£	£
Sales revenue		
Less: Cost of sales		
Opening inventory		
Production costs		
Closing inventory		
Contribution		
Fixed costs		
Profit for the period		

2 The concept of contribution

2.1 Contribution

The concept of contribution is one of the most fundamental in cost and management accounting. Contribution measures the **difference between the sales price of a unit and the variable costs of making and selling that unit**.

Contribution = Sales revenue less all variable costs

2.2 Changes in activity level

How do contribution and profit change if we double output and sales?

	10,000 units £		20,000 units £
Sales revenue 10,000 × £10	100,000	20,000 × £10	200,000
Variable costs 10,000 × £7	(70,000)	20,000 × £7	(140,000)
Contribution	**30,000**		**60,000**
Fixed overheads	(22,000)		(22,000)
Profit for the period	**8,000**		**38,000**
Contribution per unit	£3		£3
Profit per unit	£0.80		£1.90

If sales double then the total contribution doubles but total profit does not increase at the same rate. This shows that there is a **direct relationship between** the number of **sales** made and the value of **contribution** but not level of profit. There is **no direct link between profit and output.** If output doubles, profits do not necessarily double.

The contribution per unit remains constant at £3 whereas the profit per unit increases from £0.80 to £1.90. The increase in the profit per unit is because the fixed costs are being shared over more units.

What happens to profit if sales increase by one extra unit from 10,000 to 10,001?

	£
Sales revenue 10,001 × £10	100,010
Variable costs 10,001 × £7	(70,007)
Contribution	30,003
Fixed costs	(22,000)
Profit for the period	8,003

Total contribution increases £3, but the total fixed overheads do not change so **profit also goes up by £3 (i.e. the same as contribution).**

The concept of **contribution** is an extremely important one in cost and management accounting. It is important to remember that since contribution measures the **difference between sales price and the variable cost of the unit**, if a product has a positive contribution it is worth making. Any amount of contribution, however small, **goes towards paying the fixed overheads**; if enough units are made and sold such that total contribution exceeds fixed overheads then profit will start to be made.

 Marginal versus absorption costing

3.1 Comparison of absorption and marginal costing

See Chapter 7 for a recap on absorption costing.

Below is a table that compares absorption costing and marginal costing:

Absorption costing	Marginal costing
Costs are split based on **function** – production or non-production	Costs are split based on **behaviour** – variable or fixed
Inventory is valued at the **full production cost** (fixed and variable production costs)	Inventory is valued at the **variable production cost only**
Sales – cost of sales = **gross profit**	Sales – all variable costs = **contribution**
Non-production overheads are deducted after gross profit	Variable non-production overheads are excluded from the valuation of inventory but are deducted before contribution
	All fixed cost are period costs

Activity 2

The following information has been provided.

	Cost per unit £
Direct material	8.50
Direct labour	27.20
Variable production overhead	11.30
Fixed production overhead	14.00
Selling price	61.50

Required:

Calculate each of the following in £/unit:

(a)   prime cost

(b)   marginal cost

(c)   absorption cost

(d)   gross profit

(e)   contribution

4 The impact of changing inventory levels

4.1 Changing inventory levels

The cost of sales calculation in the budgeted statement of profit or loss can be broken down into 3 elements – opening inventory, production and closing inventory. The units within these elements are valued either at marginal cost or absorption cost. The value of the closing inventory is subtracted from the sum of the value of the opening inventory and production to calculate the cost of making sales.

When inventory levels increase or decrease during a period, profits will differ under absorption and marginal costing.

Increasing inventory is when closing inventory in the cost of sales is greater than opening inventory. Decreasing inventory is when opening inventory is greater than closing inventory.

- If inventory is increasing then absorption costing will give the higher profit.

- If inventory levels are decreasing then absorption costing will give the lower profit.

- If inventory levels remain constant then the profit values will be the same.

This is because:

- under **marginal costing** all the period's fixed production overheads are charged **in full** against that period's profit, whereas

- under **absorption costing** some of the period's fixed production overheads will be **carried forward** in the closing inventory value and charged to the next period's statement of profit or loss.

This is illustrated in the following example:

Example

Worked example of profit differences

	£ per unit
Sales price	£15
Prime cost	£4
Variable production costs	£2
Budgeted fixed production overheads	£40,000 per month
Budgeted production	10,000 units per month
Budgeted sales	8,000 units
Opening inventory	500 units

Required:

Produce a budgeted marginal costing and an absorption costing statement of profit or loss for a month

Solution

When calculating the profit we will need the number of units in closing inventory. This is given by:

Opening inventory units + production units – sales units

This will be 500 + 10,000 – 8,000 = 2,500 units

Marginal costing statement of profit or loss

	£	£
Sales revenue (8,000 × £15)		120,000
Opening inventory (500 × £6)	3,000	
Marginal production costs (10,000 × £6)	60,000	
Closing inventory (2,500 × £6)	(15,000)	
Marginal cost of sales		(48,000)
Contribution		72,000
Fixed costs		(40,000)
Profit for the period		32,000

The marginal cost includes the prime cost and the variable production cost. The fixed costs are charged in full against the sales for the period.

Absorption costing statement of profit or loss

	£	£
Sales revenue (8,000 × £15)		120,000
Opening inventory (500 × £10)	5,000	
Production costs (10,000 × £10)	100,000	
Closing inventory (2,500 × £10)	(25,000)	
Absorption cost of sales		(80,000)
Profit for the period		40,000

The production cost includes the prime cost of production, the variable production costs plus an amount per unit for the fixed production costs.

The fixed overhead absorbed by each unit is as follows.

$$\frac{\text{Budgeted fixed overheads}}{\text{Budgeted production}} = \frac{£40,000}{10,000} = £4 \text{ per unit}$$

4.2 Reconciliation of profits

Example continued

In the example above the absorption costing profit is £8,000 higher than the marginal costing profit. Why?

Under absorption costing:

- The opening inventory has been charged with £2,000 of fixed production cost (500 units × £4)

- The £40,000 fixed production costs have been charged to production costs (10,000 units × £4)

- £10,000 of this has then been deducted from the cost of sales as part of the closing inventory value (2,500 unit × £4)

- This means that under absorption costing only £32,000 of fixed costs has been charged in this month's statement of profit and loss (£2,000 + £40,000 – £10,000 = £32,000)

Under marginal costing:

- The full £40,000 of fixed costs as been charged to this month's statement of profit or loss

- The profit under marginal costing is £8,000 lower than under absorption costing as £8,000 more cost has been charged against revenue.

It may be necessary to calculate the absorption profit from the marginal profit or vice versa. Use the proforma below to do this:

Absorption costing profit	X
Less: Change in inventory × OAR	+/–X
Marginal costing profit	X

Note the change in inventory is calculated as the opening inventory units less the closing inventory units.

Example continued

Using the information in the example:

Absorption costing profit	£40,000
Less: Change in inventory × OAR	
(500 – 2,500) × 4	–£8,000
Marginal costing profit	£32,000

Activity 3

McTack

McTack manufactures PCs and has produced a budget for the quarter ended 31 March 20X4 (Quarter 1) using absorption costing as follows.

	£	£
Sales revenue (100 units @ £500 per unit)		50,000
Production cost of 120 units		
Materials	12,000	
Labour	24,000	
Variable overhead	6,000	
Fixed overhead	6,000	
	48,000	
Less: Closing inventory (20 × £400)	(8,000)	
		(40,000)
		10,000

Required:

Re-draft the statement of profit or loss using marginal costing principles.

	£	£
Sales revenue		
Less Cost of sales:		
Opening inventory		
Production costs		
Closing inventory	( )	
		( )
Contribution		
Fixed costs		( )
Profit for the period		

Reconcile the profits:

5 Advantages of marginal costing

5.1 Advantages of marginal costing

1 Marginal costing avoids needing to allocate, apportion, re-apportion and absorb fixed overheads (see Chapter 7).

2 Fixed costs logically relate to time and so are charged as period costs.

3 Profit figures are more consistent with fluctuating sales.

4 Used for short term decision-making (see Chapter 11).

6 Summary

Marginal costing calculates the **contribution** per unit of a product. In marginal costing units are valued at **variable production cost** and fixed overheads are accounted for as period costs.

In **absorption costing**, units are valued at **variable cost plus fixed production overheads** absorbed using a pre-determined absorption rate.

The differences in these methods give rise to different profit figures which are usually reconciled at the end of an accounting period.

Answers to chapter activities

Activity 1

There will be closing inventory of 30 units.

Opening inventory + production − sales = closing inventory

Under marginal costing, the closing inventory will be valued at the variable production cost of £8 per unit.

Marginal costing statement of profit and loss

	£	£
Sales revenue		2,280
Less: Cost of sales		
Opening inventory (20 × 8)	160	
Production costs (200 × 8)	1,600	
Closing inventory (30 × 8)	(240)	
		1,520
Contribution		760
Fixed costs		(650)
Profit for the period		110

Activity 2

(a) Prime cost per unit

	£
Direct material	8.50
Direct labour	27.20
	35.70

(b) Marginal cost per unit

	£
Prime cost	35.70
Variable production overhead	11.30
	47.00

(c) Absorption cost per unit

	£
Prime cost	35.70
Variable production overhead	11.30
Fixed production overhead	14.00
	61.00

(d) Gross profit per unit

	£
Selling price	61.50
Less Absorption cost	(61.00)
	0.50

(e) Contribution per unit

	£
Selling price	61.50
Less Marginal cost	(47.00)
	14.50

Activity 3

McTack – Budgeted profit statement quarter ended 31 March

Marginal costing format

Marginal costing statement of profit or loss

	£	£
Sales revenue (100 × £500)		50,000
Less: Cost of sales		
Opening inventory	0	
Production costs (12,000 + 24,000 + 6,000)	42,000	
Closing inventory (20 × £350)	(7,000)	
		(35,000)
Contribution		15,000
Fixed costs		(6,000)
Profit for the period		9,000

Calculation of marginal cost per unit.

Marginal cost/number of units produced = marginal cost per unit

42,000/120 = £350

Reconciliation of profits

	£
Absorption costing profit	10,000
Change in inventory × OAR (0 – 20) × £50	–1,000
Absorption costing profit	9,000

7 Test your knowledge

Workbook Activity 4

Billie Millar

The following information relates to the manufacture of product Delphinium during the month of April 2005:

Direct materials per unit	£10.60
Direct labour per unit	£16.40
Variable overheads per batch	£60,000
Fixed overheads per batch	£80,000
Number of units per batch	10,000

Task

Calculate the prime cost per unit.

Calculate the marginal cost per unit.

Calculate the absorption cost per unit.

Workbook Activity 5

Crescent Feeds Ltd have produced the following set of cost and management accounting figures for its current accounting period.

	£	
Production and sales tonnage	–	2,500 tonnes
Direct labour	102,000	
Admin overheads	16,500	
Direct materials	210,000	
Direct expenses	5,250	
Fixed production overheads	20,400	
Variable production overheads	20,000	
Selling and distribution costs (fixed)	52,300	

KAPLAN PUBLISHING

Calculate for the period:

- Prime cost
- Marginal cost
- Absorption cost
- Non-production cost
- Total cost
- Prime cost per tonne of product
- Marginal cost per tonne of product
- Absorption cost per tonne of product
- Total cost per tonne of product

Workbook Activity 6

Voliti Limited has produced the following budgeted figures for a new product it hopes to launch.

Direct material	£10 per unit
Direct labour	£5 per unit
Variable production overheads	£8 per unit
Fixed production costs	£19,500 per month
Budgeted output	6,500 units per month
Sales price	£30 per unit
Month 1	
Production	6,500
Sales	5,000

Task

Complete the statement of profit or loss for month 1 on each of the following bases, and reconcile the resulting profit figures:

(i) **Marginal costing principles**

	£	£
Sales revenue		
Less: Cost of sales		
Opening inventory		
Production costs		
Closing inventory	( )	
		( )
Contribution		
Fixed costs		( )
Profit for the period		

(ii) **Absorption costing principles**

	£	£
Sales revenue		
Cost of sales		
Opening inventory		
Production costs		
Closing inventory	( )	
		( )
Gross profit		
Non-production costs		( )
Profit for the period		

The absorption costing profit is *higher/lower** than the marginal costing profit because there are *more/less** fixed costs charged against the sales in the absorption costing statement.

*delete as appropriate

KAPLAN PUBLISHING

Short-term decision making

Introduction

There are a number of calculations that can be completed to aid decision making in the short term. Within this chapter we will consider a number of different techniques that are required in different situations.

ASSESSMENT CRITERIA

Prepare estimates of future income and costs for decision making using (5.1S):

– Relevant costs

– Break-even analysis

– Margin of safety

– Target profit

– Limiting factors

Prepare management reports in an appropriate format, presenting these within the required timescales (4.4S)

CONTENTS

1 Relevant costing
2 Cost-volume-profit (CVP) analysis
3 CVP charts
4 Limiting factors analysis

---

1 Relevant costing

1.1 The concept of relevant costing

When assisting management in **short term** decision making only costs or revenues that are **relevant** to the decision should be considered. Any form of decision-making process involves making a choice between two or more alternatives.

1.2 Relevant costs and revenues

> 🔍 **Definition**
>
> Relevant costs and revenues are those costs and revenues that **change as a direct result of a decision that is taken**.

A relevant cost is a **future, incremental cash flow** arising as direct result of a decision being taken:

- **Future costs and revenues** – costs and revenues that are going to be incurred sometime in the future due to the decision being taken.

- **Incremental costs and revenues** – any extra cost or revenue generated by the decision that would not arise otherwise e.g. an extra amount of fixed costs due only to the decision.

- **Cash flows rather than profits** – actual cash being spent or received should be used when making the decision. Profits can be manipulated by accounting concepts like depreciation. Cash flows are more reliable.

A relevant cost or revenue could also be referred to as an avoidable cost.

> 🔍 **Definition**
>
> An **avoidable cost** is any cost that would only occur as a result of taking the decision. If the decision did not go ahead then the cost would not be incurred so it is avoidable.

1.3 Non-relevant costs and revenues

Costs or revenues that can be ruled out when making a decision come under the following categories:

- **Sunk costs** – past or historic costs that cannot be changed e.g. any cost incurred due to research and development that has already been carried out will not apply after the decision has been made.

- **Committed costs** – costs that are **unavoidable** and will be incurred whether or not the project is done.

- **Non-cash flow costs** – depreciation and carrying amounts are accounting concepts, not actual cash flows and are not relevant costs

Activity 1

Which of the following is not a relevant cost/revenue?

A   Variable costs

B   Research and development costs that have already been incurred

C   Incremental fixed costs

D   Increase in sales revenue

1.4 Fixed and variable costs

It is usually assumed that a **variable cost** will be **relevant** to a decision as when activity increases the total variable cost incurred increases. There is a direct relationship between production activity and variable costs. However there are some situations where this may not be true.

Example

A company is considering a short-term pricing decision for a contract that would use 1,000 kg of material A. There are 800 kg of material A in inventory, which was bought some time ago for £3 per kg. The material in inventory could be sold for £3.50 per kg. The current purchase price of material A is £4.50.

What is the relevant cost of material A for this contract?

Solution

The cost per kg of material is considered to be a variable cost but you also need to consider whether the cost is a future cost for it to be relevant.

The company has already got 800 kg in inventory so this does not need to be purchased. The £3 per kg is an old purchase price i.e. a past or historic cost so it is not relevant. The material would therefore be valued at the current re-sale value of £3.50 per kg.

The company will need to buy a further 200 kg to complete the contract. This would be valued at the current purchase price of £4.50.

The total relevant cost of material A is:

800 kg × £3.50 = £2,800

200 kg × £4.50 = £900

Total = £3,700

Unless told otherwise variable costs and the variable element of the semi-variable costs are relevant to a decision.

Fixed costs tend to come under the umbrella of committed costs so are not relevant. Be careful though because if the fixed cost were to step up as a direct result of a decision taken then the extra cost would be relevant as it is an incremental cost.

Example

MCL Plc absorbs overheads on a machine hour rate, currently £20 per hour, of which £7 is for variable overheads and £13 is for fixed overheads. The company is deciding whether to undertake a contract in the coming year. If the contract is accepted it is estimated that the fixed costs will increase by £3,200 for the duration.

What are the relevant overhead costs for this decision?

Solution

The variable cost per hour is relevant as this cost would be avoidable of the contract were not undertaken. The relevant cost is therefore £7 per machine hour.

The fixed cost per hour is an absorption rate. This is not an indication of how much actual overheads would increase by. The £3,200 extra fixed cost is relevant as it is an incremental or extra cost.

With regards short-term decision making we assume that on the whole **fixed costs** are **non-relevant** costs so we can approach decisions using the **marginal costing technique.**

2 Cost-volume-profit (CVP) analysis

2.1 Introduction

Cost volume profit analysis looks at the link between costs, levels of activity and profits generated. It is used to make short term decisions and answer questions such as:

- how many units do we need to sell to make a certain profit?

- how many units do we need to sell to cover our costs?

- by how much will profit fall if the price is lowered by £1?

- what will happen to our profits if we rent an extra factory but find that we can operate at only half capacity?

2.2 The approach to CVP analysis

CVP analysis makes a number of assumptions as follows.

- Costs are assumed to be either **fixed** or **variable**, or at least **separable into these elements**.

- Fixed costs remain fixed throughout the activity range charted.

- Variable costs change in direct proportion to volume.

- Economies or diseconomies of scale are ignored; this ensures that **the variable cost per unit is constant**.

- Selling prices do not change with volume.

- Efficiency and productivity do not change with volume.

- It is applied to a single product or static mix of products.

- We look at the effect a change in volume has on **contribution** (not profit). Therefore we use **marginal costing**.

- Volume is the only factor affecting cost.

- Contribution per unit = selling price per unit – total variable cost per unit.

While some of the assumptions may seem unrealistic, over the short-term considered, they are often a **reasonable approximation** of the true position.

There are a number of calculations and formulas that make up CVP analysis:

- Breakeven point
- Margin of safety
- Target profit
- Profit/volume ratio

You will need to learn these formulae for the exam.

2.3 Breakeven point

> ### 🔍 Definition
>
> The **breakeven point** is the volume of sales at which neither a profit nor a loss is made.

When there is no profit or loss we can assume that total fixed costs equal total contribution:

Sales revenue – variable costs = total contribution – fixed costs = profit

- If profit is zero then total contribution must equal the fixed costs.
- Contribution per unit is constant therefore we can calculate the number of units required to break even as follows:

$$\text{Breakeven point (units)} = \frac{\text{Fixed cost}}{\text{Contribution/unit}}$$

> ### 🔆 Example
>
> **Breakeven point**
>
> Rachel's product, the 'Steadyarm', sells for £50. It has a variable cost of £30 per unit. Rachel's total fixed costs are £40,000 per annum.
>
> What is her breakeven point?
>
> **Solution**
>
> To break even we want just enough contribution to cover the total fixed costs of £40,000.
>
> We therefore want total contribution of £40,000.
>
> Each unit of sales gives contribution of £50 – £30 = £20.

Therefore the breakeven point in units:

$$= \frac{\text{Total fixed costs}}{\text{Contribution per unit}} = \frac{\text{£40,000}}{\text{£20}} = 2{,}000 \text{ units}$$

We can show that this calculation is correct as below.

	£
Total contribution (2,000 units × £20)	40,000
Total fixed costs	(40,000)
	———
Profit/loss	0
	———

Breakeven point can also be expressed in sales revenue terms. We know we have to sell 2,000 units to breakeven and we know the selling price is £50. The breakeven point in sales revenue is therefore £100,000.

	£
Sales revenue (2,000 units × £50)	100,000
Variable costs (2,000 units × £30)	(60,000)
	———
Total contribution	40,000
Total fixed costs	(40,000)
	———
Profit/loss	0
	———

2.4 Margin of safety

Definition

The **margin of safety** is the amount by which the anticipated (budgeted) sales can fall before the business makes a loss.

The margin of safety is therefore the difference between budgeted sales volume and **break-even point**. It can be expressed in absolute units or relative percentage terms.

Margin of safety (units) = Budgeted sales units – Breakeven sales units

$$\text{Margin of safety (\%)} = \frac{\text{Budgeted sales units} - \text{Breakeven sales units}}{\text{Budgeted sales unit}} \times 100$$

> ### Example
>
> **Margin of safety**
>
> Rachel's product, the 'Steadyarm', sells for £50. It has a variable cost of £30 per unit. Rachel's total fixed costs are £40,000 per annum. Rachel is expecting to achieve sales of 2,500 units.
>
> What is her margin of safety?
>
> **Solution**
>
> To calculate the margin of safety we first need to know the breakeven point in units. From the previous example we know that for Rachel to breakeven she needs to sell 2,000 units.
>
> $$= \frac{\text{Total fixed costs}}{\text{Contribution per unit}} = \frac{£40,000}{£20} = 2,000 \text{ units}$$
>
> We can then work out the margin of safety in units:
>
> = Budgeted sales units – Breakeven sales units
>
> = 2,500 – 2,000 = 500 units
>
> And then the margin of safety as a percentage of budgeted sales units
>
> $$= \frac{\text{Budgeted sales units} - \text{Breakeven sales units}}{\text{Budgeted sales unit}} \times 100$$
>
> $$= \frac{2,500 - 2,000}{2,500} \times 100 = 20\%$$
>
> Margin of safety can also be expressed in sales revenue terms. In the example above we know we have a margin of safety of 500 units and the selling price for each of these units is £50. The sales revenue margin of safety is therefore £25,000.

2.5 Achieving a target profit

A similar approach to the breakeven point calculation can be used to find the **sales volume at which a particular profit is made**.

When calculating the breakeven point we wanted to find the number of units that would mean that contribution equalled fixed costs, i.e. zero profit. Now if we know the required profit we can add this to the fixed costs to find the amount of contribution we need to cover both the fixed costs and to generate the required profit.

Sales volume to achieve a particular profit:

$$= \frac{\text{Total fixed costs} + \text{required profit}}{\text{Contribution/unit}}$$

Example

Achieving a target profit

Information as in Rachel example above but we now want to know how many units must be sold to make a profit of £12,000.

To achieve a profit of £12,000, we require sufficient contribution firstly to cover the fixed costs (£40,000) and secondly, to give a profit of £12,000. Therefore our required contribution is £52,000.

Sales volume to achieve a profit of £12,000

$$= \frac{\text{Total fixed costs} + \text{required profit}}{\text{Contribution/unit}}$$

$$= \frac{£40,000 + £12,000}{£20}$$

$$= \quad 2,600 \text{ units}$$

We can show that this is the case with a summarised statement of profit or loss account.

	£
Sales revenue (2,600 × £50)	130,000
Variable cost (2,600 × £30)	(78,000)
Total fixed costs	(40,000)
Profit	12,000

A required profit could also be achieved by changing the **selling price** rather than the sales volume.

Example

Achieving a target profit

Information as in Rachel example above but we now want to know how much the sales price needs to change to be able to make a profit of £12,000.

To achieve a profit of £12,000, we require sufficient contribution firstly to cover the fixed costs (£40,000) and secondly, to give a profit of £12,000. Therefore our required contribution is £52,000.

This means that the contribution per unit needs to be:

$$= \frac{\text{Total fixed costs} + \text{required profit}}{\text{Budgeted sales volume}}$$

$$= \frac{£40,000 + £12,000}{2,500}$$

$$= £20.80$$

This means that contribution needs to increase from £20 to £20.80 – an increase of £0.80. To do this the sales price can be increased by £0.80 to £50.80.

We can show that this is the case with a summarised statement of profit or loss account.

	£
Sales revenue (2,500 × £50.80)	127,000
Variable cost (2,500 × £30)	(75,000)
Total fixed costs	(40,000)
Profit	12,000

2.6 Profit/Volume ratio

Definition

The **P/V ratio** is a measure of the rate at which profit (or, strictly, contribution) is generated with sales volume, as measured by revenue.

An alternative name which provides a more accurate description is the contribution/sales (C/S) ratio.

$$\text{P/V ratio} = \frac{\text{Contribution per unit}}{\text{Selling price per unit}} \text{ or } \frac{\text{Total contribution}}{\text{Total revenue}}$$

It tells us what **proportion or percentage of the selling price is contributing to our fixed overhead and profits.**

If, for example, the P/V ratio was 40% this would mean that 40% of the selling price was contribution which means therefore that the remaining 60% is variable cost.

It can be **used in the breakeven point and the target profit** calculations to be able to calculate the answer **in terms of sales value** (rather than volume).

Breakeven point in sales value = $\dfrac{\text{Total fixed costs}}{\text{P/V ratio}}$

Sales value giving a profit £X = $\dfrac{\text{Total fixed costs} + \text{required profit}}{\text{P/V ratio}}$

When using the P/V ratio in calculations the **decimal format** is used rather than the percentage i.e. 0.4 rather than 40%.

 Example

P/V ratio

We return to the 'Steadyarm' example, where the product sells for £50, has a variable cost of £30 per unit and fixed costs and £40,000 per annum.

What value of sales revenue will give a profit of £12,000?

Sales value giving profit £12,000 means that the required contribution is £52,000.

$$= \dfrac{\text{Total fixed costs} + \text{required profit}}{\text{P/V ratio}}$$

$$= \dfrac{£40,000 + £12,000}{0.4 \text{ (W)}}$$

$$= £130,000$$

This corresponds with 2,600 units (as before) at £50 sales value per unit.

Working:

P/V ratio = $\dfrac{\text{Contribution}}{\text{Selling price}} = \dfrac{£20}{£50} = 0.4$

Activity 2

Camilla

Camilla makes a single product, the Wocket. During 20Y1 she plans to make and sell 3,500 Wockets and has estimated the following:

	Per unit £
Selling price	16
Material	4
Labour	6
Variable overhead	2

Total fixed costs are budgeted to be £12,000

Target profit £150,000

(a) Calculate the contribution per unit earned by each Wocket.

(b) Calculate the P/V ratio

(c) Calculate Camilla's breakeven point in units.

(d) Calculate Camilla's breakeven point in revenue.

(e) Calculate Camilla's margin of safety in units

(f) Calculate Camilla's margin of safety in revenue

(g) Calculate Camilla's margin of safety as a percentage of budgeted sales (2 decimal places)

(h) Calculate the sales revenue that Camilla would require to meet her target profit.

3.1 Breakeven charts

We can show our analysis diagrammatically in a breakeven chart.

Breakeven chart showing fixed and variable cost lines

To make the diagram clearer we can show it with only the total cost line on the graph.

Breakeven chart showing total cost line

📝 Activity 3

APSTEL Limited

The following information relates to a month's production of APSTEL Limited, a small manufacturing company mass producing a single product.

Materials per unit	£4
Labour per unit	£6
Selling price per unit	£17
Planned level of sales per month	7,000 units

Required:

(a) Read off an approximate breakeven point in sales value and units.

(b) Calculate the breakeven point in units using the formula.

(c) Calculate the margin of safety as a percentage of budgeted sales.

(d) Calculate how many units APSTEL would have to sell if they required a profit of £100,000?

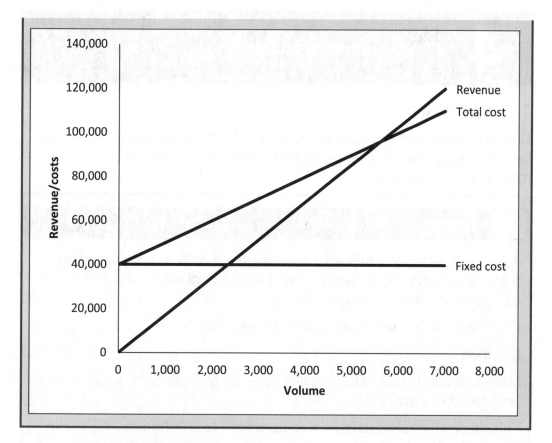

3.2   Profit-volume (P/V) chart

A P/V chart is another way of presenting the information

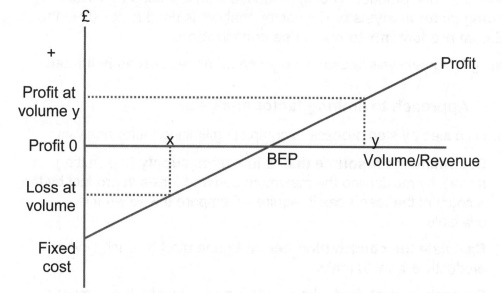

Note that at a **sales volume of nil**, the **total loss** will be the same as the business's **fixed costs**.

4 Limiting factors analysis

4.1 Introduction

During a period it may become necessary to amend production due to a lack of a resource, for example material, labour, machine time or cash may be in short supply.

Example

A company wishes to make 2,500 units in a month. Each unit requires 5 kgs of material. There is currently a shortage of material and the company can only access 10,000 kg.

How many units can the company actually make?

Solution

Maximum production would require 12,500 kg of material but there is only 10,000 kg available.

This means that production would be limited to 2,000 units (10,000 kg/ 5 kg per unit)

If more than one product is being produced then a procedure called **Limiting factor analysis** or Key factor analysis is used to calculate the **optimum product mix to maximise contribution**.

Limiting factor analysis is used if only **one** of the **resources is limited**.

4.2 Approach to limiting factor analysis

There is a step by step process to completing limiting factor analysis

- **Determine the resource that is in scarce supply** (the limiting factor), by multiplying the maximum demand for each product by the amount of the resources it requires. Compare this to what is available.

- **Calculate the contribution per unit** generated by each type of product we want to make.

- For each product divide the contribution per unit by the number of units of scarce resource needed to make one unit of that product (**contribution per limiting factor**).

- **Rank the products** from highest contribution per limiting factor to lowest contribution per limiting factor.

- **Allocate the scarce resource** to the product ranked 1 and calculate how much of the scarce resource this would use to produce the required demand.

- If there is any scarce resource remaining, follow the previous step for the product ranked 2 and so on until there is not enough scarce resource to match the demand for a product.

- Calculate how much of the remaining product can be produced with the remaining scarce resource.

- Calculate the total contribution from the new production plan and the overall profit.

🔆 Example

Truffle Ltd

Truffle Ltd makes 3 products the Dog, the Hound and the Canine. The money available to pay for the resources needed for next month's production is as follows:

Material £10,000

Labour £10,000

Variable overheads £15,000

Below are the details for a unit each product:

	Dog	Hound	Canine
	£	£	£
Selling price	10	12	15
Material cost	2	3	2
Labour cost	1	3	4
Other variable costs	2	4	4
Maximum monthly demand	1,000	1,500	1,250

Total fixed costs £9,000

What is Truffle's optimal production plan for the next month?

Solution

Step 1 – identify the limiting factor

To be able to meet the maximum demand for all the products the requirements would be as follows:

Material = (2 × 1000) + (3 × 1500) + (2 × 1250) = £9,000

Labour = (1 × 1000) + (3 × 1500) + (4 × 1250) = £10,500

Other variable costs = (2 × 1000) + (4 × 1500) + (4 × 1250) = £13,000

Therefore the labour cost is the limiting factor as there is enough cash available to cover the cost of materials and other variable costs.

Step 2 – calculate the contribution per unit

	Dog	Hound	Canine
	£	£	£
Selling price	10	12	15
Material cost	(2)	(3)	(2)
Labour cost	(1)	(3)	(4)
Other variable costs	(2)	(4)	(4)
Contribution per unit	5	2	5

Step 3 – calculate the contribution per limiting factor

	Dog	Hound	Canine
	£	£	£
Contribution per unit	5	2	5
Limiting factor per unit (labour cost per unit)	1	3	4
Contribution per limiting factor	5	0.66	1.25

Step 4 – rank the products

	Dog	Hound	Canine
	£	£	£
Contribution per limiting factor	5	0.66	1.25
Rank	1	3	2

Steps 5 to 8 – allocate the scarce supply

Product in rank order	Units	LF per unit £	Total LF £	Contribution £
Dog	1,000	1	1,000	5,000
Canine	1,250	4	5,000	6,250
Hound	1,333 (W)	3	4,000β	2,666

LF available	£10,000	
Total contribution		13,916
Less fixed costs		(9,000)
Profit		4,916

Working:

There is only £4,000 left to spend on labour once maximum demand is allocated to the other products (β = balancing amount). This means that Truffle will be able to make 1,333 complete Hounds (4,000/3 = 1,333.33).

Activity 4

ABC

ABC makes three products with the following estimated costs and revenues.

	A	B	C
Selling price (£)	20	25	30
Variable cost per unit (£)	10	11	14
Amount of material X used per unit (kg)	2	2	4
Maximum demand (units)	250	100	200

Total fixed costs £1,250

Due to a shortage in the market, only 800 kg are available.

Required:

Using limiting factor analysis complete the table below to determine the production plan that will optimise profit

	A	B	C
Selling price (£)			
Variable cost per unit (£)			
Contribution per unit (£)			
LF per unit (kg)			
Contribution per LF (£)			
Rank			

Production plan

Product in rank order	Units	LF per unit (kg)	Total LF (kg)	Contribution (£)
1				
2				
3				
		Total LF	800 kg	
			Total Contribution	
			Fixed costs	
			Profit	

Activity 5

Dunnsports

Dunnsports make a variety of sports goods. One of its product groups is cricket boots and they make a range of three styles. You are given the following data for the forthcoming quarter.

	Gower	Boycott	Willis
Selling price	£27.50	£30.00	£28.50
Direct material	£8.00	£8.50	£8.25
Direct labour at £7.50 per hour	£9.00	£9.75	£8.25
Forecast sales/production	500	510	520

Shortly after the budgeted output was agreed a machine breakdown occurred and, as parts are not available immediately, labour hours will be limited to 1,540 hours.

Required:

Complete the table below to calculate the production schedule that will optimise profit, assuming that the actual sales per product will not exceed the forecast figures quoted.

	Gower	Boycott	Willis
Selling price (£)			
Variable cost per unit (£)			
Contribution per unit (£)			
LF per unit (hours)			
Contribution per LF (£)			
Rank			

Product in rank order	Units	LF per unit (hours)	Total LF (hours)	Contribution (£)
1				
2				
3				
	Total LF	1,540		
		Total Contribution		

Activity 6

Naturo

Naturo Limited can synthesise a natural plant extract called Ipethin into one of three products. Ipethin is in short supply and the company at present is able to obtain only 1,000 kgs per period at a cost of £25 per kg.

The budgeted costs and other data for a typical period are as follows:

	Product F	Product G	Product H
Kg of Ipethin per unit	1.4	0.96	2.6
Labour hours per unit (£8 per hour)	3	8	4
Selling price per unit	£110	£150	£180
Maximum demand (units)	200	400	300

Fixed costs are £25,000 per period.

Task

Determine the preferred order of manufacture in order to maximise profit.

	F	G	H
Selling price (£)			
Variable cost per unit (£)			
Contribution per unit (£)			
LF per unit (kg)			
Contribution per LF (£)			
Rank			

Production plan

Product in rank order	Units	LF per unit (kg)	Total LF (kg)	Contribution (£)
1				
2				
3				
		Total LF	1,000 kg	
			Total Contribution	
			Fixed costs	
			Profit	

KAPLAN PUBLISHING

5 Summary

In this chapter we have considered the approaches required to make short-term decisions about operating levels. CVP analysis recognises that changes in profit arise from changes in contribution which, in turn, is directly related to activity levels. Thus, we can use contribution per unit to calculate the required activity level to achieve a particular profit level, including zero (breakeven point). The formulae are not provided in the exam so make sure you have learnt them.

Breakeven point in units

$$\frac{\text{Fixed cost}}{\text{Contribution/unit}}$$

Sales volume to achieve a particular profit

$$\frac{\text{Total fixed costs} + \text{required profit}}{\text{Contribution/unit}}$$

If we **know the breakeven point**, then we can also calculate the margin of safety.

Margin of safety (units)

$$\text{Budgeted sales units} - \text{Breakeven sales units}$$

Margin of safety (%)

$$\frac{\text{Budgeted sales units} - \text{breakeven sales units}}{\text{Budgeted sales units}} \times 100\%$$

Profit/Volume ratio or **C/S** ratio

$$\frac{\text{Contribution per unit}}{\text{Selling price}}$$

Breakeven point in **sales revenue** terms (£)

$$\frac{\text{Fixed cost}}{\text{C/S ratio}}$$

Sales revenue (£) to achieve a particular profit

$$\frac{\text{Total fixed costs} + \text{required profit}}{\text{C/S ratio}}$$

Key factor analysis is a technique that we can use when we have a resource (materials, labour or machine time, for example) that is in short supply. Scarce resources should be allocated between products on the basis of the contribution that they earn per unit of scarce resource.

Answers to chapter activities

Activity 1

B Research and development costs that have **already been incurred**.

This is a sunk cost and not relevant to a future decision.

Activity 2

(a) **Contribution per unit**

= Selling price per unit – Variable cost per unit

= £16 – £12 = **£4**

(b) **P/V ratio**

PV ratio = 4/16 = **0.25**

(c) **Breakeven point (units)**

= Total fixed costs/Contribution per unit

= £12,000/£4 = **3,000 units**

(d) **Breakeven point (revenue)**

= Breakeven point (units) × sales revenue per unit

= 3,000 units × £16 = **£48,000**

(e) **Margin of safety (units)**

= budgeted sales – breakeven point

= 3,500 – 3,000 = **500 units**

(f) **Margin of safety (revenue)**

= margin of safety (units) × sales revenue per unit

= 500 × £16 = **£8,000**

(g) **Margin of safety (%)**

= (budgeted sales – breakeven point)/budgeted sales × 100%

= (3,500 – 3,000)/3,500 × 100% = **14.29%**

(h) **Sales revenue to meet the target profit.**

(£12,000 + £150,000)/0.25 = **£648,000**

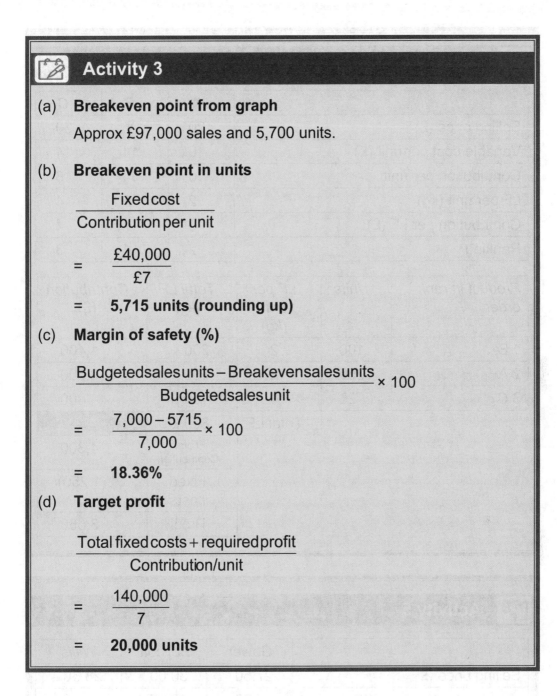

Activity 3

(a) **Breakeven point from graph**

Approx £97,000 sales and 5,700 units.

(b) **Breakeven point in units**

$$\frac{\text{Fixed cost}}{\text{Contribution per unit}}$$

$$= \frac{£40,000}{£7}$$

= **5,715 units (rounding up)**

(c) **Margin of safety (%)**

$$\frac{\text{Budgeted sales units} - \text{Breakeven sales units}}{\text{Budgeted sales unit}} \times 100$$

$$= \frac{7,000 - 5715}{7,000} \times 100$$

= **18.36%**

(d) **Target profit**

$$\frac{\text{Total fixed costs} + \text{required profit}}{\text{Contribution/unit}}$$

$$= \frac{140,000}{7}$$

= **20,000 units**

Activity 4

	A	B	C
Selling price (£)	20	25	30
Variable cost per unit (£)	10	11	14
Contribution per unit	10	14	16
LF per unit (kg)	2	2	4
Contribution per LF (£)	5	7	4
Ranking	2	1	3

Product in rank order	Units	LF per unit (kg)	Total LF (kg)	Contribution (£)
1 B	100	2	200	1,400
2 A	250	2	500	2,500
3 C	25	4	100 β	400
	Total LF	800 kg		
			Total Contribution	4,300
			Fixed costs	(1,250)
			Profit	3,050

Activity 5

	Gower	Boycott	Willis
Selling price (£)	27.50	30.00	28.50
Variable cost per unit (£)	17.00	18.25	16.50
Contribution per unit (£)	10.50	11.75	12.00
LF per unit (hours) (W)	1.2	1.3	1.1
Contribution per LF (£)	8.75	9.04	10.91
Rank	3	2	1

6 Test your knowledge

Workbook Activity 7

Product	Batman	Robin
Budgeted sales and production	500,000	750,000
Machine hours required	1,000,000	3,750,000
Sales revenue (£)	5,000,000	9,000,000
Direct materials (£)	1,000,000	2,250,000
Direct labour (£)	1,250,000	2,625,000
Variable overheads (£)	1,500,000	1,500,000
Fixed Costs £	1,000,000	2,450,000

The latest sales forecast is that 480,000 units of Product Batman and 910,000 units of Product Robin will be sold during the year.

Complete the table below to calculate the following:

(i)   budgeted breakeven sales, in units, for each of the two products

(ii) the margin of safety (in units) for each of the two products

(iii) the margin of safety as a percentage (to two decimal places)

(iv) If only Robins were made how many would be needed to make a profit of £280,000? (assume fixed costs are product specific).

Product	Batman	Robin
Fixed costs (£)		
Unit contribution (£)		
Breakeven sales (units)		
Forecast sales (units)		
Margin of safety (units)		
Margin of safety (%)		
Target profit (units)		

Workbook Activity 8

A business has a contract with a customer to produce 4,000 units of product.

Revenues and costs for 4,000 units are shown below.

Possible production level	4,000 units
	£
Sales revenue	50,000
Variable and semi-variable costs:	
Material	2,000
Labour	4,000
Overheads	6,000
Fixed costs:	
Indirect labour	12,000
Overheads	8,000
Target profit for contract	20,000

The labour cost is a semi-variable cost. The fixed cost is £2,000 and the variable cost is £0.50 per unit.

Use the table below to calculate the required number of units for this contract to achieve its target profit. Enter the contribution per unit to two decimal places.

Calculation of required number of units	£
Fixed costs	
Target profit	
Fixed cost and target profit	
Sales revenue	
Variable costs	
Contribution	
Contribution per unit	
Required number of units to achieve target profit	

Workbook Activity 9

DH is considering the purchase of a bar/restaurant which is available for £130,000. He has estimated that the weekly fixed costs will be as follows:

	£
Business rates	125
Electricity	75
Insurances	60
Gas	45
Depreciation	125
Telephone	50
Advertising	40
Postage and stationery	20
Motor expenses	20
Cleaning	10

The contribution to sales ratio is 60%.

The weekly breakeven sales value of the business is:

A   £800

B   £970

C   £850

D   £950

Workbook Activity 10

Triproduct Limited makes and sells three types of electronic security systems for which the following information is available.

Expected cost and selling prices per unit:

Product	Day scan	Night scan	Omni scan
	£	£	£
Materials	70	110	155
Manufacturing labour	40	55	70
Installation labour	24	32	44
Variable overheads	16	20	28
Selling price	250	320	460

Fixed costs for the period are £450,000 and the installation labour, which is highly skilled, is available for 25,000 hours only in a period and is paid £8 per hour.

Both manufacturing and installation labour are variable costs.

The maximum demand for the products is:

Day scan	Night scan	Omni scan
2,000 units	3,000 units	1,800 units

Determine the best production plan, assuming that Triproduct Limited wishes to maximise profit.

	Day	Night	Omni
Selling price (£)			
Variable cost per unit (£)			
Contribution per unit (£)			
LF per unit (hrs)			
Contribution per LF (£)			
Rank			

Production plan

Product in rank order	Units	LF per unit (hr)	Total LF (hr)	Contribution (£)
1				
2				
3				
		Total LF	25,000 hr	
			Total Contribution	
			Fixed costs	
			Profit	

Workbook Activity 11

Burma Limited manufactures two products: Alfie and Boris. Details about the products are as follows.

Sales price and costs per unit	Alfie	Boris
Sales price	£16.20	£22.80
Direct materials	£4.00	£6.00
Direct labour	£2.00	£4.00
Fixed production overheads per unit based on labour hour	£3.00	£6.00
Variable selling costs	£0.50	£0.50
Maximum sales units	10,000 units	15,000 units

Direct materials cost £2 per kilo, and direct labour costs £10 per hour.

In the coming year it is expected that the supply of labour will be limited to 4,000 hours.

Fixed production overhead rates have been calculated using the maximum expected number of labour hours available in the coming period.

State how many units of each product Burma Limited should produce in order to maximise profit.

	Alfie	Boris
Selling price (£)		
Variable cost per unit (£)		
Contribution per unit (£)		
LF per unit (hrs)		
Contribution per LF (£)		
Rank		

Production plan

Product in rank order	Units	LF per unit (hr)	Total LF (hr)	Contribution (£)
1				
2				
		Total LF	4,000 hr	
			Total Contribution	
			Fixed costs	
			Profit	

Long-term decision making

12

Introduction

In this chapter the focus is on long-term investment decisions – usually lasting **more than one year**. This could vary from the decision to build a new factory to whether or not to discontinue a product range.

The investment appraisal techniques that are discussed in this chapter are payback period, net present cost, net present value and internal rate of return.

ASSESSMENT CRITERIA	CONTENTS
Prepare estimates of future income and costs for decision making using (5.1S): – Payback – Discounted cash flow Prepare management reports in an appropriate format, presenting these within the required timescales (4.4S)	1 Long-term investments 2 Predicting future cash flows 3 Payback period 4 Discounting 5 Net present value/cost 6 Internal rate of return 7 Practice question

1 Long-term investments

1.1 Introduction

The key characteristic of a capital investment project is the tying up of capital for a number of years, or for the long term, in order to earn profits or returns over the period.

1.2 What will the capital be invested in?

The most common investment you will encounter will be in **tangible non-current assets**, such as a new machine, factory or premises from which to operate a new service business.

Other intangible forms of investment include **research and development**, **patent rights or goodwill** obtained on the purchase of an existing business.

1.3 What form will the returns take?

The purchase of a new non-current asset will often be with the intention of starting a new line of business – say the manufacturing of a new product, or the provision of a new or extended service. The returns will be the **net income** generated by the new business.

Alternatively, the investment may be to benefit the existing operations, such that **sales are increased** (where existing products/services are improved technologically or in quality) or **costs are reduced** (where production processes are updated or personnel reorganised). The returns will be measured as the **increase in net income or net reduction in costs** resulting from the investment.

1.4 Authorisation for a capital project

For projects involving a significant amount of capital investment, **authorisation** will be required. This authorisation will usually be given by the main board, or a sub-committee formed from the board for this purpose. Smaller projects (such as the replacement of an existing machine) may be within the authorisation limits of the manager of the area of business involved.

1.5 Importance of non-financial factors

Although these appraisal methods will usually give a basis for a **recommendation as to whether or not the project should be accepted,** they will only be able to take account of monetary costs and benefits. **Qualitative factors** will also need to be considered when reaching a final decision – such as possible effects on staff morale (for example, if the project involves increased automation or considerable overtime), the environment, customer satisfaction and the business's status/reputation.

Predicting future cash flows

2.1 Introduction

Any potential investment will need to be evaluated with regards the costs and revenues that will occur i.e. the net cash flow received from the investment activity. This will involve estimating the cash flows for sales, costs, capital expenditure and disposal proceeds.

2.2 The cash flows under consideration

When estimating future cash flows we want to identify what difference the project will make therefore we only consider **future incremental** cash flows to be relevant, e.g. if a new machine was to be purchased, the factory rent may be unaffected so would not need to be included when assessing the investment, but the purchase cost of the new machine is relevant so would be included.

As well as knowing what the future cash flows will be, we also need to know when they will occur. The time the investment starts is called time or year 0 or $t = 0$. Subsequent future cash flows are assumed to happen at year-ends, e.g. all of the sales revenues and costs for the first year are assumed to be paid at the end of the first year this is called time or year 1 or $t = 1$.

If we do this for all the future cash flows of the project, then we will typically end up with a table like the following:

	t = 0 £000	Year 1 (t = 1) £000	Year 2 (t = 2) £000	Year 3 (t = 3) £000	Year 4 (t = 4) £000	Year 5 (t = 5) £000
Initial Investment	(100)					
Scrap value						30
Sales revenues		40	50	60	50	40
Variable costs		(10)	(12)	(15)	(13)	(11)
Net cash flow	(100)	30	38	45	37	59

3 Payback period

3.1 Calculation

 Definition

The **payback period** is the length of time a project takes to recoup the initial money invested in it. This is the time which elapses until the invested capital is recovered.

If the annual cash flows are constant, then the calculation is very straightforward e.g. if £100,000 is invested and £20,000 cash in received each year, then it will take 100/20 = 5 years to recover the investment cost.

However, if the annual cash flows vary, then we need to calculate the cumulative net position at the end of each year.

Example

A machine costs £100,000 now. We expect the following cash flows:

	Year 1 (t = 1) £000	Year 2 (t = 2) £000	Year 3 (t = 3) £000	Year 4 (t = 4) £000	Year 5 (t = 5) £000
Scrap value					30
Sales revenues	40	50	60	50	40
Variable costs	(10)	(12)	(15)	(13)	(11)

Calculate the payback period for the investment.

Solution

Time	Net cash flow £000	Cumulative position £000	Working to calculate the cumulative position
t = 0	(100)	(100)	
t = 1	30	(70)	(100) + 30
t = 2	38	(32)	(70) + 38
t = 3	45	13	(32) + 45
t = 4	37	50	13 + 37
t = 5	59	109	50 + 59

From this table we can see that the initial investment would be recovered sometime in the third year as this is when the cumulative position initially becomes positive.

If cash flows are assumed to occur at the end of each year the payback period would 3 years.

If we assume that cash flows accrue evenly through the year i.e. there is an equal amount of sales revenue each month and an equal amount of costs each month, we are then able to estimate at what point during the year break even occurs.

From the figures above we can see that the outstanding amount at the start of year 3 is £32,000 (*) and that during the third year there is a total of £45,000 (**) cash flow. See extract of table below:

Time	Net cash flow £000	Cumulative position £000
t = 2	38	**(32)***
t = 3	**45***	13

The payback period is therefore calculated as follows:

Calculate the cash flow per month

£45,000/12 = £3,750

Calculate how many months are needed to cover remaining investment

£32,000/£3,750 = 8.533 months

Payback is 2 years and 8½ months

This could also be calculated as follows:

= $2\,^{32}/_{45}$ or 2.71 years

0.71 of a year is 8½ months

Note: In the exam the payback period is rounded **up** to the nearest whole month. The payback period is therefore 2 years and 9 months.

The payback period is then compared with the target payback that has been set, e.g. this company may have decided only to accept projects with paybacks lower than four years, in which case this project is acceptable.

Activity 1

A machine costs £100,000 now. We expect net cash flows of £30,000 in one year's time, £40,000 in two years' time, £60,000 in three years' time and £10,000 in four years' time.

Calculate the payback period for the investment by filling in the table below:

Time	Net cash flow £000	Cumulative Cash flow £000
t = 0	(100)	
t = 1	30	
t = 2	40	
t = 3	60	
t = 4	10	

Payback is _____ years and _____ months

Activity 2

Highscore Ltd manufactures cricket bats. They are considering investing £30,000 in a new delivery vehicle which will generate savings compared with sub-contracting out the delivery service. The vehicle will have a life of six years, with zero scrap value.

The accounting technician and the transport manager have prepared the following estimates relating to the savings.

The net cash flows from the project are:

Year	£
1	9,000
2	11,000
3	10,000
4	10,500
5	10,200
6	10,100

Calculate the payback period in year(s) and months.

3.2 Advantages of payback period

(a) It is simple to calculate.

(b) It is understandable for non-financial managers

(c) It is **less affected by uncertainty** as the cash flows that are being considered are earlier forecasts.

(d) It is very useful in specific circumstances such as when the company has **liquidity problems** i.e. if cash is only available for a limited length of time it provides an estimate of how long cash will be tied up in the investment for.

3.3 Disadvantages of payback period

(a) **Flows outside the payback period are ignored**. If we consider the previous example, if the cash flow in the fifth year had been £20,000 the payback period would be unaltered at 2 years 8½ months.

(b) The **timing of flows within the payback period** are ignored. If, again for the same example, the first two years' receipts had been:

1st year £50,000

2nd year £20,000

again the payback period would be unaltered at 2 years 8½ months.

(c) It **ignores the time value of money** i.e. the interest that capital can earn. We shall see the relevance of this in the next sections on discounted cash flow.

(d) It does not provide a monetary value for the return available from the investment.

4 Discounting

4.1 The time value of money

A key concept in long-term decision-making is that money received today is worth more than the same sum received in the future, i.e. it has a **time value.**

Suppose you were offered £100 now or £100 in one year's time. Even though the sums are the same, most people would prefer the money now. The £100 in the future is effectively worth less to us than £100 now – the timing of the cash makes a difference.

The main reasons for this are as follows:

- **Investment opportunities**: the £100 received now could be deposited into a bank account and earn interest. It would therefore grow to become worth more than £100 in one year.

- **Inflation**: the £100 now will buy more goods than £100 in one year due to inflation increasing the cost of goods.

- **Cost of capital**: the £100 received now could be used to reduce a loan or overdraft and save interest.

- **Risk**: the £100 now is more certain than the offer of money in the future.

To do calculations using the time value of money it needs to be expressed as an interest rate (often known as a cost of capital, a required return or a **discount rate**)

Suppose we felt that £100 now was worth the same to us as £110 offered in one year's time due to the factors above. We could say that our time value of money was estimated at 10% per annum.

Therefore £100 now is worth the same as £110 offered in one year. Alternatively we say that the £110 in one year has a present value of £100 now. This process of taking future cash flows and converting them into their equivalent present value now is called **discounting**.

To calculate the present value of any future cash flow we multiply the cash flow by a suitable discount factor (or present value factor):

Present value = future cash flow × discount factor

Discount factors are provided in the assessment so you do not need to be able to calculate them but you will need to know how to use them.

For example, with a 10% discount rate, the discount factor for a cash flow at t=1 is 0.909. Thus the offer of receiving £110 in one year's time is worth in today's terms

Present value = £110 × 0.909 = £99.99

The use of the discount rate enables more accurate prediction of the return an investment will give. Future incremental cash flows can be discounted to present values and the values can then be netted off against the initial investment to see what the overall return from the investment will be.

5 Net present value/cost

5.1 Net Present Value (NPV)

🔍 Definition

The net present value is the net benefit or loss of benefit in present value terms from an investment opportunity. The NPV represents the surplus funds earned on a project.

There is a step by step procedure for completing an NPV calculation:

Step 1 Calculate the future incremental net cash flows.

Step 2 Discount the net cash flows so they are in today's terms (present values).

Step 3 Add up the present values and add them to the initial investment out flow to give a net present value or NPV.

Step 4 If the NPV is positive, then it means that the cash inflows are worth more than the outflows and the project should be accepted.

💡 Example

A machine costs £100,000 now. We expect the following cash flows:

	Year 1 (t = 1) £000	Year 2 (t = 2) £000	Year 3 (t = 3) £000	Year 4 (t = 4) £000	Year 5 (t = 5) £000
Scrap value					30
Sales revenues	40	50	60	50	40
Variable costs	(10)	(12)	(15)	(13)	(11)

Calculate the net present value of the investment if a discount factor of 10% is used.

Solution

	t = 0 £000	Year 1 (t = 1) £000	Year 2 (t = 2) £000	Year 3 (t = 3) £000	Year 4 (t = 4) £000	Year 5 (t = 5) £000
Net cash flow	(100)	30	38	45	37	59
Discount factor at 10%	1.000	0.909	0.826	0.751	0.683	0.621
Present value	(100)	27.3	31.4	33.8	25.3	36.6

The Net Present Value = (100) + 27.3 + 31.4 + 33.8 +25.3 + 36.6 = 54.4

The NPV = £54,400 positive, so the project should be undertaken.

Activity 3

A machine costs £80,000 to buy now. The predicted sales revenue and operating costs for the following 4 years are as follows:

Year	Sales revenue £	Operating cost £
1	40,000	20,000
2	70,000	20,000
3	80,000	40,000
4	90,000	80,000

The rate of interest applicable is 15%. Should we accept or reject the machine?

The relevant present value factors are:

	Year 1	Year 2	Year 3	Year 4
15%	0.870	0.756	0.658	0.572

	Year 0	Year 1	Year 2	Year 3	Year 4
Capital expenditure					
Sales revenues					
Operating costs					
Net cash flow					
PV Factor	1.000	0.870	0.756	0.658	0.572
Discounted cash flow					
Net present value					

The net present value is *positive/negative**

*delete as appropriate

Activity 4

Machine A costs £100,000, payable immediately. Machine B costs £120,000, half payable immediately and half payable in one year's time.

The net cash flows expected are as follows.

	A £	B £
at the end of 1 year	20,000	–
at the end of 2 years	60,000	60,000
at the end of 3 years	40,000	60,000
at the end of 4 years	30,000	80,000
at the end of 5 years	20,000	–

With interest at 5%, which machine should be selected?

The relevant present value factors are:

	Year 1	Year 2	Year 3	Year 4	Year 5
5%	0.952	0.907	0.864	0.823	0.784

Machine A

	Year 0	Year 1	Year 2	Year 3	Year 4	Year 5
Capital expenditure						
Net cash flow						
PV Factor	1.000	0.952	0.907	0.864	0.823	0.784
Discounted cash flow						
Net present value						

The net present value of machine A is *positive/negative**

*delete as appropriate

Machine B

	Year 0	Year 1	Year 2	Year 3	Year 4	Year 5
Capital expenditure						
Net cash flow						
PV Factor	1.000	0.952	0.907	0.864	0.823	0.784
Discounted cash flow						
Net present value						

The net present value of machine B is *positive/negative**

*delete as appropriate

Machine *A/B** should be selected as it has the *higher/lower** NPV

*delete as appropriate

5.2 Net present cost

In some cases you may be asked to look at only the **operating costs** of an investment rather than the costs and revenues associated with the investment. In this case the step by step procedure is exactly the same but you will need to decide which investment is cheapest to run.

Activity 5

Machine A costs £100,000, payable immediately. Machine B costs £80,000, payable immediately. The running costs expected are as follows.

	A £	B £
at the end of 1 year	20,000	20,000
at the end of 2 years	50,000	30,000
at the end of 3 years	30,000	40,000
at the end of 4 years	20,000	50,000
at the end of 5 years	10,000	60,000

With interest at 8%, which machine should be selected?

The relevant present value factors are:

	Year 1	Year 2	Year 3	Year 4	Year 5
8%	0.926	0.857	0.794	0.735	0.681

Machine A

	Year 0	Year 1	Year 2	Year 3	Year 4	Year 5
Capital expenditure						
Net cash flow						
PV Factor	1.000	0.926	0.857	0.794	0.735	0.681
Discounted cash flow						
Net present cost						

Machine B

	Year 0	Year 1	Year 2	Year 3	Year 4	Year 5
Capital expenditure						
Net cash flow						
PV Factor	1.000	0.926	0.857	0.794	0.735	0.681
Discounted cash flow						
Net present cost						

Machine A/B* should be selected as it has the *higher/lower** net present cost

*delete as appropriate

5.3 Advantages of NPV/NPC

(a) It considers the **time value of money**.

(b) It uses cash flows which are less subjective than profits. Profit measures rely on such things as depreciation and other policies which are to a certain extent subjective.

(c) It considers the **whole life** of the project.

(d) It provides a monetary value for the return from an investment.

5.4 Disadvantages of NPV/NPC

(a) Cash flows are future predictions and we are **unable to predict** the future with accuracy.

(b) Discounted cash flow as a concept is **more difficult** for a non-financial manager to understand.

(c) It may be difficult to **decide on which discount rate** to use when appraising a project.

6 Internal rate of return

6.1 The internal rate of return (IRR)

> ### 🔍 Definition
>
> The **IRR** calculates the **rate of return** (or discount rate) that one project is expected to achieve if it **breaks even** i.e. no profit or loss is made. The IRR is therefore the point where the **NPV of an investment is zero**.

For one investment, a graph of NPV against discount rate looks like the following:

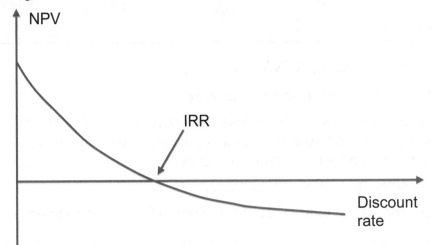

As the discount rate gets higher, the NPV gets smaller and then becomes negative. The cash flows are being discounted by a higher percentage therefore the present value of the cash flows becomes less.

The internal rate of return (IRR) is the discount rate that will cause the cash flow of a project to have a net present value equal to zero.

To decide on whether to invest using the IRR you need to compare the IRR with the discount rate that the company would like to use. If the chosen discount rate was somewhere between 10% and 15%, and the IRR of a project was 22% then we can still accept the project as our rate is less than the IRR, giving a positive NPV.

> **Activity 6**
>
> If the company's cost of capital is 16% and the IRR is 14% the investment should go ahead.
>
> True or false?

6.2 Calculation of the IRR

The approximate IRR of a project can be estimated by considering how close the NPVs are to zero.

The method used to estimate the IRR is as follows:

- Calculate two NPVs for the investment at different discount rates.
- Estimate the IRR with reference to the NPV values.

> **Example continued**
>
> A machine costs £150,000 now. We expect the following cash flows:
>
> | | Year 1 (t = 1) £000 | Year 2 (t = 2) £000 | Year 3 (t = 3) £000 | Year 4 (t = 4) £000 | Year 5 (t = 5) £000 |
> |---|---|---|---|---|---|
> | Scrap value | | | | | 30 |
> | Sales revenues | 40 | 50 | 60 | 50 | 40 |
> | Variable costs | (10) | (12) | (15) | (13) | (11) |
>
> Estimate the IRR of the investment.
>
> **Solution**
>
> 1   NPV with a discount rate of 10% = £4,400
>
> 2   NPV at a discount rate of 20% = -£31,000
>
> 3   Estimate the IRR
>
>   The IRR will be closer to 10% then 20% as £4,400 is closer to zero than -£31,000. As indicated by the diagram below:
>
> | £50,000 | £4,400 | £0 | £31,000 | -£50,000 |
> |---|---|---|---|---|
> | | 10% | | 20% | |
>
> From this we could estimate the IRR as approximately 11% or 12%.

The IRR of an investment can also be calculated using linear interpolation i.e. it uses two known points on a graph and joins them with a straight line. The point where the line crosses the x-axis will be calculated to provide the IRR.

The method used to calculate the IRR is as follows:

- Calculate two NPVs for the investment at different discount rates

- Use the following formula to find the IRR:

$$IRR\ (\%) = L + \frac{N_L}{N_L - N_H} \times (H - L)$$

Where:

L = Lower rate of interest

H = Higher rate of interest

N_L = NPV at lower rate of interest

N_H = NPV at higher rate of interest

Example

A machine costs £150,000 now. We expect the following cash flows:

	Year 1 (t = 1) £000	Year 2 (t = 2) £000	Year 3 (t = 3) £000	Year 4 (t = 4) £000	Year 5 (t = 5) £000
Scrap value					30
Sales revenues	40	50	60	50	40
Variable costs	(10)	(12)	(15)	(13)	(11)

Calculate the IRR of the investment.

Solution

1   NPV with a discount rate of 10% = £4,400 positive

2   NPV at a discount rate of 20% = £31,000 negative

3   Using the formula – you need to remember the rules of maths. Remove the brackets first, then deal with and division or multiplication and finally addition and subtraction (BODMAS).

$$IRR = L + \frac{N_L}{N_L - N_H} \times (H - L)$$

$$IRR = 10 + \frac{4,400}{4,400 - -31,000} \times (20 - 10)$$

$$IRR = 10 + \frac{4,400}{35,400} \times 10$$

$$IRR = 10 + \quad 0.1243 \quad \times 10$$

$$IRR = 10 + \quad 1.243 \quad = 11.24\%$$

Activity 7

A business undertakes high-risk investments and requires a minimum expected rate of return of 17% per annum on its investments.

A proposed capital investment has the following expected cash flows:

	£
Year 0	(50,000)
Year 1	18,000
Year 2	25,000
Year 3	20,000
Year 4	10,000

1   Calculate the NPV using 15% cost of capital and 20% cost of capital.

The relevant present value factors are:

	Year 1	Year 2	Year 3	Year 4
15%	0.870	0.756	0.658	0.572
20%	0.833	0.694	0.579	0.482

NPV @ 15%

	Year 0	Year 1	Year 2	Year 3	Year 4
Capital expenditure					
Net cash flow					
PV Factor	1.000	0.870	0.756	0.658	0.572
Discounted cash flow					
Net present value					

NPV @ 20%

	Year 0	Year 1	Year 2	Year 3	Year 4
Capital expenditure					
Net cash flow					
PV Factor	1.000	0.833	0.694	0.579	0.482
Discounted cash flow					
Net present value					

2   Using the NPVs you have calculated, estimate the IRR of the project.

3   Should the company proceed with the investment?

6.3   Advantages of IRR

(a)   It considers the **time value of money** as NPVs are used in the calculation process.

(b)   It uses cash flows which are less subjective than profits. Profit measures rely on such things as depreciation and other policies which are to a certain extent subjective.

(c)   It considers the **whole life** of the project.

(d)   It provides a **percentage return** that is easier for non-financial managers to understand.

(e)   It can be calculated without deciding on the desired cost of capital

6.4   Disadvantages of IRR

(a)   Cash flows are future predictions and we are **unable to predict** the future with accuracy.

(b)   It does not provide a monetary value for the return available from the investment.

6.5   Conflict between Payback, NPV and IRR

NPV is considered the most robust of the project appraisal techniques so if there is a conflict between payback, NPV and IRR then the result of the NPV should be used to make the final decision with regards investment.

7 Practice question

Activity 8

Mickey

Mickey is considering two mutually-exclusive projects with the following details.

	A £	B £
Initial investment	450,000	100,000
Year 1	200,000	50,000
Year 2	150,000	40,000
Year 3	100,000	30,000
Year 4	100,000	20,000
Year 5	100,000	20,000

At the end of the five years each project has a scrap value. Project A's scrap value is £20,000 and Project B's scrap value is £10,000.

1 Calculate the payback period of each project.

2 Calculate the NPV of each project to the nearest £000 using a cost of capital of 10%.

The relevant present value factors are:

	Year 1	Year 2	Year 3	Year 4	Year 5
10%	0.909	0.826	0.751	0.683	0.621

KAPLAN PUBLISHING

Project A

	Year 0	Year 1	Year 2	Year 3	Year 4	Year 5
Capital expenditure						
Net cash flow						
PV Factor	1.000	0.909	0.826	0.751	0.683	0.621
Discounted cash flow						
Net present value						

Project B

	Year 0	Year 1	Year 2	Year 3	Year 4	Year 5
Capital expenditure						
Net cash flow						
PV Factor	1.000	0.909	0.826	0.751	0.683	0.621
Discounted cash flow						
Net present value						

If Project A is appraised using a cost of capital of 20% the NPV is £25,000 negative. If Project B is appraised using a cost of capital of 20% the NPV is £8,500 positive.

3   Calculate the IRR of each project.

4   Which project should Mickey invest in and why?

8   Summary

In this chapter we have considered the mechanics, the advantages and the disadvantages of various investment appraisal techniques. In the context of an examination, you must be able to **calculate** the **payback period, the net present value and the IRR of a project.**

The payback period calculates how long it will take to recover the initial investment in a project. The Net Present Value, on the other hand, is an appraisal technique that takes the time value of money into account and calculates the return from an investment in monetary terms.

The IRR of a project is the discount rate at which a project has a NPV equal to zero. A cost of capital (or discount rate) which is less than the IRR will give rise to a positive NPV (and is therefore considered to be an 'acceptable investment').

If there are conflicts between payback, NPV and IRR investment appraisal methods then the NPV is the strongest measure so the **NPV result will overrule the payback and IRR.**

Answers to chapter activities

Activity 1

Time	Cash flow £000	Cumulative position £000	Working £000
t = 0	(100)	(100)	
t = 1	30	(70)	(100) + 30
t = 2	40	(30)	(70) + 40
t = 3	60	30	(30) + 60
t = 4	10	40	30 + 10

Payback period is **2** years and **6** months

$$= 2\,^{30}\!/_{60}\ \text{or 2.5 years}$$

Or

£60,000/12 = £5000

£30,000/£5000 = 6 months

Activity 2

The payback period is **3** Year(s) and **0** Months

Year	Cash flow	Cumulative cash flow
0	(30,000)	(30,000)
1	9,000	(21,000)
2	11,000	(10,000)
3	10,000	0

Activity 3

	Year 0	Year 1	Year 2	Year 3	Year 4
Capital expenditure	(80,000)				
Sales revenue		40,000	70,000	80,000	90,000
Operating costs		(20,000)	(20,000)	(40,000)	(80,000)
Net cash flow	(80,000)	20,000	50,000	40,000	10,000
PV Factor	1.000	0.870	0.756	0.658	0.572
Discounted cash flow	(80,000)	17,400	37,800	26,320	5,720
Net present value	7,240				

The net present value is *positive*.

Activity 4

Machine A

	Year 0	Year 1	Year 2	Year 3	Year 4	Year 5
Capital expenditure	(100,000)					
Net cash flow	(100,000)	20,000	60,000	40,000	30,000	20,000
PV Factor	1.000	0.952	0.907	0.864	0.823	0.784
Discounted cash flow	(100,000)	19,040	54,420	34,560	24,690	15,680
Net present value	48,390					

The net present value of machine A is *positive*.

Machine B

	Year 0	Year 1	Year 2	Year 3	Year 4	Year 5
Capital expenditure	(60,000)	(60,000)				
Net cash flow	(60,000)	(60,000)	60,000	60,000	80,000	0
PV Factor	1.000	0.952	0.907	0.864	0.823	0.784
Discounted cash flow	(60,000)	(57,120)	54,420	51,840	65,840	0
Net present value	54,980					

The net present value of machine B is *positive*.

Machine B has the higher NPV therefore the return from using this machine is better than machine A. Machine B should be selected.

Activity 5

Machine A

	Year 0	Year 1	Year 2	Year 3	Year 4	Year 5
Capital expenditure	100,000					
Net cash flow	100,000	20,000	50,000	30,000	20,000	10,000
PV Factor	1.000	0.926	0.857	0.794	0.735	0.681
Discounted cash flow	100,000	18,520	42,850	23,820	14,700	6,810
Net present cost	206,700					

Machine B

	Year 0	Year 1	Year 2	Year 3	Year 4	Year 5
Capital expenditure	80,000					
Net cash flow	80,000	20,000	30,000	40,000	50,000	60,000
PV Factor	1.000	0.926	0.857	0.794	0.735	0.681
Discounted cash flow	80,000	18,520	25,710	31,760	36,750	40,860
Net present cost	233,600					

Machine *A* should be selected as it has the *lower* net present cost.

Activity 6

False. The IRR is lower than the cost of capital therefore the investment will have broken even at 14% and be a negative NPV at 16%.

Activity 7

1   Calculate the NPV using 15% cost of capital and 20% cost of capital.

NPV @ 15%

	Year 0	Year 1	Year 2	Year 3	Year 4
Capital expenditure	(50,000)				
Net cash flow	(50,000)	18,000	25,000	20,000	10,000
PV Factor	1.000	0.870	0.756	0.658	0.572
Discounted cash flow	(50,000)	15,660	18,900	13,160	5,720
Net present value	3,440				

NPV @ 20%

	Year 0	Year 1	Year 2	Year 3	Year 4
Capital expenditure	(50,000)				
Net cash flow	(50,000)	18,000	25,000	20,000	10,000
PV Factor	1.000	0.833	0.694	0.579	0.482
Discounted cash flow	(50,000)	14,994	17,350	11,580	4,820
Net present value	−1,256				

2   Using the NPVs you have calculated, estimate the IRR of the project

$$\text{IRR} = L + \frac{N_L}{N_L - N_H} \times (H - L)$$

$$\text{IRR} = 15 + \frac{3,440}{3,440 - {-1,256}} \times (20 - 15)$$

$$\text{IRR} = 15 + \frac{3,440}{4,696} \times 5$$

$$\text{IRR} = 15 + \quad 0.7325 \quad \times 5$$

$$\text{IRR} = 15 + \quad 3.663 \quad = 18.7\%$$

3   Should the company proceed with the investment?

The IRR of the project is 18.7%. The company requires a return of 17%. The IRR is higher than the required return therefore the company should invest.

Activity 8

1   Calculate the payback period for each project

Project A

	Cash flow	Cumulative cash flow
Year 0	(450,000)	(450,000)
Year 1	200,000	(250,000)
Year 2	150,000	(100,000)
Year 3	100,000	0

Payback is 3 years

Project B

	Cash flow	Cumulative cash flow
Year 0	(100,000)	(100,000)
Year 1	50,000	(50,000)
Year 2	40,000	(10,000)
Year 3	30,000	20,000

Payback is 2 years 4 months

2   Calculate the NPV for each project

Project A

	Year 0	Year 1	Year 2	Year 3	Year 4	Year 5
Capital expenditure	(450)					
Net cash flow	(450)	200	150	100	100	120
PV Factor	1.000	0.909	0.826	0.751	0.683	0.621
Discounted cash flow	(450)	182	124	75	68	75
Net present value	74					

Project B

	Year 0	Year 1	Year 2	Year 3	Year 4	Year 5
Capital expenditure	(100)					
Net cash flow	(100)	50	40	30	20	30
PV Factor	1.000	0.909	0.826	0.751	0.683	0.621
Discounted cash flow	(100)	45	33	23	14	19
Net present value	34					

3   Calculate the IRR of each project

Project A

$$IRR = 10 + \frac{74}{74 - -25} \times (20 - 10)$$

IRR = 17.5%

Project B

$$IRR = 10 + \frac{34}{34 - 8.5} \times (20 - 10)$$

IRR = 23.3%

4   Which project should Mickey invest in and why?

Project A should be invested in.

Project B has a shorter payback period and higher IRR but the NPV of Project A is the greater therefore providing the better return for the investment. NPV is the more robust of the investment appraisal techniques used as it considers the whole life of the project, includes the effect of the time value of money and also provides an absolute value for the return from the investment.

9 Test your knowledge

Workbook Activity 9

Whitby Engineering Factors are considering an investment in a new machine tool with an estimated useful life of five years.

The investment will require capital expenditure of £50,000 and the accounting technician has prepared the following estimates of cash flow over the five-year period:

Year	£
1	18,000
2	20,000
3	21,000
4	22,000
5	18,000

The firm's cost of capital is considered to be 12% and it uses this rate to appraise any future projects.

Required:

Prepare an appraisal of the project using the discounted cash flow (NPV method) technique and payback method

	Year 0	Year 1	Year 2	Year 3	Year 4	Year 5
Capital expenditure						
Net cash flow						
PV Factor	1.000	0.893	0.797	0.712	0.636	0.567
Discounted cash flow						
Net present value						

The net present value is *positive/negative**

*delete as appropriate

The payback period is   Year(s) and   Months

Accept/reject* investment

*delete as appropriate

Workbook Activity 10

An investment project has the following expected cash flows over its three-year life span.

Year	Cash flow £
0	(285,400)
1	102,000
2	124,000
3	146,000

Task

Calculate the net present value of the project at a discount rate of 20%.

	Year 0	Year 1	Year 2	Year 3
Capital expenditure				
Net cash flow				
PV Factor	1.000	0.833	0.694	0.579
Discounted cash flow				
Net present value				

The net present value is *positive/negative**

*delete as appropriate

The payback period is   Year(s) and   Months

*Accept/reject** investment

*delete as appropriate

Workbook Activity 11

Martinez Limited makes a single product, the Angel.

Martinez Limited has a long-term contract to supply a group of customers with 10,000 units of Angel a year for the next three years.

Martinez is considering investing in a new machine to manufacture the Angel. This machine will produce 10,000 units a year, which have a profit of £8 per unit. The machine will cost £220,000 and will last for the duration of the contract. At the end of the contract the machine will be scrapped with no resale value.

Task

Calculate the present value of the machine project if a 10% discount rate is used.

	Year 0	Year 1	Year 2	Year 3
Capital expenditure				
Net cash flow				
PV Factor	1.000	0.909	0.826	0.751
Discounted cash flow				
Net present value				

The net present value is *positive/negative**

*delete as appropriate

The payback period is _____ Year(s) and _____ Months

Accept/reject* investment

*delete as appropriate

Workbook Activity 12

Loamshire County Council operates a library service.

In order to reduce operating expenses over the next four or five years, there is a proposal to introduce a major upgrade to the computer system used by the library service. Two alternative projects are under examination with different initial outlays and different estimated savings over time. The computer manager has prepared the following schedule:

	Project A £	Project B £
Initial outlay	75,000	100,000
Annual cash savings		
1st year	20,000	30,000
2nd year	30,000	45,000
3rd year	30,000	45,000
4th year	25,000	40,000
5th year	20,000	–

Assume that the cash savings occur at the end of the year, even though in practice they would be spread over the year. From a technical point of view, both systems meet the librarian's specification. It is assumed that there will be no further savings after year 5. The county uses the net present value method for evaluating projects at a 10% discount rate.

Task

Project A

	Year 0	Year 1	Year 2	Year 3	Year 4	Year 5
Capital expenditure						
Net cash flow						
PV Factor	1.000	0.909	0.826	0.751	0.683	0.621
Discounted cash flow						
Net present value						

The net present value is *positive/negative**

*delete as appropriate

The payback period is　　　　　　Year(s) and　　　　　　Months

Project B

	Year 0	Year 1	Year 2	Year 3	Year 4
Capital expenditure					
Net cash flow					
PV Factor	1.000	0.909	0.826	0.751	0.683
Discounted cash flow					
Net present value					

The net present value is *positive/negative**

*delete as appropriate

The payback period is　　　　　　Year(s) and　　　　　　Months

Invest in *A/B**

*delete as appropriate

Workbook Activity 13

A transport company is considering purchasing an automatic vehicle-cleansing machine. At present, all vehicles are cleaned by hand.

The machine will cost £80,000 to purchase and install in year 0 and it will have a useful life of four years with no residual value.

The company uses a discount rate of 10% to appraise all capital projects.

The cash savings from the machine will be:

Year	£
0	–
1	29,600
2	29,200
3	28,780
4	28,339

Task

As assistant management accountant, you are asked to carry out an appraisal of the proposal to purchase the machine and prepare a report to the general manager of the company. Your report should contain the following information:

(1) the net present value of the cash flows from the project

(2) the payback period of the proposal

(3) a recommendation as to whether or not the proposal should be accepted.

	Year 0	Year 1	Year 2	Year 3	Year 4
Capital expenditure					
Net cash flow					
PV Factor	1.000	0.909	0.826	0.751	0.683
Discounted cash flow					
Net present value					

The net present value is *positive/negative**

*delete as appropriate

The payback period is   Year(s)

*Accept/reject** project

*delete as appropriate

Workbook Activity 14

A company is considering setting up a small in-house printing facility.

Machines costing £14,400 will be purchased in year 0. They will last for four years and will have no value at the end of this time.

The cash savings associated with the machines will be:

Year	£
0	–
1	6,920
2	6,920
3	6,920
4	6,920

Task

(a) Calculate the net present value of the cash flows from the proposal, using a 12% discount rate over four years.

Assume that all cash flows occur at the end of the year.

(b) Calculate the payback period for the proposal assuming that cash flows occur evenly through the year.

	Year 0	Year 1	Year 2	Year 3	Year 4
Capital expenditure					
Net cash flow					
PV Factor	1.000	0.893	0.797	0.712	0.636
Discounted cash flow					
Net present value					

The net present value is *positive/negative**

*delete as appropriate

The payback period is   Year(s) and   Months

Accept/reject* project

*delete as appropriate

Workbook Activity 15

Data

RBG plc is a large quoted company using a 25% rate of interest for appraising capital projects. One of its divisional directors has put forward plans to make a new product, the AI. This will involve buying a machine specifically for that task. The machine will cost £600,000 and have a life of 5 years. However, because of the nature of the product, the machine will have no residual value at any time.

The annual cash flows will be as follows:

	£
Sales revenues	380,000
Material costs	90,000
Labour costs	30,000
Overhead costs	20,000

Task

You are asked to appraise the divisional director's proposal by calculating:

(a)   the net present value

(b)   the payback period

	Year 0	Year 1	Year 2	Year 3	Year 4	Year 5
Capital expenditure						
Net cash flow						
PV Factor	1.000	0.800	0.640	0.512	0.410	0.328
Discounted cash flow						
Net present value						

The net present value is *positive/negative**

*delete as appropriate

The payback period is   Year(s) and   Months

Further information

The IRR is 28%

The new product *should be/should not be** purchased

*delete as appropriate

WORKBOOK ACTIVITIES
ANSWERS

Workbook Activities Answers

2 Cost classification

📝 Workbook Activity 10

Direct costs are:

C   Costs that relate directly to a unit

📝 Workbook Activity 11

Cost	Direct	Indirect
Machine operators wages	☑	
Supervisors wages		☑
Resin for golf balls	☑	
Salesmen's salaries		☑

📝 Workbook Activity 12

A semi-variable cost is:

D   A cost that contains both a fixed and a variable element

📝 Workbook Activity 13

D   Pure fixed costs remain exactly the same in total regardless of the activity level.

Workbook Activity 14

C

	£
Cost of 25,000 units	21,000
Less cost of 10,000 units	12,000
Difference = variable cost of 15,000 units	9,000

$$\text{Variable cost per unit} = \frac{\pounds 9,000}{15,000} = 60\text{p each}$$

Fixed costs = total cost – variable costs

Fixed costs = £21,000 – £(25,000 × 0.6) = £6,000

Therefore total cost for 40,000

	£
Variable (40,000 × 0.6)	24,000
Fixed	6,000
	30,000

Workbook Activity 15

The sales revenue per unit if the contract is for 4,000 units

    50,000/4,000 = £12.50

The variable cost per unit if the contract is for 4,000 units

    (2,000 + 4,000 + 6,000)/4,000 = £3.00

The fixed cost per unit if the contract is for 4,000 units

    (12,000 + 8,000)/4,000 = £5.00

The total cost if the contract is for 6,000 units

    (£3.00 × 6,000) + (12,000 + 2,000) + (8,000) = £40,000

The total profit if the contract is for 6,000 units

    (£12.50 × 6,000) – £40,000 = £35,000

Workbook Activity 16

BUDGETED COST SCHEDULE		YEAR 20X9		
		ACTIVITY (Packets)		
	150,000	175,000	200,000	225,000
Description	£	£	£	£
Variable costs				
Direct material	12,000	14,000	16,000	18,000
Direct labour	9,000	10,500	12,000	13,500
Packing costs	1,500	1,750	2,000	2,250
Fixed costs:				
Depreciation costs	12,000	12,000	12,000	12,000
Rent and rates	26,000	26,000	26,000	26,000
Supervisory costs	12,000	12,000	12,000	12,000
Administration costs	8,000	8,000	8,000	8,000
Total costs	80,500	84,250	88,000	91,750
Cost per packet (2 decimal places)	0.54	0.48	0.44	0.41

The cost per packet has **decreased** because the fixed cost per unit has **decreased**.

Workbook Activity 17

Sheds sold and produced	500	750	1,000
Sales revenue	8,000	12,000	16,000
Variable costs:			
Direct materials	800	1,200	1,600
Direct labour	760	1,140	1,520
Overheads	1,440	2,160	2,880
Semi-variable costs	900		
Variable element		1,125	1,500
Fixed element		150	150
Fixed cost	700	700	700
Total cost	4,600	6,475	8,350
Total profit	3,400	5,525	7,650
Profit per shed (to 2 decimal places)	6.80	7.37	7.65

3 Inventory

Workbook Activity 7

Goods received note	Document completed by stores on receipt of goods.
Purchase order	Form completed by the purchasing department to order supplies.
Purchase requisition	Form completed by the stores department detailing inventory requirements.
Stores record card	Document completed to show the movement of inventory.
Delivery note	Form received with goods on delivery
Purchase invoice	Details the amount due to be paid and the date payment is due by

Workbook Activity 8

Stores Record Card FIFO

Material: Pizza

Code: 1626

Date	Details	Receipts		Issues			Inventory	
		Units	£	Units	Price	£	Units	£
1 Dec	Balance b/f						200	180
3 Dec	Receipt	800	800				200	180
							800	800
							1,000	980
7 Dec	Issue			200	0.9	180		
				200	1.0	200	600	600
				400		380	600	600
14 Dec	Issue			350	1.0	350	250	250
20 Dec	Receipt	1,200	1,140				250	250
							1,200	1,140
							1,450	1,390
21 Dec	Issue			250	1.0	250		
				160	0.95	152	1,040	988
				410		402		
28 Dec	Issue			475	0.95	451	565	537

Workbook Activity 9

Stores Record Card AVCO

Material: Component AB3

Code: 010203

Date	Receipts			Issues			Inventory	
	Units	Cost	£	Units	Cost	£	Units	£
1 Sept							75	3,000
1 Sept	100	40.00	4,000				175	7,000
10 Sept	75	42.00	3,150				250	10,150
15 Sept				60	40.60	2,436	190	7,714
20 Sept				55	40.60	2,233	135	5,481
23 Sept	45	42.00	1,890				180	7,371
30 Sept				50	40.95	2,048	130	5,323

Weighted average price 10th September = 10,150 ÷ 250 = £40.60 per unit

Value of issues: £2,463 + £2,233 + 2,048 = £6,744

Closing inventory valuation: £5,323

Workbook Activity 10

Reorder level:

(Maximum usage per period × maximum delivery period) + buffer

   (50 × 5) + 20 = 270 units

Economic order quantity:

$\sqrt{[(2 \times 50.63 \times 50 \times 50)/5]}$ = 225 units

Maximum inventory level:

Reorder level + Reorder quantity – (minimum usage in minimum delivery period)

   = 270 + 225 – (30 × 3) = 405 units

Minimum inventory level:

Reorder level – (average usage in average reorder period)
   = 270 – (50 × 5) = 20 units

Workbook Activity 11

Stores Record Card FIFO

Material: Protective gloves

Code: 1607

Date	Details	Receipts		Issues			Inventory	
		Pairs	£	Pairs	Price	£	Pairs	£
1 Jan	Balance b/f						150	300
7 Jan	Purchases	40	76				150	300
							40	76
							——	——
							190	376
15 Jan	Issues			30	2	60	120	240
							40	76
							——	——
							160	316
29 Jan	Issues			35	2	70	85	170
							40	76
							——	——
							125	246

Workbook Activity 12

Stores Record Card

Material: Sugar **Month:** May 20X8

Date	Receipts			Issues			Balance	
	Quantity	Price £	Total £	Quantity	Price £	Total £	Quantity	Total £
1/5 Balance							2,420	12,584
7/5	2,950	5.500	16,226				5,370	28,810
11/5	3,200	5.700	18,239				8,570	47,049
14/5				4,105	5.490	22,536	4,465	24,513
21/5	1,535	5.400	8,289				6,000	32,802
27/5				1,800	5.467	9,841	4,200	22,961
30/5				2,600	5.467	14,214	1,600	8,747

The double entry for the issue on the 27 May is

D   Dr Production, Cr Materials

Workbook Activity 13

FIFO

Issue = (500 × 1.20) + (450 × 1.30) + (50 × 1.50) = £1,260

Closing inventory = (600 + 585 + 900) – £1260 = £825

LIFO

Issue = (600 × 1.5) + (400 × 1.3) = £1,420

Closing inventory = (600 + 585 + 900) – £1,420 = £665

AVCO

Issue = (600 + 585 + 900)/(500 + 450 + 600) × 1,000 = £1,345

Closing inventory = (600 + 585 + 900) – £1,345 = £740

4 Labour

Workbook Activity 9

C

Gross wage:

Basic pay 45 hrs @ £6	£270.00
Overtime 5 hrs @ £3	£15.00

Bonus:

25 doors × 2 hours = 50 hours allowed
Time taken 45 hours
Time saved – 5 hours × £3

	£15.00
	£300.00

Workbook Activity 10

B

Basic pay 10,500 hrs @ £7	£73,500
Overtime 1,500 hrs @3.5	£5,250
Overtime 1,000 hrs @ £7	£7,000
	£85,750

5 Expenses

Workbook Activity 2

RFB plc makes wheels for a variety of uses: wheelbarrows, carts, toys, etc. Complete the following form by putting a tick for each of the cost items into the appropriate column.

	Capital expenditure	Revenue expenditure
Repairs to machinery		☑
Purchase of new delivery vehicle	☑	
Depreciation of delivery vehicle		☑
Vehicle tax for new vehicle		☑
Installation of air conditioning unit	☑	
Redecoration of office		☑

KAPLAN PUBLISHING

6 Basic variance analysis

 Workbook Activity 7

Batches sold and produced	1,000	1,500	2,000
Sales revenue	80,000	120,000	160,000
Variable cost			
Direct materials	8,000	12,000	16,000
Direct labour	7,600	11,400	15,200
Overheads	14,400	21,600	28,800
Fixed cost	7,000	7,000	7,000
Total cost	37,000	52,000	67,000
Total profit	43,000	68,000	93,000
Profit per batch (to 2 decimal places)	43.00	45.33	46.50

	Flexed budget	Actual	Variance value	Favourable or Adverse
Volume sold	1,200	1,200		
	£	£	£	
Sales revenue	96,000	100,000	4,000	F
Less costs:				
Direct materials	9,600	9,000	600	F
Direct labour	9,120	9,300	180	A
Overheads	17,280	17,500	220	A
Fixed cost	7,000	7,100	100	A
Profit for the period	53,000	57,100	4,100	F

7   Overheads

Workbook Activity 10

Step 1: Calculate budgeted overhead absorption rate (OAR):

OAR = £5 per hour

Step 2: Calculate absorbed overhead

Absorbed overhead = £5 × 10,000 hours

= £50,000

Step 3: Compare overhead absorbed with actual overhead incurred

Absorbed overhead = £50,000 > actual overhead £48,000

therefore £2,000 over-absorption

Workbook Activity 11

Overhead analysis sheet

	Basis	Total	Machine 1	Machine 2	Assembly	Packaging
Dep'n	Carrying amount	80,000	32,000	8,000	24,000	16,000
Rent and rates	Square meters	120,000	30,000	12,000	24,000	54,000
Indirect labour cost	Allocated	97,900	40,500	18,300	12,400	26,700
Assembly costs	Allocated	15,600	–	–	15,600	–
TOTAL		313,500	102,500	38,300	76,000	96,700

Workbook Activity 12

What is the budgeted fixed overhead absorption rate for the division for July 20Y0, using the most appropriate basis of absorption?

B £40.00

£400,000 ÷ 10,000

What is the value of the overhead absorbed into production?

C £360,000

£40 × 9,000

What is the under- or over absorption for the division?

D £90,000 under

£450,000 – £360,000

What is the double entry for the above?

B Dr Statement of profit or loss £90,000, Cr Production overheads £90,000

Workbook Activity 13

Production overhead control account

	£		£
Actual overhead	11,600	Absorbed overhead	11,290
		Under-absorbed costing SOPL	310
	11,600		11,600

Workbook Activity 14

	Mixing £	Baking £	Packing £
Budgeted overhead absorption rate	£2.50 per £1 direct labour	£14 per machine hour	£12.50 per labour hour

PRODUCTION OVERHEAD SCHEDULE			
Month: November 1998			
	Mixing £	Baking £	Packing £
Budgeted overheads	164,000	228,900	215,000
Actual overheads	171,500	224,000	229,000
Overhead absorbed	159,250	225,400	200,000

	Mixing £	Baking £	Packing £
Over-absorbed overheads		1,400	
Under-absorbed overheads	12,250		29,000

Production overhead control account

	£		£
Actual overhead	624,500	Absorbed overhead	584,650
		Under absorbed	39,850
	624,500		624,500

8 Job, batch and service costing

 Workbook Activity 4

Jetprint Limited

	10,000 leaflets	20,000 leaflets
	£	£
Artwork	65.00	65.00
Machine setting	88.00	88.00
Paper	125.00	250.00
Ink and consumables	40.00	80.00
Printers' wages	32.00	64.00
General fixed overheads (W)	100.00	200.00
Total cost	450.00	747.00

Workings:

$$OAR = \frac{£15,000}{600} = £25 \text{ per hour}$$

10,000 leaflets £25 × 4 hours = £100

20,000 leaflets £25 × 8 hours = £200

9 Process costing

Workbook Activity 14

Process soft drink

	kg	£		kg	£
Material	1,000	90,300	Normal loss	30	1,920
Labour		4,960	Output	990	97,218
Overhead		1,914			
Abnormal gain	20	1,964			
	1,020	99,138		1,020	99,138

$$\text{Normal cost of normal output} = \frac{97,174 - 1,920}{1,000 - 30}$$

$$= \text{£98.20 per kg}$$

Cost of output $= 990 \times £98.20 = £97,218$

Cost of abnormal gain $= 30 \times £98.20 = £1,920$

Workbook Activity 15

Process 1

	Litres	£		Litres	£
Direct material	10,000	50,000	Normal loss	500	500
Direct labour		4,000	Output	9,300	58,247
Overhead		6,000	Abnormal loss		
			(W1)	200	1,253
	10,000	60,000		10,000	60,000

Scrap account

	Litres	£		Litres	£
Process	500	500	Cash		700
Abnormal loss	200	200			
		700			700

Abnormal loss/gain account

	Litres	£		Litres	£
Process	200	1,253	Scrap	200	200
			SOPL		1,053
		1,253			1,253

Working 1:

Normal cost of normal output = $\dfrac{59,500}{9,500}$ = £6.2631 per litre.

Therefore, output and the abnormal loss are both costed at £6.2631 per litre.

Workbook Activity 16

Work-in-progress valuation

Statement of equivalent units and statement of cost

Element of cost	Comp output	WIP	Equivalent units	Cost £	Cost per unit
Direct materials	4,750	250	5,000	12,350	£2.47
Direct labour	4,750	150	4,900	1,225	£0.25
Overhead	4,750	150	4,900	1,862	£0.38
					£3.10

Workbook Activity 17

Equivalent units		Material	Conversion
	Completed Output	1,200	1,200
	Total EU	1,200	1,200
Costs			
	OWIP	48,000	34,800
	Period	120,000	78,000
	Total cost	168,000	112,800
Cost per EU		£140.00	£94.00

Workbook Activity 18

OWIP	+	Started	=	Completed
250	+	2,950	=	3,200

The completed units consist of 250 OWIP that were completed this period and then a further 2,950 units that were started and finished in this period.

To complete the OWIP no more material is required but 40% more conversion is needed.

Equivalent units		Material	Conversion
	OWIP to complete	0	100
	Completed Output	2,950	2,950
	Total EU	2,950	3,050
Costs			
	Period	135,700	97,600
	Total cost	135,700	97,600
Cost per EU		£46.00	£32.00

10 Marginal costing

Workbook Activity 4

Calculate the prime cost per unit.

10.60 + 16.40 = £27.00

Calculate the marginal cost per unit.

27.00 + (60,000 ÷ 10,000) = £33.00

Calculate the absorption cost per unit.

33.00 + (80,000 ÷ 10,000) = £41.00

Workbook Activity 5

• Prime cost (210,000 + 102,000 + 5,250)	£317,250
• Marginal cost (317,250 + 20,000)	£337,250
• Absorption cost (337,250 + 20,400)	£357,650
• Non-production cost (16,500 + 52,300)	£68,800
• Total cost (357,650 + 68,800)	£426,450
• Prime cost per tonne (317,250 ÷ 2,500)	£126.90
• Marginal cost per tonne (337,250 ÷ 2,500)	£134.90
• Absorption cost per tonne (357,650 ÷ 2,500)	£143.06
• Total cost per tonne (426,450 ÷ 2,500)	£170.58

Workbook Activity 6

(i) Marginal costing principles

	£	£
Sales revenue		150,000
Less: Cost of sales		
Opening inventory	0	
Production costs	149,500	
Closing inventory	(34,500)	
		(115,000)
Contribution		35,000
Fixed costs		(19,500)
Profit for the period		15,500

(ii) Absorption costing principles

	£	£
Sales revenue		150,000
Cost of sales		
Opening inventory	0	
Production costs	169,000	
Closing inventory	(39,000)	
		(130,000)
Gross profit		20,000
Non-production costs		(0)
Profit for the period		20,000

The absorption costing profit is **higher** than the marginal costing profit because there are **less** fixed costs charged against the sales in the absorption costing statement.

The difference of £4,500 is the increase in inventory of 1,500 units × the £3 per unit OAR for fixed overheads.

11 Short-term decision making

Workbook Activity 7

Product	Batman	Robin
Fixed costs (£)	1,000,000	2,450,000
Unit contribution (£)	2.50	3.50
Breakeven sales (units)	400,000	700,000
Forecast sales (units)	480,000	910,000
Margin of safety (units)	80,000	210,000
Margin of safety (%)	16.67%	23.08%
Target profit (units)		780,000

Unit contribution

Calculate the revenue and each variable cost per unit based on budget.
Sales revenue less variable costs = contribution

Batman   £10 – (2 + 2.50 + 3) = £2.50

Robin   £12 – (3 + 3.5 + 2) = £3.50

Target profit

$$\frac{2,450,000 + 280,000}{£3.50} = 780,000 \text{ units of Robin}$$

Workbook Activity 8

Calculation of required number of units	£
Fixed costs (12,000 + 8,000 + 2,000)	22,000
Target profit	20,000
Fixed cost and target profit	42,000
Sales revenue	50,000
Variable costs (2,000 + (4,000 × 0.5) + 6,000)	10,000
Contribution	40,000
Contribution per unit	10.00
Required number of units to achieve target profit	4,200

Workbook Activity 9

D   £950

Weekly fixed costs are £570; C/S ratio is 0.6 therefore weekly breakeven sales £570/0.6 = £950.

Workbook Activity 10

	Day scan £	Night scan £	Omni scan £
Selling price	250	320	460
Variable costs	(150)	(217)	(297)
Contribution per unit	100	103	163
Installation hours required	3	4	5.5
Contribution per installation hour	£33.33	£25.75	£29.64
Production priority	1st	3rd	2nd

Best production plan

	Units	Hours used
Day scan to maximum demand	2,000 (× 3)	6,000
Omni scan to maximum demand	1,800 (× 5.5)	9,900

This leaves (25,000 – 6,000 – 9,900) = 9,100 installation labour hours for Night scan.

Therefore production of Night scan = $\dfrac{9,100}{4}$ = 2,275 units

	Day scan	Omni scan	Night scan	Total
Units	2,000	1,800	2,275	
	£	£	£	£
Contribution	200,000	293,400	234,325	727,725
Fixed costs				(450,000)
Maximum profit				277,725

Workbook Activity 11

	Alfie	Boris
Selling price (£)	16.20	22.80
Variable cost per unit (£)	6.50	10.50
Contribution per unit (£)	9.70	12.30
LF per unit (hrs)	0.2	0.4
Contribution per LF (£)	48.50	30.75
Rank	1	2

Product in rank order	Units	LF per unit (hr)	Total LF (hr)	Contribution (£)
1 Alfie	10,000	0.2	2,000	97,000
2 Boris	5,000	0.4	2,000	61,500
		Total LF	4,000 hr	
			Total contribution	158,500
			Fixed costs	60,000 (W1)
			Profit	98,500

Working:

(W1) **Fixed production overheads**

Using (say) product A: fixed overheads per unit = £3; Labour hours per unit = 0.2.

Thus fixed overheads per hour = £3/0.2 = £15.

Maximum hours available = 4,000.

Fixed production overheads budgeted at 4,000 × £15 = £60,000.

12 Long-term decision making

Workbook Activity 9

	Year 0	Year 1	Year 2	Year 3	Year 4	Year 5
Capital expenditure	(50,000)					
Net cash flow	(50,000)	18,000	20,000	21,000	22,000	18,000
PV Factor	1.000	0.893	0.797	0.712	0.636	0.567
Discounted cash flow	(50,000)	16,074	15,940	14,952	13,992	10,206
Net present value	21,164					

The net present value is *positive*

The payback period is **2** Year(s) and **7** Months

Year	Cash flow	Cumulative cash flow
0	(50,000)	(50,000)
1	18,000	(32,000)
2	20,000	(12,000)
3	21,000	9,000
4	22,000	

12,000/21,000 × 12 = 7 months

Accept

Workbook Activity 10

	Year 0	Year 1	Year 2	Year 3
Capital expenditure	(285,400)			
Net cash flow	(285,400)	102,000	124,000	146,000
PV Factor	1.000	0.833	0.694	0.579
Discounted cash flow	(285,400)	84,966	86,056	84,534
Net present value	(29,844)			

The net present value is *negative*

The payback period is   **2**   Year(s) and   **5**   Months

Year	Cash flow	Cumulative cash flow
0	(285,400)	(285,400)
1	102,000	(183,400)
2	124,000	(59,400)
3	146,000	86,600

59,400/146,000 × 12 = 5 months

This project has a negative NPV but still pays back within the life of the project. This project should be **rejected** as when the time value of money is considered there is not a return from the investment.

Workbook Activity 11

	Year 0	Year 1	Year 2	Year 3
Capital expenditure	(220,000)			
Net cash flow	(220,000)	80,000	80,000	80,000
PV Factor	1.000	0.909	0.826	0.751
Discounted cash flow	(220,000)	72,720	66,080	60,080
Net present value	(21,120)			

The net present value is *negative*

The payback period is   **2**   Year(s) and   **9**   Months

Year	Cash flow	Cumulative cash flow
0	(220,000)	(220,000)
1	80,000	(140,000)
2	80,000	(60,000)
3	80,000	20,000

60,000/80,000 × 12 = 9 months

This project has a negative NPV but still pays back within the life of the project. This project should be **rejected** as when the time value of money is considered there is not a return from the investment.

Workbook Activity 12

Project A

	Year 0	Year 1	Year 2	Year 3	Year 4	Year 5
Capital expenditure	(75,000)					
Net cash flow	(75,000)	20,000	30,000	30,000	25,000	20,000
PV Factor	1.000	0.909	0.826	0.751	0.683	0.621
Discounted cash flow	(75,000)	18,180	24,780	22,530	17,075	12,420
Net present value	19,985					

The net present value is *positive*

The payback period is   **2**   Year(s) and   **10**   Months

Year	Cash flow	Cumulative cash flow
0	(75,000)	(75,000)
1	20,000	(55,000)
2	30,000	(25,000)
3	30,000	5,000

25,000/30,000 × 12 = 10 months

Project B

	Year 0	Year 1	Year 2	Year 3	Year 4
Capital expenditure	(100,000)				
Net cash flow	(100,000)	30,000	45,000	45,000	40,000
PV Factor	1.000	0.909	0.826	0.751	0.683
Discounted cash flow	(100,000)	27,270	37,170	33,795	27,320
Net present value	25,555				

The net present value is *positive*

The payback period is   **2**   Year(s) and   **7**   Months

Year	Cash flow	Cumulative cash flow
0	(100,000)	(100,000)
1	30,000	(70,000)
2	45,000	(25,000)
3	45,000	20,000

25,000/45,000 × 12 = 7 months

Project **B** should be invested in.

Project B should be recommended as it has the higher discounted cash flow, therefore the higher return from the investment. Payback is a cruder method of assessing future cash flows. No account is taken of flows after the payback period and equal weight given to flows within the payback period.

Workbook Activity 13

	Year 0	Year 1	Year 2	Year 3	Year 4
Capital expenditure	(80,000)				
Net cash flow	(80,000)	29,600	29,200	28,780	28,339
PV Factor	1.000	0.909	0.826	0.751	0.683
Discounted cash flow	(80,000)	26,906	24,119	21,614	19,356
Net present value	11,995				

The net present value is **positive**

The payback period is **2** Year(s) and **9** Months

Year	Cash flow	Cumulative cash flow
0	(80,000)	(80,000)
1	29,600	(50,400)
2	29,200	(21,200)
3	28,780	7,580

21,200/28,780 × 12 = 9 months

Accept

Workbook Activity 14

	Year 0	Year 1	Year 2	Year 3	Year 4
Capital expenditure	(14,400)				
Net cash flow	(14,400)	6,920	6,920	6,920	6,920
PV Factor	1.000	0.893	0.797	0.712	0.636
Discounted cash flow	(14,400)	6,180	5,515	4,927	4,401
Net present value	6,623				

The net present value is *positive*

The payback period is **2** Year(s) and **1** Month

Year	Cash flow	Cumulative cash flow
0	(14,400)	(14,400)
1	6,920	(7480)
2	6,920	(560)
3	6,920	6,360

560/6,920 × 12 = 1 month

Accept

Workbook Activity 15

	Year 0	Year 1	Year 2	Year 3	Year 4	Year 5
Capital expenditure	(600,000)					
Net cash flow	(600,000)	240,000	240,000	240,000	240,000	240,000
PV Factor	1.000	0.800	0.640	0.512	0.410	0.328
Discounted cash flow	(600,000)	192,000	153,600	122,880	98,400	78,720
Net present value	45,600					

The net present value is *positive*

The payback period is **2** Year(s) and **6** Months

Year	Cash flow	Cumulative cash flow
0	(600,000)	(600,000)
1	240,000	(360,000)
2	240,000	(120,000)
3	240,000	120,000

$120,000/240,000 \times 12 = 6$ months

The new product *should be* **purchased**

MOCK ASSESSMENT

Mock Assessment Questions

Task 1

The following information is available for product ZYQ:

Annual demand – 1,250,000 kilograms

Annual holding cost per kilogram – £5

Fixed ordering cost – £2

(a) Calculate the Economic Order Quantity (EOQ) for ZYQ.

_____

The inventory record shown below for product ZYQ for the month of April has only been fully completed for the first three weeks of the month.

(b) Complete the entries in the inventory record for the two receipts on 24 and 28 April that were ordered using the EOQ method.

(c) Complete ALL entries in the inventory record for the two issues in the month and for the closing balance at the end of April using the AVCO method of issuing inventory.

Inventory record for product ZYQ. (Show the costs per kilogram (kg) in £ to 3 decimal places, and the total costs in whole £.)

Date	Receipts			Issues			Balance	
	Quantity (kg)	Cost per kg (£)	Total cost (£)	Quantity (kg)	Cost per kg (£)	Total cost (£)	Quantity (kg)	Total cost (£)
Balance as at 22 April							900	1,125
24 April		1.275						
26 April				800				
28 April		1.475						
30 April				750				

(d) Using the LIFO method, the issue of 800 kg to production on the 26 April would be valued at a total of _____.

Task 2

What are the correct entries into the Journal below to record the following FOUR accounting transactions?

1   Receipt of ZYQ into inventory paying on credit.

2   Issue of ZYQ from inventory to production.

3   Receipt of ZYQ into inventory paying immediately by BACS.

4   Return of ZYQ from production to inventory.

The choices are:

- Dr Bank, Cr Inventory

- Dr Trade payables' control, Cr Inventory

- Dr Inventory, Cr Bank

- Dr Inventory, Cr Trade payables' control

- Dr Inventory, Cr Production

- Dr Production, Cr Inventory

Transaction 1	
Transaction 2	
Transaction 3	
Transaction 4	

Task 3

Below is a weekly timesheet for one of Icon Ltd's employees, who is paid as follows:

- For a basic six-hour shift every day from Monday to Friday – basic pay.

- For any overtime in excess of the basic six hours, on any day from Monday to Friday – the extra hours are paid at time-and-a-half (basic pay plus an overtime premium equal to half of basic pay).

- For three contracted hours each Saturday morning – basic pay.

- For any hours in excess of three hours on Saturday – the extra hours are paid at double time (basic pay plus an overtime premium equal to basic pay).

- For any hours worked on Sunday – paid at double time (basic pay plus an overtime premium equal to basic pay).

Complete the columns headed Basic pay, Overtime premium and Total pay. (*Notes* – Zero figures should be entered in cells where appropriate).

Employee's weekly timesheet for week ending 7 April

Employee: G. Michael			Cost Centre: Assembly			
Employee number: P851			Basic pay per hour: £12.00			
	Hours spent on production	Hours worked on indirect work	Notes	Basic pay (£)	Overtime premium (£)	Total pay (£)
Monday	6	2	10am–12am cleaning of machinery			
Tuesday	2	4	9am–1pm customer care course			
Wednesday	8					
Thursday	6					
Friday	6	1	3–4pm health and safety training			
Saturday	6					
Sunday	3					
Total	37	7				

Task 4

Icon Ltd's budgeted overheads for the next financial year are:

	£	£
Depreciation of machinery		974,850
Power for machinery		541,000
Rent and rates		104,500
Light and heat		23,100
Indirect labour costs:		
Maintenance	101,150	
Stores	36,050	
Administration	240,100	
Total indirect labour cost		377,300

The following information is also available:

Department	Carrying amount of machinery	Machinery power usage (KwH)	Floor space (square metres)	Number of employees
Assembly	4,200,000	298,800		15
Finishing	1,800,000	199,200		10
Maintenance			18,000	4
Stores			10,800	3
Administration			7,200	8
Total	6,000,000	498,000	36,000	40

Overheads are allocated or apportioned on the most appropriate basis. The total overheads of the support cost centres are then reapportioned to the two production centres using the direct method.

- 78% of the maintenance cost centre's time is spent maintaining machinery in the Assembly and the remainder in the Finishing.

- The stores cost centre makes 70% of its issues to the Assembly, and 30% to the Finishing.

- Administration supports the two production centres equally.

- There is no reciprocal servicing between the three support cost centres.

Complete the apportionment table using the data on this page.

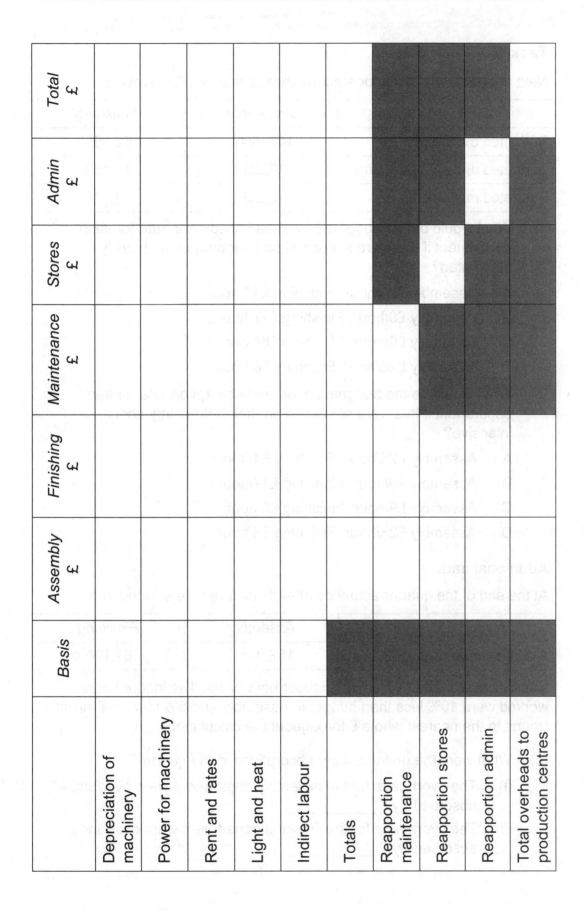

	Basis	Assembly £	Finishing £	Maintenance £	Stores £	Admin £	Total £
Depreciation of machinery							
Power for machinery							
Rent and rates							
Light and heat							
Indirect labour							
Totals							
Reapportion maintenance							
Reapportion stores							
Reapportion admin							
Total overheads to production centres							

Task 5

Next quarter Icon Ltd's budgeted overheads and activity levels are:

	Assembly	Finishing
Budgeted overheads (£)	147,224	62,900
Budgeted direct labour hours	16,358	10,483
Budgeted machine hours	5,258	3,700

(a) What would be the budgeted overhead absorption rate for each department if this were set based on their both being heavily automated?

    A   Assembly £28/hour, Finishing £17/hour

    B   Assembly £9/hour, Finishing £17/hour

    C   Assembly £9/hour, Finishing £6/hour

    D   Assembly £28/hour, Finishing £6/hour

(b) What would be the budgeted overhead absorption rate for each department if this were set based on their both being labour intensive?

    A   Assembly £28/hour, Finishing £17/hour

    B   Assembly £9/hour, Finishing £17/hour

    C   Assembly £9/hour, Finishing £6/hour

    D   Assembly £28/hour, Finishing £6/hour

Additional data

At the end of the quarter actual overheads incurred were found to be:

	Assembly	Finishing
Actual overheads (£)	152,841	61,100

Overheads were recovered on a labour hour basis. The labour hours worked were 10% less than budget in Assembly and 5% more in Finishing (round to the nearest whole £ throughout the calculation).

(c) What were the under or over absorptions in the quarter?

    (i)   The overheads for the assembly department were over/under* absorbed by £ _____.

    (ii) The overheads for the finishing department were over/under* absorbed by £ _____.

Task 6

Icon Ltd has prepared a forecast for the next quarter for one of its small wooden parts, ZYG. This component is produced in batches and the forecast is based on selling and producing 1,500 batches.

One of the customers of Icon Ltd has indicated that it may be significantly increasing its order level for component ZYG for the next quarter and it appears that activity levels of 1,800 batches and 2,000 batches are feasible.

The semi-variable costs should be calculated using the high-low method. If 3,000 batches are sold the total semi-variable cost will be £14,000, and there is a constant unit variable cost up to this volume.

Complete the table below and calculate the estimated profit per batch of ZYG at the different activity levels.

Batches produced and sold	1,500	1,800	2,000
	£	£	£
Sales revenue	45,000		
Variable costs:			
Direct materials	7,500		
Direct labour	9,000		
Overheads	6,000		
Semi-variable costs:	11,000		
Variable element			
Fixed element			
Total cost	33,500		
Profit for the period	11,500		
Profit per batch (to 2 decimal places)	7.67		

Task 7

Product ZYQ has a selling price of £52 per unit with a total variable cost of £38 per unit. Icon Ltd estimates that the fixed costs per quarter associated with this product are £84,000.

(a) Calculate the budgeted breakeven, in units, for product ZYQ.

(b) Calculate the budgeted breakeven, in £, for product ZYQ.

£

(c) Complete the table below to show the budgeted margin of safety in units, and the margin of safety percentage if Icon Ltd sells 8,000 units or 9,000 units of product ZYQ.

Units of ZYQ sold	8,000 units	9,000 units
Margin of safety (units)		
Margin of safety percentage		

(d) If Icon Ltd wishes to make a profit of £21,000, how many units of ZYQ must it sell?

units

(e) If Icon Ltd increases the selling price of ZYQ by £1, what will be the impact on the breakeven point and the margin of safety, assuming no change in the number of units sold?

A   The breakeven point will decrease and the margin of safety will increase.

B   The breakeven point will stay the same but the margin of safety will decrease.

C   The breakeven point will decrease and the margin of safety will stay the same.

D   The breakeven point will increase and the margin of safety will decrease.

Task 8

The Finishing department of Icon Ltd uses process costing for some of its products. Following are details for the month of April.

The component requires the input of three different materials:

Material ZY1 – 400kg @ £1.66 per kilogram

Material ZY2 – 300kg @ £1.50 per kilogram

Material ZY3 – 200kg @ £0.60 per kilogram

(a) Complete the table below (to two decimal places) to show the total cost of the material input into the process.

Materials	£
Material ZY1	
Material ZY2	
Material ZY3	
Total	

Icon Ltd estimates that the process will require two employees to work 38 hours per week for 4 weeks. These employees were paid £9 per hour.

Overheads are absorbed on the basis of £14 per labour hour.

(b) Calculate the total labour cost and total overhead cost for April.

The total labour cost is: £ _____.

The total overhead cost is: £ _____.

(c) Calculate the total quantity and value of inputs into the process in April.

The total quantity of material input into the process is: _____ kg.

The total value of inputs into the process is: £ _____.

Icon Ltd expects a normal loss of 4% during this process, which it then sells for scrap at 50p per kg.

(d) Calculate the total scrap value of the normal loss, state your answer to 2 decimal places.

The total scrap value of the normal loss is £ _____,

(e) Calculate the cost per kilogram of output assuming a normal loss of 4%. Your answer must be stated to four decimal places.

The cost per kilogram of output assuming a normal loss is £ _____.

(f)   Complete the sentences below, using the options listed, to identify the correct accounting entries. Enter your answer two 2 decimal places.

If the process results in an output of 850 kilograms there will be an *abnormal loss/an abnormal gain* of _____ kg.

This will have a total value of £ _____.

Task 9

Icon Ltd has the following original budget and actual performance for product ZYG for the year ending 31 April.

	Budget	*Actual*
Volume sold	10,000	12,000
	£000	£000
Sales revenue	2,000	2,500
Less costs:		
Direct materials	350	415
Direct labour	400	470
Overheads	980	1,180
Profit from operations	270	435

Both direct materials and direct labour are variable costs, but the overheads are fixed.

Complete the table below to show a flexed budget and the resulting variances against this budget for the year. Show the actual variance amount, for sales and each cost, in the column headed 'Variance' and indicate whether this is Favourable or Adverse by entering F or V in the final column. If neither F nor V, enter 0.

	Flexed	Actual	Variance	Favourable (F) or Adverse (A).
Volume sold		12,000		
	£000	£000	£000	
Sales revenue		2,500		
Less costs:				
Direct materials		415		
Direct labour		435		
Overheads		1,180		
Profit from operations		470		

Task 10

One of the painting machines in the Finishing department is nearing the end of its working life and Icon Ltd is considering purchasing a replacement machine.

Estimates have been made for the initial capital cost, sales revenue and operating costs of the replacement machine, which is expected to have a working life of three years:

	Year 0 £000	Year 1 £000	Year 2 £000	Year 3 £000
Capital expenditure	1,900			
Other cash flows:				
Sales revenue		1,620	1,860	2,300
Operating costs		1,120	1,150	1,190

The company appraises capital investment projects using a 15% cost of capital.

(a) Complete the table below and calculate the net present value of the proposed replacement machine (to the nearest £000).

	Year 0 £000	Year 1 £000	Year 2 £000	Year 3 £000
Capital expenditure				
Sales revenue				
Operating costs				
Net cash flows				
PV factors	1.0000	0.8696	0.7561	0.6575
Discounted cash flows				
Net present value				

The net present value is **positive / negative**.

(b) Calculate the payback of the proposed replacement machine to the nearest whole month.

The payback period is _____ Year(s) and _____ Months

(c) What is the approximate internal rate of return (IRR) of the project?

A   0%

B   10%

C   15%

D   20%

2 Mock Assessment Answers

Task 1

(a) The EOQ is $\sqrt{\dfrac{2 \times 2 \times 1{,}250{,}000}{5}}$ = 1,000 kg

(b) and (c)

Inventory record for ZYQ

| Date | Receipts | | | Issues | | | Balance | |
	Kg	Cost per kg (£)	Total cost (£)	Kg	Cost per kg (£)	Total cost (£)	Quantity (kg)	Total cost (£)
Balance as at 22 April							900	1,125
24 April	1,000	1.275	1,275				1,900	2,400
26 April				800	1.263	1,010	1,100	1,390
28 April	1,000	1.475	1,475				2,100	2,865
30 April				750	1.364	1,023	1,350	1,842

(d)   800 × 1.275 = £1,020

Task 2

Transaction 1	Dr Inventory, Cr Trade payables' control
Transaction 2	Dr Production, Cr Inventory
Transaction 3	Dr Inventory, Cr Bank
Transaction 4	Dr Inventory, Cr Production

Task 3

Employee's weekly timesheet for week ending 7 April

Employee: G Michael			Profit Centre: Assembly			
Employee number: P851			Basic pay per hour: £12.00			
	Hours spent on production	Hours worked on indirect work	Notes	Basic pay (£)	Overtime premium (£)	Total pay (£)
Monday	6	2	10am–12am cleaning of machinery	96	12	108
Tuesday	2	4	9am–1pm customer care course	72	–	72
Wednesday	8			96	12	108
Thursday	6			72	–	72
Friday	6	1	3–4pm health and safety training	84	6	90
Saturday	6			72	36	108
Sunday	3			36	36	72
Total	37	7		528	102	630

Task 4

	Basis	Assembly £	Finishing £	Maintenance £	Stores £	Admin £	Total £
Depreciation of machinery	Carrying amount	682,395	292,455				974,850
Power for machinery	KwH	324,600	216,400				541,000
Rent and rates	M²			52,250	31,350	20,900	104,500
Light and heat	M²			11,550	6,930	4,620	23,100
Indirect labour	All			101,150	36,050	240,100	377,300
Totals		1,006,995	508,855	164,950	74,330	265,620	2,020,750
Reapportion maintenance		128,661	36,289	(164,950)			
Reapportion stores		52,031	22,299		(74,330)		
Reapportion admin		132,810	132,810			(265,620)	
Total overheads to production centres		1,320,497	700,253				2,020,750

Task 5

(a)   The correct answer is A.

(b)   The correct answer is C.

(c)   What were the under or over absorptions in the quarter?

   (i)   The overheads for the assembly department were under absorbed by £20,343

      16,358 hours × 0.9 = 14,722 hours

      14,722 × £9 = £132,498 absorbed overhead

   (ii)   The overheads for the finishing department were over absorbed by £4,942

      10,483 hours × 1.05 = 11,007 hours

      11,007 × 6 = £66,042 absorbed overhead

Task 6

Batches produced and sold	1,500	1,800	2,000
	£	£	£
Sales revenue	45,000	54,000	60,000
Variable costs:			
Direct materials	7,500	9,000	10,000
Direct labour	9,000	10,800	12,000
Overheads	6,000	7,200	8,000
Semi-variable costs:	11,000		
Variable element		3,600	4,000
Fixed element		8,000	8,000
Total cost	33,500	38,600	42,000
Profit for the period	11,500	15,400	18,000
Profit per batch (to 2 decimal places)	7.67	8.56	9.00

Task 7

(a)   6,000 units

(b)   £312,000

(c)

Units of ZYQ sold	8,000 units	9,000 units
Margin of safety (units)	2,000	3,000
Margin of safety percentage	25%	33%

(d)   7,500 units

(e)   The correct answer is A.

Task 8

(a)   Complete the table below (to two decimal places) to show the total cost of the material input into the process.

Materials	£
Material ZY1	664
Material ZY2	450
Material ZY3	120
Total	1,234

(b)   Calculate the total labour cost and total overhead cost for April.

The total labour cost is: £2,736

The total overhead cost is: £4,256

(c)   Calculate the total quantity and value of inputs into the process in April.

The total quantity of material input into the process is: 900 kg

The total value of inputs into the process is: £8,226.

(d)   Calculate the total scrap value of the normal loss, state your answer to 2 decimal places.

The total scrap value of the normal loss is: £18

(e)   Calculate the cost per kilogram of output assuming a normal loss of 4%. Your answer must be stated to four decimal places.

The cost per kilogram of output assuming a normal loss is: £9.5000

(f)   Complete the sentences below, using the options listed, to identify the correct accounting entries. Enter your answer two 2 decimal places.

If the process results in an output of 850 kilograms there will be an *abnormal loss* of 14.00kg.

This will have a total value of £133.00.

Task 9

	Flexed	Actual	Variance	Favourable (F) or Adverse (A).
Volume sold	12,000	12,000		
	£000	£000	£000	
Sales revenue	2,400	2,500	100	F
Less costs:				
Direct materials	420	415	5	F
Direct labour	480	435	45	F
Overheads	980	1,180	200	A
Profit from operations	520	470	50	A

Task 10

(a)

	Year 0 £000	Year 1 £000	Year 2 £000	Year 3 £000
Capital expenditure	(1,900)			
Sales income		1,620	1,860	2,300
Operating costs		(1,120)	(1,150)	(1,190)
Net cash flows	(1,900)	500	710	1,110
PV factors	1.0000	0.8696	0.7561	0.6575
Discounted cash flows	(1,900)	435	537	730
Net present value	(198)			

The net present value is **negative**.

(b) The payback period is **2** years and **8** months.

Year	Cash flow	Cumulative cash flow
0	(1,900)	(1,900)
1	500	(1,400)
2	710	(690)
3	1,110	420

(690/1,110) × 12 = 7.5 months

(c) 10%

The NPV is negative at 15% so the IRR will be lower.

Glossary

Term	Description
Abnormal gain	The amount by which normal loss exceeds actual loss.
Abnormal loss	The amount by which actual loss exceeds normal loss.
Absorption costing	Inventory units are valued at variable cost plus fixed production overheads absorbed using a pre-determined absorption rate.
Batch costing	The costing system used for a business where production is made up of different product batches of identical units.
Bonus scheme	A day rate combined with a bonus based on output achieved.
Breakeven point	The level of activity required to make no profit and no loss.
Buffer inventory	Inventory held to cover variations in: – lead time, and – demand during the lead time. Sometimes defined as 'inventory held in excess of average units demanded in average lead time'.
Capital expenditure	Expenditure on the purchase or improvement of non-current assets, appearing in the statement of financial position.
Contribution	Sales revenue less variable cost of sales.
Cost absorption	The charging of overhead costs to cost units.
Cost accounting	The analysis of costs and revenues to provide useful information to assist the management accounting function.
Cost allocation	The charging of overhead costs to the specific cost centre that incurred them.
Cost apportionment	The splitting of shared overhead costs between relevant cost centres using an appropriate basis.

Term	Description
Cost centre	A location, function, activity or item of equipment in respect of which costs are accumulated.
Cost coding	The allocation of a unique code to costs, usually on the source documentation, to allow accurate and detailed analysis.
Cost unit	An individual unit of product or service for which costs can be separately ascertained.
Cost-volume-profit (CVP) analysis	Analysis of the effects of changes of volume on contribution and profit.
Depreciation	An annual internal charge to the statement of profit or loss that spreads the net cost of a non-current asset over the number of years of its useful life.
Direct costs	Costs that can be related directly to a cost unit.
Direct expenses	Expenses that can be related specifically to a cost centre.
Discounted cash flow	An investment appraisal technique which discounts future cash flows to a present value.
Economic batch quantity (EBQ)	To minimise the total of the inventory costs.
Economic order quantity (EOQ)	The quantity to be ordered/produced.
Equivalent unit	The number of whole units to which a partially completed unit is equivalent (= physical units × percentage completion).
Expenses	Items of expenditure that are not labour or materials related.
FIFO	A method of valuing issues of inventory that assumes that issues are made from the oldest inventory available (First In First Out).
Financial accounting	The production of an historic record of transactions presented in a standard format for use by parties external to the business.
Fixed costs	Costs that vary with time, not activity level.
Idle time	Paid for, but non-productive, hours.

KAPLAN PUBLISHING

Term	Description
Integrated bookkeeping system	A bookkeeping system whereby ledger accounts are kept that provide the necessary information for both costing and financial accounting.
Internal rate of return	The rate of interest which will cause the stream of cash flows discounted at that rate of interest to have a nil net present value.
Job costing	The costing system used for a business where production is made up of individual, different, large jobs.
Key factor analysis	The technique of allocating resources between products according to contribution per unit of resource.
Lead time	The time between an order for goods being placed and the receipt of that order.
LIFO	A method of valuing issues of inventory that assumes that issues are made from the newest inventory available (Last In First Out).
Management accounting	The generation, presentation and interpretation of historic, budgeted and forecast information for management for the purposes of planning, control and decision-making.
Margin of safety	The amount by which the level of activity can fall below budget before a loss is made.
Marginal costing	Inventory units are valued at variable production cost; fixed overheads are accounted for as period costs.
Normal loss	The level of expected loss of input from a process.
Over/under absorption (recovery)	Where the amount of overhead absorbed into cost units, using the pre-determined absorption rate, is more/less than the overheads actually incurred.
P/V (C/S) ratio	The ratio of contribution to sales value.
Payback period	The amount of time it takes for an investment project to recover the cash cost of the original investment.
Piecework rates	Where a constant fixed amount is paid per unit of output.

Term	Description
Present value	The value at today's date of an amount of cash received/paid at some time in the future, taking account of the compound interest earned over the relevant period.
Re-order level	The quantity of inventory in hand at the time when a new order is placed.
Re-order quantity	The quantity of inventory ordered. (Be careful to distinguish between re-order level and re-order quantity.)
Revenue expenditure	Expenditure on goods and services that will be charged to the statement of profit or loss.
Secondary apportionment	The re-apportionment of service cost centres' overhead costs to production cost centres.
Semi-variable costs	Costs with both a fixed and variable element.
Inventory control	The method of ensuring that the right quantity of the right quality of inventory is available at the right time and the right place.
Inventory control levels	Key inventory quantities that assist in inventory control, including re-order level, economic order quantity (EOQ), minimum and maximum inventory levels.
Stock-outs	Occasions when one or more items of inventory are needed but there are none in inventory.
Stores record card	A record kept for each inventory line, detailing receipts, issues and balance on hand, in terms of both physical quantities and monetary value.
Timesheet	A record of how an employee has spent his/her time, split between jobs/clients and non-productive time.
Usage	The quantity of items required for sale (in the case of goods for resale) or production (in the case of components or raw materials) in a given period.
Variable costs	Costs that vary in direct proportion to the level of activity.
Weighted average cost	A method of valuing issues of inventory that takes account of the relative quantities of inventory available purchased at different prices.

INDEX

A

Abnormal gain, 200, 204, 214

    loss, 200, 202, 211

    loss/gain account, 211

Absorption, 143, 154

    costing, 170, 249

    rate, 154

Apportionment, 143, 144

AVCO, 56, 225

Average cost, 225

B

Batch costing, 188

Behaviour, 15

Bonus schemes, 95

Breakeven charts, 275

Breakeven point, 268

Budgets, 122

C

C/S ratio, 272

Capital expenditure, 115

Clock cards, 87

Closing work in progress (CWIP), 218

Continuous operation costing, 186, 198

Contribution, 246, 247

Cost accounting, 3

Cost

    cards, 7

    centre(s), 4, 5

    classification, 12

    object, 4

    units, 4

Cost-volume-profit analysis (CVP), 267

Credit note, 45

D

Degrees of completion, 219

Delivery note, 43

Direct

    cost, 14

    expenses, 112

    labour, 98

    method, 150

Discounting, 304

E

Economic order quantity (EOQ), 51

Element, 12

Employee records, 84

Equivalent units (EU), 218

Expenses, 112

F

First in, first out FIFO, 56, 225, 227

Fixed budget, 122

Fixed costs, 17

Flexed budget, 124

Function, 13

G

Goods

    received note, 43

    requisition note, 39

    returned note, 45

Guaranteed minimum, 94

H

High-low method, 23

Holding costs, 47

I

Indirect

cost, 15

expenses, 113

labour, 98

Internal rate of return (IRR), 312

Inventory

account, 68

control, 50

valuation and profit, 65

Investment centre, 6

J

Job card, 186

Job costing, 186

L

Labour cost account, 100

Labour variances, 130

Last in, first out (LIFO), 56

Limiting factor analysis, 278

Long-term investments, 298, 299

Losses, 200

m

Management accounting, 2

Management information, 3

Margin of safety, 269

Marginal costing, 246, 249, 255

Material variances, 129

Maximum inventory, 53

Minimum inventory, 53

N

Nature, 14

Net present cost, 306, 310

Net present value (NPV), 306

Non relevant costs, 265

Non-production overheads, 142, 172

Normal loss, 200, 201

O

Opening work in progress (OWIP), 225

Ordering costs, 48

Over absorption, 162

Overhead absorption rate (OAR), 155, 157, 162

Overheads, 15, 113

Overtime, 89

payment, 89

premium, 89, 99

P

P/V ratio, 272

Payback period, 300

Piecework, 92

Present value, 305

Prime cost, 14

Process costing, 198

Production overheads, 142

Production overheads account, 167

Profit centre, 6

Profit-volume (P/V) chart, 277

Profit/volume ratio, 272

Purchase

invoice, 44

order, 42

requisition, 40

Purchasing, 38

R

Reapportionment, 148

Relevant costing, 264

Remuneration systems, 88

Re-order level, 51

Responsibility centres, 5

Revenue centre, 5

Revenue expenditure, 115

S

Sales variances, 129

Scrap account, 211

Scrap value, 206

Semi-variable costs, 19

Service cost units, 190

Service costing, 190

Specific order costing, 186

Step down method, 152

Stepped fixed costs, 18. 22

T

Target profit, 270

Time value of money, 304

Timesheets, 87

U

Under absorption, 162

V

Variable costs, 16

Variance analysis, 126

W

Weighted average, 56